HOTEL MANAGEMENT AND TOURISM

HOTEL MANAGEMENT AND TOURISM

Ravindra Verma

CENTRUM PRESS
NEW DELHI-110002 (INDIA)

CENTRUM PRESS
H.O.: 4360/4, Ansari Road, Daryaganj,
New Delhi-110002 (India)
Tel: 23278000, 23261597, 23255577, 23286875
B.O.: No. 1015, Ist Main Road, BSK IIIrd Stage,
IIIrd Phase, IIIrd Block, Bangalore-560085 (INDIA)
Tel: 080-41723429
Email: centrumpress@gmail.com
Visit us at: www.centrumpress.com

Hotel Management and Tourism

First Edition, 2010

ISBN 978-93-80540-94-8

PRINTED IN INDIA

Printed at Balaji Offset, Delhi.

Contents

Preface

Tourism is travel for recreational, leisure or business purposes. The World Tourism Organization defines tourists as people who travel to and stay in places outside their usual environment for more than twenty-four hours and not more than one consecutive year for leisure, business and other purposes not related to the exercise of an activity remunerated from within the place visited. There has been an upmarket trend in the tourism over the last few decades, especially in Europe, where international travel for short breaks is common. Tourists have high levels of disposable income, considerable leisure time, are well educated, and have sophisticated tastes. There is now a demand for a better quality products, which has resulted in a fragmenting of the mass market for beach vacations; people want more specialised versions, quieter resorts, family-oriented holidays or niche market-targeted destination hotels.

The World Tourism Organization forecasts that International tourism will continue growing at the average annual rate of 4 %. With the advent of e-commerce, tourism products have become one of the most traded items on the internet. Tourism products and services have been made available through intermediaries, although tourism providers (hotels, airlines, etc.) can sell their services directly. This has put pressure on intermediaries from both on-line and traditional shops.

It has been suggested there is a strong correlation between tourism expenditure per capita and the degree to which countries play in the global context· Not only as a result of the important economic contribution of the tourism industry, but also as an indicator of the degree of confidence with which global citizens leverage the resources of the globe for the benefit of their local economies. This is why any projections of growth in tourism may serve as an indication of the relative influence that each country will exercise in the future.

Tourism and hospitality industry reached the zenith in twentieth century. And with emergence of liberalisation and globalization concepts, this is the real industry of future—having vast scope and potential. The present book intends to bring together authentic information on diverse aspects of hotel, hospitality and tourism management.

—*Ravindra Verma*

1

Brief History of the Hotel Industry

Hotel

A hotel is an establishment that provides paid lodging on a short-term basis. The provision of basic accommodation, in times past, consisting only of a room with a bed, a cupboard, a small table and a washstand has largely been replaced by rooms with modern facilities, including en-suite bathrooms and air conditioning or climate control. Additional common features found in hotel rooms are a telephone, an alarm clock, a television, and Internet connectivity; snack foods and drinks may be supplied in a mini-bar, and facilities for making hot drinks. Larger hotels may provide a number of additional guest facilities such as a restaurant, a swimming pool or childcare, and have conference and social function services. Hotels rooms are usually numbered to allow guests identify their room.

Some hotels offer meals as part of a room and board arrangement. In the United Kingdom, a hotel is required by law to serve food and drinks to all guests within certain stated hours; to avoid this requirement it is not uncommon to come across *private hotels* which are not subject to this requirement. In Japan, capsule hotels provide a minimized amount of room space and shared facilities.

In the United Kingdom, Australia, Canada and Ireland (and rarely in some parts of the United States), the word may also refer to a pub or bar and might not offer accommodation. In India and Bangladesh, the word may also refer to a restaurant.

Etymology

The word *hotel* is derived from the French *hotel* (coming from *hote* meaning *host*), which referred to a French version of a townhouse or any other building seeing frequent visitors, rather than a place offering accommodation. In contemporary French usage, *hotel* now has the same meaning as the English term, and *hotel particulier* is used for the old meaning. The French spelling, with the circumflex, was also used in English, but is now rare. The circumflex replaces the 's' found in the earlier *hostel* spelling, which over time took on a new, but closely related meaning. Grammatically, hotels usually take the definite article-hence "The Astoria Hotel" or simply "The Astoria".

Classification

The cost and quality of hotels are usually indicative of the range and type of services available. Due to the enormous increase in tourism worldwide during the last decades of the 20th century, standards, especially those of smaller establishments, have improved considerably. For the sake of greater comparability, rating systems have been introduced, with the one to five stars classification being most common and with higher star ratings indicating more luxury.

Hotels are independently assessed in traditional systems and these rely heavily on the facilities provided. Some consider this disadvantageous to smaller hotels whose quality of accommodation could fall into one class but the lack of an item such as an elevator would prevent it from reaching a higher categorization. In some countries, there is an official body with standard criteria for classifying hotels, but in many others there is none. There have been attempts at unifying the classification system so that it becomes an internationally recognized and reliable standard but large differences exist in the quality of the accommodation and the food within one category of hotel, sometimes even in the same country. The American Automobile Association (AAA) and their affiliated bodies use diamonds instead of stars to express hotel and restaurant ratings levels.

Hotels are also classified by service type ranging for all-inclusive full-service resorts that cater to vacationers to small limited service hotels that cater to transient business travellers. The main categories of hotels are as follows;

- Full Service Upscale :
  - *Examples include Conrad Hotels, Ritz Carlton, Four Seasons Hotels, and JW Marriott*
- Full Service :
  - *Examples include Hilton, Marriott, Doubletree, and Hyatt*
- Select Service :
  - *Examples include Courtyard by Marriott and Hilton Garden Inn*
- Limited Service :
  - *Examples include Hampton Inn, Fairfield Inn, Days Inn, and La Quinta Inn*
- Extended Stay :
  - *Examples include Homewood Suites by Hilton, Residence Inn by Marriott, and Extended Stay Hotels*
- Timeshare :
  - *Examples include Marriott Vacation Club, Westgate Resorts, and Disney Vacation Club*
- Destination Club.

Historic Hotels

Some hotels have gained their renown through tradition, by hosting significant events or persons, such as Schloss Cecilienhof in Potsdam, Germany, which derives its fame from the Potsdam Conference of the World War II allies Winston Churchill, Harry Truman and Joseph Stalin in 1945. The Taj Mahal Palace & Tower in Mumbai is one of India's most famous and historic hotels because of its association with the Indian independence movement. Some establishments have given name to a particular meal or beverage, as is the case with the Waldorf Astoria in New York City, United States where the Waldorf Salad was first created or the Hotel Sacher in Vienna, Austria, home of the Sachertorte. Others have achieved fame by association with dishes or cocktails created on their premises, such as the Hotel de Paris where the crepe Suzette was invented or the Raffles Hotel in Singapore, where the Singapore Sling cocktail was devised.

A number of hotels have entered the public consciousness through popular culture, such as the Ritz Hotel in London, United Kingdom, through its association with Irving Berlin's song, 'Puttin' on the Ritz'. The Algonquin Hotel in New York City is famed as the meeting place of the literary group, the Algonquin Round Table, and Hotel Chelsea, also in New York City, has been the subject of a number of songs and the scene of the stabbing of Nancy Spungen (allegedly by her boyfriend Sid Vicious). The Waldorf Astoria and Statler hotels in New York City are also immortalized in the names of Muppets Statler and Waldorf.

The luxurious Grand Hotel Europe in Saint Petersburg, Russia achieved fame with its inclusion in the James Bond film GoldenEye.

Unusual Hotels

Many hotels can be considered destinations in themselves, by dint of unusual features of the lodging or its immediate environment:

Treehouse Hotels

Some hotels are built with living trees as structural elements, for example the Costa Rica Tree House in the Gandoca-Manzanillo Wildlife Refuge, Costa Rica; the Treetops Hotel in Aberdare National Park, Kenya; the Ariau Towers near Manaus, Brazil, on the Rio Negro in the Amazon; and Bayram's Tree Houses in Olympos, Turkey.

Bunker Hotels

The Null Stern Hotel in Teufen, Appenzellerland, Switzerland and the Concrete Mushrooms in Albania are former nuclear bunkers transformed into hotels.

Cave Hotels

Desert Cave Hotel in Coober Pedy, South Australia and the Cuevas Pedro Antonio de Alarcon (named after the author) in Guadix, Spain, as well as several hotels in Cappadocia, Turkey, are notable for being built into natural cave formations, some with rooms underground.

Capsule Hotels

Capsule hotels are a type of economical hotel that are found in Japan, where people sleep in stacks of rectangular containers.

Ice and Snow Hotels

The Ice Hotel in Jukkasjarvi, Sweden, and the Hotel de Glace in Duschenay, Canada, melt every spring and are rebuilt each winter; the Mammut Snow Hotel in Finland is located within the walls of the Kemi snow castle; and the Lainio Snow Hotel is part of a snow village near Yllas, Finland.

Garden Hotels

Garden hotels, famous for their gardens before they became hotels, include Gravetye Manor, the home of garden designer William Robinson, and Cliveden, designed by Charles Barry with a rose garden by Geoffrey Jellicoe.

Underwater Hotels

Some hotels have accommodation underwater, such as Utter Inn in Lake Malaren, Sweden. Hydropolis, project cancelled 2004 in Dubai, would have had suites on the bottom of the Persian Gulf, and Jules Undersea Lodge in Key Largo, Florida requires scuba diving to access its rooms.

Other Unusual Hotels

- The Library Hotel in New York City, is unique in that each of its ten floors is assigned one category from the Dewey Decimal System.
- The Burj al-Arab hotel in Dubai, United Arab Emirates, built on an artificial island, is structured in the shape of a boat's sail.
- The Jailhotel Löwengraben in Lucerne, Switzerland is a converted prison now used as a hotel.
- The Luxor, a hotel and casino on the Las Vegas Strip in Paradise, Nevada, United States due to its pyramidal structure.
- The Liberty Hotel in Boston, used to be the Charles Street Jail.
- Built in Scotland and completed in 1936, The former ocean liner RMS *Queen Mary* in Long Beach, California, United States uses its first-class staterooms as a hotel, after retiring in 1967 from Transatlantic service.

Resort Hotels

Some hotels are built specifically to create a captive trade, example at casinos and holiday resorts. Though of course hotels have always been built in popular desinations, the defining characteristic of a resort hotel is that it exists purely to serve another attraction, the two having the same owners. In Las Vegas there is a tradition of one-upmanship with luxurious and extravagant hotels in a concentrated area known as the Las Vegas Strip.

This trend now has extended to other resorts worldwide, but the concentration in Las Vegas is still the world's highest: nineteen of the world's twenty-five largest hotels by room count are on the Strip, with a total of over 67,000 rooms.

In Europe Centre Parcs might be considered a chain of resort hotels, since the sites are largely man-made (though set in natural surroundings such as country parks) with captive trade, whereas holiday camps such as Butlins and Pontin's are probably not considered as resort hotels, since they are set at traditional holiday destinations which existed before the camps.

Railway Hotels

Frequently, expanding railway companies built grand hotels at their termini, such as the Midland Hotel, Manchester next to the former Manchester Central Station and in London the ones above St Pancras railway station and Charing Cross railway station also in London is the Chiltern Court Hotel above Baker Street tube station and Canada's grand railway hotels. They are or were mostly, but not exclusively, used by those travelling by rail.

Motels

A motel (Motor Hotel) is a hotel which is for a short stay, usually for a night, for motorists on long journeys. It has direct access from the room to the vehicle (for example a central parking lot around which the buildings are set), and is built conveniently close to major roads and intersections.

World Record Setting Hotels

Largest

In 2006, Guinness World Records listed the First World Hotel in Genting Highlands, Malaysia as the world's largest hotel with a total of 6,118 rooms.

Oldest

According to the Guinness Book of World Records, the oldest hotel still in operation is the Hoshi Ryokan, in the Awazu Onsen area of Komatsu, Japan which opened in 718.

Tallest

Burj Al Arab in United Arab Emirates is the tallest building used exclusively as a hotel. However, the Rose Tower, also in Dubai, which has already topped Burj Al Arab's height at 333 m (1,093 ft.), will take away this title upon its opening.

Hotel Rooms as an Investment

Some hotels sell individual rooms to investors. The buyer is allowed to stay in the room without charge or at a reduced rate for a given number of days each year. The investor is paid a share of the takings for the room. Rooms can be sold on a leasehold basis, sometimes on a 999 year lease. Room owners are free to sell at any time.

Living in Hotels

A number of public figures have notably chosen to take up semi-permanent or permanent residence in hotels.

- Actor Richard Harris lived at the Savoy Hotel while in London. Hotel archivist Susan Scott recounts an anecdote that when he was being taken out of the building on a stretcher shortly before his death he raised his hand and told the diners "it was the food".

Fictitious Hotels

Hotels have been used as the settings for television programmes such as the British situation comedies Fawlty Towers and I'm Alan Partridge, the British soap opera Crossroads, and in films such as the Bates Motel in Hitchcock's 1960 film Psycho.

In an increasingly competitive employment arena, African Americans must prepare for and secure strong, definite jobs which lead them to long-term realistic career options and opportunities.

One of the fastest growing sectors of the economy of our time is the hospitality industry. The hospitality industry alone is a multi-billion dollar and growing enterprise. It is exciting, never boring and offers unlimited opportunities. The hospitality industry is diverse enough for people to work in different areas of interest and still be employed within the hospitality industry. Think about this: It makes sense to prepare for a job in which you have numerous opportunities for advancement, because it is an economic advantage for you in the long run.

The hospitality industry pays those well who have prepared well.

Hospitality management involves the planning, organizing, directing and controlling of human and material resources within the lodging, restaurant, travel and tourism, institutional management, recreational management and meeting and convention planning industries. All of these separate yet related segments of the hospitality industry are interrelated to deliver kind and generous services to guests.

The hospitality industry is one of the oldest businesses in history. People have always gone out to eat sometimes and travelled for work or leisure purposes. However, the face of the hospitality industry has changed drastically. Brenda Scott, president and CEO of the Mobile, Ala., Convention and Visitors Corporation, agrees and says; demographically the world is changing. By the year 2000, 45-50 percent of the workforce and consumers will be non-white. Not only has the industry expanded to include areas such as tourism and meeting and convention planning, but also the face of the workforce in substantial positions has expanded to include all races and colors. The explosion of growth in the hospitality industry demands highly qualified people trained in hospitality management to fill rapidly opening positions.

Although African Americans have had a wealth of experience in hospitality, it has not always been positive. In the past African Americans have usually performed in low-level managerial positions in hospitality operations holding positions from the lowest realm in service to now having the realistic opportunity of becoming general managers.

The present hospitality industry is extraordinarily healthy and viable and as a result offers excellent opportunities for African Americans in each of the segments; restaurant management, lodging management, recreational management, travel and tourism, meeting and convention planning and institutional management. Scott announces good news: the opportunities are there. The globalization of the hospitality industry creates the availability of jobs in virtually every city in the world. Ed Moore, Jr., regional recruiter for Applebee's International says the restaurant industry is a wonderful field to be in, especially in the 90s. He further states, oftentimes young adults think of flipping burgers when they think of the business. That is not all there is to it. There are positions in middle management as well as the corporate office. We are talking about jobs that range from $26,000 to $100,000 plus. In the growing field of hospitality, it is projected that by the year 2000 an additional two million people will fill new jobs in the industry. According to the U.S. Department of Labour, in the next decade nine out of ten new jobs created will be in the service industry. Through the year 2000, positions for hotel managers are expected to grow faster than the average for all occupations, as reported in the Occupational Outlook Handbook, a publication of the U.S. Department of Labour. It is estimated by Kelley Notes that by the turn of the century the lodging industry will create over 500,000 additional entry-level positions. Kelley Notes also estimates in less than a decade, travel and tourism will become the nation's number one employer with one of every five Americans working in some segment of the hospitality industry.

African Americans do well to actively prepare themselves and aggressively seek employment in the hospitality industry. They should especially investigate opportunities in meeting and convention planning, and travel and tourism. These two areas are hot spots of the industry and presently offer outstanding opportunities for prepared students.

To help African Americans prepare for a successful hospitality career, completing a college degree in hospitality management and/or related area is a great beginning. Phillip Cunningham, general manager of the Tuskegee University Kellogg Conference Centre, believes that success for African Americans in the hospitality industry means being flexible in business and in personal life, understanding the true meaning of customer and employee service, and knowing the job that you are asking others to perform. In addition says Cunningham, with the onslaught of public held hotel companies, today's industry professional must understand how to make a profit. Having great customer skills no longer promotes you to the top. A degree in hospitality management with a strong emphasis in business administration strengthens your preparation for the industry. In additional to classroom preparation, junior and senior students especially should seek hands-on opportunities such as internships, shadowing experiences and mentoring relationships. Internships are very beneficial to students in that they provide immediate access to the real work world and also are the time for students to make mistakes as they learn. These experiences also provide the graduate with a strong level of preparedness for entry-level positions.

Moore contends that students must be prepared and learn as much as possible while still in school. He feels that their education should give them a good solid background before they seek employment in the industry. For those who have properly prepared themselves, entry-level positions may include but are not limited to manager trainee internships, unit manager, food and beverage director, operations manager, sales and marketing, human resources, front office supervisor, executive housekeeper, director of housekeeping, controller, conference manager, rooms divisions manager, travel consultant, meeting planner, events planner, and the assistant manager position in all segments of the industry, etc. In planning and preparing for a successful career in hospitality, take advantage of in-house management training programs and seek mentors which will increase the potential of a steady and timely progression in hospitality. Students obtaining degrees in hospitality are prepared to seek employment in hotels, restaurants, travel and tourism destinations, convention and visitors bureaus, health care facilities, airlines, recreational facilities, and management/contract services, etc.

Successful African Americans in hospitality recognize their role and the importance of mentoring incoming students interested in hospitality management. According to Phillip Cunningham, historically African Americans have not achieved the same level of success in the industry, due to the lack of corporate mentors. It is extremely important to identify people who can help you achieve your goals. Often this means the mentor takes on additional responsibilities without being paid, works more than 50 hours a week, and moves from city to city. Scott agrees that mentoring as well as helping to place students is a responsibility that all successful role models in the industry should take on. She further charges herself as well as fellow colleagues to, assist students' progression in the industry by making opportunities available and by developing outreach programs to disseminate information to students and professionals.

Although competition is tough, well-prepared students can expect steady opportunities for advancement. However, explains Scott, students can compete by participating in internships and working any and every job available in the industry. She also says, if students are to progress upward to managerial level positions, they need practical experience and must have a positive attitude. Overall she feels the most important thing a student can do to be successful is, plan and prepare, have a willingness to work, and be passionate about your career. The industry is very demanding but rewarding and appreciates those who have paid their dues so to speak. Hospitality companies are looking for confident, well-adjusted individuals with good communication and interviewing skills. In his role as a regional recruiter, Ed Moore, Jr. states, verbal skills are of concern and that students should learn how to articulate well. However, he continues, one of the glaring areas of concern that I have noticed is students are not ready for the interview. This is something that you will need to practice with an experienced person or professional.

Recognizing a shortage of African Americans in key positions in the industry, African-American college graduates are zealously sought and offered substantial positions. To help the industry achieve its goals, many historically Black colleges and universities serve as clearing houses for qualified African-American graduates in hospitality management. This affords colleges and universities the opportunity to maintain ongoing relationships with industry personnel as well as receive constant feedback on the expectations of industry regarding entering employees.

Interested in a career in hospitality management? Where do you go from here? First, complete your college degree in hospitality management and/or related major. Work whenever and wherever possible in any segment of the hospitality industry, be flexible, find a dedicated and concerned mentor in the segment of the industry which interests you most, and talk to successful African Americans in the industry, organizations, and who are in positions of leadership in the field of hospitality management.

The following organizations listed focus primarily on the needs and concerns of African Americans and other people of colour in the industry, as well as serve as a clearinghouse for information and opportunities for students, faculty and the industry.

Preparation inside and outside of the classroom is vital to a progressive and successful career path in the hospitality industry. The opportunities are great, advancement is realistic, and success is attainable.

A Brief History

The history of hotels is intimately connected to that of civilisations. Or rather, it is a part of that history. Facilities offering guests hospitality have been in evidence since early biblical times. The Greeks developed thermal baths in villages designed for rest and recuperation. Later, the Romans built mansions to provide accommodation for travellers on government business. The Romans were the first to develop thermal baths in England, Switzerland and the Middle East. Later still, caravanserais appeared, providing a resting place for caravans along Middle Eastern routes. In the Middle Ages, monasteries and abbeys were the first establishments to offer refuge to travellers on a regular basis. Religious orders built inns, hospices and hospitals to cater for those on the move.

From antiquity to the Middle Ages-The history of hotels is intimately connected to that of civilisations. Or rather, it is a part of that history. Facilities offering guests hospitality have been in evidence since early biblical times. The Greeks developed thermal baths in villages designed for rest and recuperation. Later, the Romans built mansions to provide accommodation for travellers on government business. The Romans were the first to develop thermal baths in England, Switzerland and the Middle East.

Later still, caravanserais appeared, providing a resting place for caravans along Middle Eastern routes. In the Middle Ages, monasteries and abbeys were the first establishments to offer refuge to travellers on a regular basis. Religious orders built inns, hospices and hospitals to cater for those on the move.

Inns multiplied, but they did not yet offer meals. Staging posts were established for governmental transports and as rest stops. They provided shelter and allowed horses to be changed more easily. Numerous refuges then sprang up for pilgrims and crusaders on their way to the Holy Land.

Travelling then became progressively more hazardous. At the same time, inns gradually appeared in most of Europe. Some of them have remained famous, for example, l' Auberge des Trois Rois in Basle, which dates from the Middle Ages.

Around 1200, staging posts for travellers and stations for couriers were set up in China and Mongolia.

In Europe, or more precisely in Belgium, l' Auberge Cour Saint Georges opened in Gant, while the Angel Inn was built at

Grantham in Lincolnshire, England. The start of the hotel industry- In France, at the beginning of the fifteenth century, the law required that hotels keep a register. English law also introduced rules for inns at that time. At the same time, around 1500 thermal spas were developed at Carlsbad and Marienbad.

During this epoch, more than 600 inns were registered in England. Their architecture often consisted of a paved interior court with access through an arched porch. The bedrooms were situated on the two sides of the courtyard, the kitchen and the public rooms at the front, and the stables and storehouses at the back. The first guide books for travellers were published in France during this period.

An embryonic hotel industry began to develop in Europe. Distinctive signs were hung outside establishments renowned for their refined cuisine. At the end of the 1600s, the first stage coaches following a regular timetable started operating in England. Half a century later, clubs similar to English gentlemen's clubs and masonic lodges began to appear in America.

In Paris in the time of Louis XIV, the Place Vendome offered the first example of a multiple-use architectural complex, where the classical facades accommodated boutiques, offices, apartments and also hotels.

In the nineteenth century, hotels take over the town-The industrial revolution, which started in the 1760s, facilitated the construction of hotels everywhere, in mainland Europe, in England and in America.

In New York first of all, and then in Copenhagen, hotels were established in city centres.

At the beginning of the 1800s, the Royal Hotel was built in London. Holiday resorts began to flourish along the French and Italian rivieras.

In Japan, Ryokan guest houses sprang up. In India, the government-run Dak bungalows provided reliable accommodation for travellers. The Tremont House in Boston was the first deluxe hotel in a city centre. It offered inside toilets, locks on the doors and an "a la carte" menu.

The Holt Hotel in New York City was the first to provide its guests with a lift for their luggage.

In 1822, in Venice, a certain Giuseppe Dal Niel transformed an old palace into a hotel and gave it his name, "Le Danieli". As trains began to replace horse-drawn transport, highway inns for stage coaches started to decline.

During this period, the Shepheards Hotel in Cairo was founded, the result of a complete transformation of an ancient city-centre harem.

L'Hôtel des Bergues was built in the spring of 1834 on the shore of the Lake of Geneva. One of its founders, Guillaume Henri Dufour, became a famous Swiss general. In 1840, Hotel des Trois Couronnes was established in Vevey in Switzerland and the Baur au Lac in Zurich, fully refurbished since 1995.

In New York, the New York Hotel was the first to be equipped with private bathrooms.

The "Bayerischer Hof" was built in Munich in 1841, followed in 1852 by the "Vier Jahreszeiten". These two famous establishments were completely renovated after the Second World War.

Le Grand Hotel Paris-The inauguration of the Grand Hotel in Paris took place on 5 May 1862 in the presence of the Empress Eugenie. The orchestra, directed by Jacques Offenbach, played the Traviata. This building was designed by the architect Alfred Armand, in order to "show the élite of travellers from all over the world the progress made under the Second Empire by the sciences, arts and industry".

The exterior facades with their high arched doors and their Louis XIV windows were in the style required for the surroundings of the Opera. The greatest names in painting and decoration participated in the completion of this hotel, the grandest in Europe in its dimensions, luxury and installations. The first hydraulic lift was installed in this hotel. "Lighting was supplied by 4000 gas jets; heating by 18 stoves and 354 hot air vents.

In 1890, the entire hotel was equipped with electric lighting.

Due to the installation of steam central heating in 1901, baskets of wood were no longer sold on the floors. Some years later the hotel was renovated. Further renovation took place in 1970 and 1985. In 1982, it became a member of the Intercontinental chain.

Since 1992 the hotel has been equipped with a central Building Management System.

In June 2003, Le Grand Hotel Paris has reopened its doors following an eighteen-month multi-million dollar renovation.

The Fifth Avenue Hotel in New York City was the first in that period to provide lifts for its guests. 1869 saw the inauguration, near Cairo, of the Mena House, an oasis of calm and luxury, at the foot of the famous pyramids of Cheops, Chephren and Mikerinos.

In 1870, the Palmer House Hotel in Chicago was the grandest of all hotels. Its structure, the first of its kind, was fire-resistant.

In 1873, the Palais de Würtemberg in Vienna was transformed into a superb luxury residence for the notables of the epoch, hotel Imperial. Kings and queens became regular visitors to what is without doubt the finest example of the refined architecture of the Ringstrasse in Vienna. It is said that Richard Wagner directed the first productions of "Tannhäuser" and "Lohengrin" there. Two years later in 1875, the Grand Hotel Europe opened its doors in St Petersburg. This prestigious place where Tchaikoswky spent his honeymoon and where Shostakovich played a sonata for Prokofiev in his suite.

In 1880, the Sagamore Hotel on Lake George in the state of New York was the very first to provide electricity in all its rooms.

The first school for hoteliers was founded in Lausanne, Switzerland in 1890 by J. Tschumi, Director of the Beau Rivage in Lausanne, and A.R. Armleder, the "father" of the Richemond in Geneve.

In Monte Carlo, hotel Hermitage opened its doors in 1896, offering its guests the refined and luxurious atmosphere enjoyed by the rich at the close of the nineteenth century. Shortly afterwards, the Victoria Hotel in Kansas City offered bathrooms with every room. The Netherland Hotel in New York City then became the first to provide all its guests with their own telephone.

In Athens in 1874, Stathis Lampsas, a chef by profession, realised his dream by building hotel Grande Bretagne. Athens was suffering at that time from a shortage of water. It is said that the personnel bought water from carriers in the street to bring to the 80 bedrooms and... the two bathrooms. Of course, the establishment has undergone several renovations since that time.

In 1894, the Grand Hotel became the first Italian hotel to boast an electricity supply.

The Swiss hotelier Caspar Badrutt opened the famous Palace de Saint Moritz in 1896. In 1898, Cesar Ritz, from the Valais in Switzerland, who became, to quote the famous phrase of King Edward VII, the "king of hoteliers and hotelier to kings", opened the hotel which bears his famous name in the Place Vendôme in Paris.

The twentieth century: the age of prosperity-The early years of the twentieth century were rich in new hotels which rapidly became prestigious.

Edouard Niiermans, the "architect of palaces", transformed the Villa "Eugenie", the summer residence of the Emperor Napoleon III and his wife Eugénie de Montijo, in 1900. In 1905, he built hotel du Palais in Biarritz. In 1913 his "Negresco" was opened in Nice, in the presence of seven kings!

In Madrid, King Alphonse XIII was anxious that the capital should have a luxurious and prestigious hotel, and as a result the Ritz was inaugurated in 1910. Seville paid its own homage to the king by opening a splendid establishment, constructed by the architect Jose Espiau, the Alphonso XIII. Not to be outdone, Barcelona inaugurated its own Ritz in 1919. This was equipped with an unheard of luxury at that time, bathrooms with hot as well as cold water!

We could also cite, among many other hotels built in the same period, the Ritz and Savoy in London, the Beau Rivage Palace in Lausanne, le Négresco in Nice, the Plaza in New York, the Metropole in Brussels, the Plaza-Athene and hotel de Crillon in Paris, the Taj Mahal in Bombay and so on. The latter was renovated in 1972 by the Inter-Continental chain.

The prosperous nineteen-twenties saw a veritable boom in the hotel industry. Numerous hotels were established in this decade. In 1923, the architects Marchisio and Prost constructed a hotel in some wonderful gardens in the heart of Marrakech in Morocco, and for decades it was considered the most beautiful hotel in the world: La Mamounia. Winston Churchill helped to forge its reputation by becoming a frequent guest.

Hotels were built not only in cities, but also in the mountains. The first ski resorts in Switzerland (Saint-Moritz, Gstaad, Montana, etc.) welcomed tourists (often English ones) to some very comfortable establishments.

The worldwide depression which followed in 1929 did not prevent the construction of the famous Waldorf Astoria in New York. This was the greatest hotel edifice of those troubled times.

After the war, the fifties saw the second boom in the hotel industry. The Club Mediterranée (G. Trigano) created the now famous, but then revolutionary concept of the club village. These years were also notable for the construction of the first casino hotels. This was also the time when the airline companies began to develop their own hotels.

In the sixties, new tourist resorts flourished around the Mediterranean. From Spain to Greece and from the Balearics to Yugoslavia, numerous city and beach hotels opened their doors to summer guests hungry for relaxation and a good dose of sunshine. Portugal and the Scandinavian countries soon followed their lead.

Hotels for Business People

1970 saw the beginning of the construction of hotels for business people. This movement was supported by several factors. First of all, there was the will of the airline companies to extend their efforts in the domain of hotels.

Then there was the sudden prosperity, due to black gold, of Middle Eastern countries which attracted business people from the entire world. This engendered an important business travel trend-not limited to this region alone-which initiated the development of hotels primarily designed for business people in Middle-Eastern cities like Dubai, Abu Dhabi, Riyadh and Jeddah, to mention only the most important.

Hotel chains, attentive to their customers' wishes, started to offer an increasingly varied range of services. Their rooms became more spacious and the cuisine more refined.

Gradually, too, various first class hotels (among them former palaces and city centre hotels) which had fallen into disrepair began systematic renovation programmes.

The end of the seventies, when China opened its doors to foreign tourists, also saw the first congresses of international hotel experts.

The third hotel industry boom-The third boom in the hotel industry began in 1980, marked by more inventive marketing and the development of hotels increasingly adapted to a particular type of clientele.

This trend prompted the construction of hotels near airports, hotels for conferences, health hotels, ski holiday hotels, holiday villages and marina hotels. The first Property Management Systems (Fidelio, Hogatex, etc.) appear in the hospitality market.

In Istanbul in 1984, work began on the renovation and transformation into a hotel of the prestigious sultans' residence, the Ciragan Palace in Istanbul. The resulting hotel is no less prestigious than the Ciragan Palace was. Managed by the Kempinski chain, it opened its 322 rooms to guests in 1991.

The first administrative hotel management systems, offering hotels greater independence from human resources, then appeared on the market. The hotel industry was becoming more and more competitive. Business travellers and retired people became important target customers.

In the eighties, too, the Far East began to prepare itself to welcome both business people and the tourists who were beginning to discover the countries of the rising sun, such as China, South Korea, Thailand and Japan. The international chains (American for the most part) prepared expansion plans for Europe, the Middle and Far East which were mainly aimed at congress participants and business people.

The nineties: technology starts to make an impact-The early nineties were characterised by a recession in the hotel business, without doubt caused by reductions in multinationals' travel budgets and the growing crisis in the Gulf.

The Gulf War helped to create great insecurity for both individuals and business. 1991 is considered to be the black year of the hotel trade. It forced hoteliers to become more creative in finding ways of attracting guests (special programmes, offers for "frequent travellers", high performance reservation systems) and thus emerge from the crisis with the minimum damage.

For the first time, the environment and energy conservation played an important role in the marketing activities of numerous chains (thanks in part to the green movement) and even helped to win the loyalty of numerous clients while safeguarding assets at the same time. Reservation systems became more efficient and offered the hotelier a new dimension in the creation of customer loyalty, the database. The records of each guest's individual history have helped create individualised marketing programmes and have enabled hotels to satisfy a guest's personal needs from the moment of his arrival.

Hotel Adlon Berlin is a legend reborn. From its opening in 1907, until it was destroyed in 1945, it was a symbol of Berlin, a lavish host for royalty, heads of government, stage and screen stars, and the greats of literature and science. Now, it has been rebuilt (1997) on its original site, the corner of Unter den Linden and Pariser Platz, facing the Brandenburg Gate. Outside, it is a virtual replica of the original; inside it is testimony to what smart hotel operators (in this case the Kempinski group) can accomplish with an investment of $260 million. The hotel's 337 rooms and suites are the ultimate in luxury. Interiors, designed by England's Ezra Attia and Sweden's Lars Malmquist, dazzle with marble, sandstone, stained glass, gold leaf, stuccowork, cherry wood panelling, and damask draperies. This hotel is today equipped with the most advanced technology with regards to the Room Management System communicating with the Property Management System.

Since 1992, the most important international chains have been vying with each other in ever greater imaginative feats related to the vital process of renovating their establishments worldwide. Technology has started to take its rightful place in hotel administration (simplification of check-in and check-out procedures, global reservation systems, marketing management etc.). In 1995, the first Hotel Room Management System is launched at the European level. It is linked to the most popular Property Management Systems to make the front desk more efficient and near to the guests.

At International Technology Forums, speakers unanimously, underlined the impact of technology on hotel rooms.

Hotel chains have been searching for alliances and some of them. For example: Holyday Inn, Intercontinental, and Crown Plaza have merged to form Six continents hotels Chain; Marriot absorbed Renaissance and Ramada International; Sol Melia opened a new line of Boutique hotels, Accor signed several joint ventures in the East and the Far East, etc.) Forte acquired Meridian to reinforce its global position. Starwoods (Sheraton) absorbed the

Italian chain and Westin. The main expansion zones for the hotel industry in 1994 remained Asia (particularly China and India), the Middle East (above all, the United Arab Emirates and Egypt) and Latin America.

In Europe, hotel enterprises in the eastern countries (Russia, Croatia, Slovakia, etc.) decided to renovate dilapidated palaces built at the turn of the century. All the European capitals started to invest in preparations for the major event of this fin de siecle period, that is, the celebration of our entry into the third millennium.

The 3 star hotel Millennium enjoying top level of On-line Room Management System is situated at the best site in Opatija at the Mediterranean coast. Opatija in Croatia corresponds, in terms of reputation, to the level of St. Moritz in Switzerland.

Capitals throughout the world were busy developing the necessary infrastructure to welcome the millions of tourists for the celebration of this event.

Major hotel chains are drawing up development plans in almost all parts of Europe. These plans primarily involve the renovation of numerous prestigious hotels in both western and eastern European countries. Gradually, the great capitals of Europe have been endowed with hotels boasting three, four and five stars, offering quality services, innovative architecture, style, charm, and interior design (city Boutique hotels). Specialised hotels offer wellness programs including health and beauty centres, personalised services and treatments, anti-stress, revitalising, regenerating programs, etc.

Extravaganza-In 1995 construction began in Dubai of one of the most ambitious and prestigious tourist complexes in the region, the Jumeirah Beach Hotels (Jumeirah Beach hotel, Burj Al Arab, etc.). These comprise several establishments capable of satisfying the needs of average tourists, business people and those who can afford real luxury. The talk now is of six-and seven-star hotels, a surprising designation which is nevertheless perfectly justified by the luxury of the bedrooms and the facilities they offer, the impeccable service, the high degree of modern technology, as well as the beauty of the surroundings and the high-quality environment.

In 2004, another Emirate, Abu Dhabi, will welcome the delegates of the Gulf Council Countries. in the new Conference Palace Hotel (CPH). This superior construction has been specified "to offer the most outstanding services with a challenging 9 star definition"... We will, of course, report on it on a later stage.

On-line in seconds, work surf, communicate-everywhere-Today in 2003, travellers, mostly businessmen, carry their personal PC to make presentations, communicate with their office, via e-mails, etc. One possibility offered to them today consists in the use of so-called Pad offering, in particular,

- Cable-free and universal access to Internet or intranet, wherever you happen to be
- Brilliant colour touch screen
- Ready to go in seconds (instant on)
- Freedom in the selection of transmission standards by interchangeable PC cards
- Unlimited flexibility by open platform Windows CE 3.0
- Comprehensive office software package
- Virtual keyboard and handwriting recognition

For sure, new technologies are continuously offering innovative and more comfortable ways to the traveller.

The 160 rooms 5 star Palafitte Hotel in Monruz Neuchatel(CH) offers the visitors of the Swiss Expo 2002 a vision of sò called in-room available technologies.

Hotel Management

Seeing to every aspect of operations and functions of the hotel is hotel management. This is spearheaded by the General Manager of the hotel with his able and efficient team of departmental heads. The General Manager is responsible to direct, guide and motivate staff in the day to day operations and will oversee the general operations and diligently monitor all operating costs of the hotel. The Hotel Management is dedicated to improve the performance through cost-effective operations.

Team work is an important element in hotel management, as one department cannot function without the support and help of the other departments of the hotel. They constantly plan out new ways and methods to improve the standards and guest experiences. The hotels periodically plan out special promotions and events to allure more guests to the hotel. Hotel management is a strenuous task. From the outset it may be an exciting, people oriented career, but with the hotel industry growing with each passing day, and hotels competing with each other, the demands made by guests, their thinking and value for money expectation increases. Thus, the management has to be prepared to meet this ever increasing demand to sustain and maintain a steady income. "One Room vacant per day is revenue lost forever". As such the managers are on their toes, round the clock to see that the guest is satisfied. Their prime objective is to build a reputation by exceeding the expectations of the guest and the proprietor of the hotel, whereby not only guest satisfaction is achieved but also succeeding in obtaining investment returns to the owner.

Each departmental head is expected to guide their respective staff, for the smooth functioning of the hotel. Co-ordination and cooperation with each other is an important element. Where guest satisfaction and experiences are the key factors, each department sees to the need of the guest with utmost care. No two days will be the same in a hotel.

As such the management has to come up with ideas to see that the guest is happy and content. Some hotels have theme nights, whereby, the guests are given a different kind of experience and food. The management, who works round the clock, are dedicated and committed to ensure that new ideas and methods are brought forward. On a daily basis, the management meets to discuss how best the hotel should function, and to rectify and find solutions to any issue that they have come up with, seeing to guest needs, staff issues, day to day operations of the hotel, costing and budgeting and special events.

To achieve this comprehensive task, motivation and recognition is required. Hospitality is one industry where employees are recognized for their contribution and service. The management records and maintains the achievements of the staff, and they are duly rewarded as individuals and teams. Motivating and keeping the morale of the staff high is very important. As such the management works in a very friendly and cordial manner with the staff, and gives a hand whenever the need arises. There is open dialog all the time between the management and the staff, whereby the staff is able to approach their respective managers without any hesitation. Management continually encourages the staff to work as a team, and hospitality is one industry where 'team work' plays an important role in the functioning of an organization.

Though being a 24-7 job, and the hard work done behind the scene rarely noticed, the success of the Hotel speaks volumes and is all due to the dedicated and committed and effective management.

Hotel Industry in India

Hotel Industry in India has witnessed tremendous boom in recent years. Hotel Industry is inextricably linked to the tourism industry and the growth in the Indian tourism industry has fuelled the growth of Indian hotel industry. The thriving economy and increased business opportunities in India have acted as a boon for Indian hotel industry. The arrival of low cost airlines and the associated price wars have given domestic tourists a host of options. The 'Incredible India' destination campaign and the recently launched 'Atithi Devo Bhavah' (ADB) campaign have also helped in the growth of domestic and international tourism and consequently the hotel industry.

In recent years government has taken several steps to boost travel & tourism which have benefited hotel industry in India. These include the abolishment of the inland air travel tax of 15%; reduction in excise duty on aviation turbine fuel to 8%; and removal of a number of restrictions on outbound chartered flights, including those relating to frequency and size of aircraft. The government's recent decision to treat convention centres as part of core infrastructure, allowing the government to provide critical funding for the large capital investment that may be required has also fuelled the demand for hotel rooms.

The opening up of the aviation industry in India has exciting opportunities for hotel industry as it relies on airlines to transport 80% of international arrivals. The government's decision to substantially upgrade 28 regional airports in smaller towns and privatization & expansion of Delhi and Mumbai airport will improve the business prospects of hotel industry in India.

Substantial investments in tourism infrastructure are essential for Indian hotel industry to achieve its potential. The upgrading of national highways connecting various parts of India has opened new avenues for the development of budget hotels in India. Taking advantage of this opportunity Tata group and another hotel chain called 'Homotel' have entered this business segment.

According to a report, Hotel Industry in India currently has supply of 110,000 rooms and there is a shortage of 150,000 rooms fueling hotel room rates across India. According to estimates demand is going to exceed supply by at least 100% over the next 2 years. Five-star hotels in metro cities allot same room, more than once a day to different guests, receiving almost 24-hour rates from both guests against 6-8 hours usage. With demand-supply disparity, hotel rates in India are likely to rise by 25% annually and occupancy by 80%, over the next two years. This will affect the competitiveness of India as a cost-effective tourist destination.

To overcome, this shortage Indian hotel industry is adding about 60,000 quality rooms, currently in different stages of planning and development, which should be ready by 2012. Hotel Industry in India is also set to get a fillip with Delhi hosting 2010 Commonwealth Games. Government has approved 300 hotel projects, nearly half of which are in the luxury range. The future scenario of Indian hotel industry looks extremely rosy. It is expected that the budget and mid-market hotel segment will witness huge growth and expansion while the luxury segment will continue to perform extremely well over the next few years.

Hotel Management Tips for General Managers

Your education and experience provided you with a structured picture of what the business end of your hotel requires, and you continue to enrich yourself through additional training, seminars and workshops. Employee needs are much more basic, and while your first idea may be to give your employees raises and benefits to make them happy, employees expect only respect, honesty, recognition, job enrichment, and feedback to feel fulfilled. Employee morale is emotion based. Here are some management tips to help you as general manager.

Hotel Management Tips for General Managers 1

Get out of your office. Employees need to feel connected to their managers, and it is difficult to create this connection and trust with someone who is always behind closed doors. It is important to be visible!

Hotel Management Tips for General Managers 2

What are you good at? Focusing on your strengths will make your job fulfilling and give you the recognition you deserve. Putting a primary focus on your weakness will only take the pleasure out of your job. No one looks forward to doing things they aren't great at.

Hotel Management Tips for General Managers 3

Don't wait. Don't put off important discussions, meetings, or the elimination of employees. The longer you wait, the more difficult it becomes to face the challenges that you've been putting off.

Hotel Management Tips for General Managers 4

The right qualities make the right hires. Do not hire employees who do not suit the job you are hiring for. It becomes a waste of your time and theirs and can jeopardize the morale of others.

Hotel Management Tips for General Managers 5

Problems are opportunities! Every obstacle you face can lead to amazing breakthroughs, so never see issues as a problem. Looking for the opportunity to learn and grow from it.

Hotel Management Tips for General Managers 6

When employees feel challenged to produce, you will get the best results. Create fun competition to encourage your employees to excel better than where your numbers currently are.

Hotel Management Tips for General Managers 7

Quality service is what customers expect, so caring for your employees will ensure that your customers are well taken care of. Happy employees provide quality in their work.

Hotel Management Tips for General Managers 8

Don't gloat about your success. As a General Manager, it is important to know that your success comes directly from the success of your employees and the way they handle the customers. Praise your employees when you're doing exceptionally well and it will show that you appreciate working with them.

Hotel Management Tips for General Managers 9

Mistakes shouldn't just be cleaned up. The proper management of your hotel should include eliminating as many mistakes as possible to ensure that your hotel is running to the best of its ability.

Hotel Management Tips for General Managers 10

Listening and communication is key! As General Manager, it is important to listen and communicate effectively with employees, associates and customers in order to foresee any challenges and find solutions.

Hotel Management Tips for General Managers 11

How are you caring for your employees? Listen to your employees needs, give them feedback on what they can do to improve their production, and provide them with training to help them grow.

Hotel Management Tips for General Managers 12

Attention to the details creates success. As General Manager, it is important to pay attention to the details that go into the daily maintenance of the hotel environment. When you pay attention to details, you can catch any obstacles as they occur.

Hotel Management Tips for General Managers 13

"Reprimand in private, praise in public." Employees want respect most of all, and calling out your employees mistakes in front of their co-workers belittles them and takes down their respect.

2

Markets and Services

Concepts of Service Quality Measurement in Hotel Industry

The domination of the service sector today is confirmed by the fact that 70% of the world GDP is realized in the service sector. The same sector sees the concentration of 70% of workforce.

In order to ensure and keep the quality expected by today's customer/tourist, we need to differentiate two aspects of quality in general with particular attention to tourism, namely: design quality and the quality of conformity with design. The design quality is a concept implying the presentation of products/services directed to the needs of the clients. The hotel company can satisfy the demands of the client (tourist) only if they are included in its design, i.e. in order to do that, his demands need to be included or "built into" the product/service of the hotel. The hotels do market research in order to determine who their customers are and which of their demands require special attention.

The quality of conformity with the design completes the first aspect because it represents the level to which the product/service meets the demands of the market. The quality represents the satisfaction of the client's needs and in order to achieve it and keep it in time, we not only need a continuous research into the demands of the clients but also of our own capabilities. Such an approach would ensure the pursuing of constant improvements according to the demands of the clients.

The harsh competition on tourist market requires the development of a new approach to management known as TQM–Total Quality Management. When introducing the quality management system, hotel companies use various approaches adapted to their business conditions. The following part of the paper describes the most common service quality measurement criteria, in particular the model of internal service quality and the Servqual model.

Review of the Literature

Service quality is a way to manage business processes in order to ensure total satisfaction to the customer on all levels (internal and external). It is an approach that leads to an increase of competitiveness, effectiveness and flexibility of the entire company.

Benefits arising from a high quality are reflected in a more competitive positioning on the market, but also in a better business result. This statement can be proved by measuring the increase of profitability and market share. The results of a research carried out in the USA on a sample of 2600 companies in the period between 1987 and 2002, show a direct connection between the level of quality of goods and services and their financial performances. As a matter of fact, it was observed that all indicators of success of a company, like market share, return on investments, property turnover coefficient, show significantly more value in companies with a higher level of goods and services.

The efficiency of the whole system is possible only if we monitor and analyse the demands of the customers, as well as define and control the process and implement constant improvements.Quality is a complex term, made up of several elements and criteria.

All quality elements or criteria are equally important in order to obtain one hundred percent quality. If only one element of quality is missing, the complete quality of product or service is impossible to obtain.

Besides the mentioned general elements of quality, the product or service have to satisfy specific elements of quality, according to the demands of the profession in their pertaining activity. Today quality is the result of growing and increasingly diverse needs of the consumers, along with a highly increasing competition, market globalization and the development of modern technology. Problems in service quality measurement arise from a lack of clear and measurable parameters for the determination of quality. It is not the case with product quality since products have specific and measurable indicators like durability, number of defective products and similar, which make it relatively easy to determine the level of quality.

The most important characteristics of services, separating them neatly from products, are the impossibility to separate production from consumption; the impossibility to store services; their non material quality; transience and heterogeneity.

The impossibility to separate production from consumption and the impossibility to store services implicitly includes a simultaneous production and consumption, which is characteristic for most services. Since the services are performances, ideas or concepts rather than objects, they cannot be seen in the same way as products and are, therefore, characterized by their being immaterial. Furthermore, it is impossible to preserve services, which raises the issue of harmonizing offer and demand for services. The same service can be provided by different persons in an institution, and each of them might provide it in their own way so that heterogeneity also counts among characteristics of services that differentiate them from products.

The quality system is based on principles such as commitment of the management, focus on the customers, employees and facts, constant improvement and co-operation of all the participants to the process.

Research carried out in 101 companies in the service provision field (Zemke, Schaff, 1989) show the following results:

- Managers are "obsessed" with listening to the changeable wishes, needs and expectations of their customers, and the wish to respond to them.
- A solidly defined strategy of servicing "inspired by consumers" is created by managers in their companies, and transferred to the staff.
- Managers develop and maintain a *customer-friendly* system of providing services.
- Managers look for, and then inspire and develop staff that is in direct contact with consumers.

Two basic approaches to service quality have been identified in the early nineties of the twentieth century. The first approach is "technical" and product oriented, while the second approach is customer related. These two approaches have been recognized as results of managerial efforts to consider the aspect of quality when providing services from two angles: on one hand, the manager tends to abide by the set standards, while on the other, he wishes to satisfy the customer. The first approach is production oriented and tends to the consistency of service by impeding or minimizing the influence of the personnel directly involved in providing a service.

The service providing process is defined as a standard performance. The role of the staff providing services is reduced to the realization of the defined performance and the staff's discretion, i.e. its influence on the performance itself is minimized. In that way we can achieve maximum efficiency. Such a "product based" approach to the process of service provision is the result of the managerial view on this process as a series of elements that require a trained coordination and control, while the service itself is strictly standardized. The "product based" approach is contradictory to the aspirations of the consumers to be treated as individual people with marked personal tendencies and expectations. Besides, such an approach, "industrial" and cliche, is in contrast with the wish of the consumer to find warm and friendly manners when *consuming* the service. The second approach is consumer oriented. Expectations are the basis for satisfaction. After consuming the service, they compare their earlier expectations with experience. Results can range from satisfaction to dissatisfaction. The consumer anticipates the service standards in his expectations. Wilkie claims: "The seed of the consumer's dissatisfaction is sown in the pre-purchase stage, before reaching the decision to purchase." According to this, the consumer creates his own, individual *benchmark*, and the rating of his satisfaction is the result of his after purchase state.

Normann, the creator of the concept "moment of truth", points out that the first generation of researchers in the field of service sector management, had the task to determine the specificities of the services as opposed to other sectors, which paved the way for the second generation of researchers who focused on the relations in the service industry, the behaviour when providing service and service design, with the aim to optimize the "moment of truth". On the basis of the above exposed thesis, the understanding of service quality is based on the *paradigm of service.* In that sense, the service sector company manager looks for a "balance between the human factor and technology, between expenses and profit and, after all, between quality and productivity" (Gummesson, 1993).

The organization has to strive for success. When the set goals are achieved, we set other goals, striving for higher levels of product, processes and service efficiency. Accepting the concept of constant improvement means changing the management style. A total quality cannot be a program of changes with a set duration, it is a continuous, constant process. The questions set before the organization are the following: How do you keep up the constant striving for new improvement? What kind of measures and revisions of the business process do you have to use? How do you convince the employees that the business success and survival of the organizations can only occur if all employees accept constant actions to improve all their activities in the organizations? A successful organization constantly identifies and tackles the causes of problems or potential problems that employees have in doing their jobs. For that reason every employee has to be trained to identify such problems. The management and the employees must work together on implementing suitable corrective and preventive measures.

Each business process is subject to variability. Process variability is considered a normal phenomenon that is usually counted on. Parameter variability in the field of transformation of incoming values into outcoming values of the process affects the variability of the entire business process. For example, a lack of a specific product on the supplies market may require a substitution with another product of similar characteristics. Departure from the usual process (*variability*) can affect the quality of meals as results of a process, the timing of a process cycle, expenses of process quality, the level of satisfaction of the consumer/user with the process result.

Each episode of variability and a departure from the optimal process does not necessarily have a negative impact on the quality level of the process results. However, if the process is moving away from its optimal course so much as to get close to the acceptable limit or it has surpassed the limit, cost incur due to poor quality. The process becomes too expensive, jeopardizing the quality of the results and thus seriously risking dissatisfaction on the part of the client/consumer, in other words, it becomes irrational.

Service Quality Measurement in Hotel Industry

In order to achieve rationality the models of business excellence also, in a way, determine whether the criteria have been met, but the evaluation of business excellence is based not only on the fulfilment of the set criteria but also on the determination of the level up to which the criteria have been fulfilled (systems of points).

When analyzing the quality of service it is desirable to analyse the largest possible number of companies supplying the same type of service. As we already mentioned, if a company carries out a research and finds that the results are negative, it can interpret this information in the wrong way and conclude that it provides services in a totally wrong way. On the other hand, when analyzing a large number of companies, it is possible to compare data and obtain a realistic picture of the position of an individual company compared to others regarding quality.

The upper part of the model includes phenomena tied to the consumer, while the lower part shows phenomena tied to the supplier of services. The expected service is the function of earlier experiences of the consumer, their personal needs and oral communication. Communication with the market also influences the expected service. Experienced service, here called perceived service, is the result of a series of internal decisions and activities. The management's perceptions of the consumer's expectations is the guiding principle when deciding on the specifications of the quality of service that the company should follow in providing service. If there are differences or discrepancies in the expectations or perceptions between people involved in providing and consuming services, a "service quality gap" can occur, as shown in image 1. Since there is a direct connection between the quality of service and the satisfaction of clients in hotel industry, it is important for the company to spot a gap in the quality of service.

The first possible gap is the knowledge gap. It is the result of the differences in managing knowledge and their real expectations. This gap can lead to other gaps in the process of service quality and is, among other things, caused by:

- incorrect information in market researches and demand analysis;
- incorrect interpretations of information regarding expectations;
- lack of information about any feedback between the company and the consumers directed to the management;
- too many organizational layers that hinder or modify parts of information in their upward movement from those involved in contact with the consumers.

The second possible gap is that of standard. It is the result of differences in managing knowledge of the client's expectations and the process of service provision (delivery).

This gap is the result of:

- mistakes in planning or insufficient planning procedures;
- bad management planning;
- lack of clearly set goals in the organization; and
- insufficient support of the top management to service quality planning.

The management can be right in evaluating the client's expectations and develop business methods to satisfy these expectations, without the employees being correct in providing service. For example, a restaurant can order the waiters to serve the customers in two minutes after they sit at the table. Nevertheless, the waiters can ignore that specification and talk between them on the side.

The fourth possible gap is the communication gap arising when there is a difference between the delivered service and the service that the company promised to the clients via external communications.

The reasons are:

- the planning of communication with the market is not integrated with the services;
- lack or insufficient coordination between traditional marketing and procedures;
- organizational performance not in keeping with the specifications, while the policy of communication with the market abides by the given specifications; and

- tendency to exaggerate in accordance with exaggerated promises.

Should any of the mentioned gaps arise, the "service gap" will also appear because the real service will not satisfy the client's expectations. Hotel companies try to detect the "service gap" with survey questionnaires. Gap analysis is the file conducteur for the management to find the causes of problems regarding quality and to find suitable ways to remove such gaps. For this reason the first four gaps are also called organizational or internal gaps.

Although there are several models (scales) for the measurement of service quality and the satisfaction of customers, they are often too generalized or ad hoc, and as such hard to apply in the hotel industry. As opposed to TQM, which began before all in companies that dealt with products, due to the specificities of services (the basic are: impalpability, inseparability from provider

and receiver of service, impossibility of storage), a specific concept called Servqual (SERVices QUALity Model) was created. 8 The Servqual model offers a suitable conceptual frame for the research and service quality measurement in the service sector. The model has been developed, tested and adapted during various researches in cooperation with the Marketing Science Institute from Texas and numerous companies operating in the service sector. The model is based on the definition of quality as a comparison of the expected and the obtained as well as a consideration of gaps in the process of service provision. Servqual is based on the client's evaluation of service quality. The described concept is based on the gap between expectations and perception of the clients. Service quality represents a multidimensional construction.

The choice of the most important characteristics was an issue dealt with in various ways. One of these is a logical attempt to work out a list of desirable attributes from the basic needs of the clients. A variant of a scale containing desirable characteristics of services, known as Servqual scale, is currently quite popular in literature. It was developed in marketing circles with the aim to measure service quality (Bakoviæ, Lazibat). In the original Servqual instrument, Parasuraman et al. (1985) define service quality through ten dimensions which they sum up in five in 1988:

1) Reliability,

2) Assurance,
3) Tangibles,
4) Empathy,
5) Responsiveness.

Each of the listed dimensions has different features. Just like dimensions have different influence on the final service quality, so do these features have different influence on the grading of success of a single dimension. Despite its popularity and wide application, Servqual is exposed to numerous criticisms, from both the conceptual and the operational aspect.

Theoretical Criticism

- pattern objections: Servqual is based rather on an affirmation pattern than on the pattern of understanding; it does not manage to tie in with proved economical, statistical and psychological theories.
- Gap model: there is little evidence that the consumer evaluates service quality in the sense of perception – expectation gaps.
- Direction to the process: Servqual is directed to the process of service delivery and not to the result of service experience.
- Dimensionality: the five dimensions of Servqual are not universal; the number of dimensions that encompass service quality is connected to the context; there is a high degree of inter-correlation between RATER dimensions. RATER is a mnemonic acronym where R = reliability, A = assurance, T = tangibles, E = empathy and R = responsiveness. Operative criticism:
- Expectations: the term of expectations has multiple meanings; in evaluating services consumers use standards instead of expectations; Servqual cannot measure the absolute expectations of service quality.
- Content of the elements: four out of five elements cannot encompass the variability inside each dimension of service quality.
- Moment of truth: the consumer's rating of the service can vary from one to the next moment of truth.

- Polarity: the reverse polarity of the scale elements causes wrong reactions.
- Scale grading: Likert's scale with 7 ratings is inadequate.
- Dual administration: dual administration of instruments causes boredom and confusion.

The most important criticism of Servqual was the usage of gap analysis results (difference between expectations and perception of the received service) in measuring service quality.

Comparing the expectation-perception gaps with perception only, called Servperf, Cronin and Taylor concluded that measurement of service quality based only on perception was enough.

Servqual Model in Croatian Hotel Industry

The Faculty for Tourist and Hospitality Management in Opatija constructed an empirical model for the measurement of service quality in hotel industry on the model of hospitality on the Opatijska Riviera. Its use shall be simple and effective in hotel practice.

The aims of the research were:

a) Evaluate expectations and perceptions of hotel guests on the studied sample,

b) Evaluate and calculate the Servqual gap,

c) Test the reliability of the Servqual model in hotel industry,

d) Determine the dimensions of service quality in hotel industry by applying the method of factor analysis.

From a practical point of view, the research intended to test the adapted Servqual model for the measurement of service quality of hotel guests (Markoviæ: 2005).

It represents the difference between the average ratings of perceptions and the average expectations ratings. The wider the gap, the greater the difference between expectations and perception.

The results of the quantitative application of the Servqual model in Croatian hotel industry show that the expectations of hotel guests are higher than their perception. This proves the existence of a negative Servqual gap. It is visible that tourists from Great Britain have the highest total expectations, followed by guests from Australia and USA, while the Japanese tourists have the least expectations. Compared to clients in other services, "reliability" and an "impeccable" service is important to all hotel guests, regardless of their country of origin. Hotel guests prioritize this dimension, and so should hotel managers and personnel.

Dimensions of Countries

The need for the application of Servqual model in hotel industry is confirmed by the fact that, in the observed sample, hotel managers do not know the expectations of their guests because the dimensions of service quality they consider most important, do not match those that are most important for the clients, which is confirmed by the total Servqual gap.

Conclusion

Servqual can be widely applied, not only in science but also in practice in various services. The aim of the scientists is to work out and test useful instruments for managers in order to help them determine those organizational variables (policy, staff, structure, technology, processes) that will guarantee the best service quality with minimal costs. This methodology can assist hotel managers in assessing the position of the hotel regarding its competition and strategic and operative decision-making.

In hotel industry, service quality, as an extremely subjective category, is crucial to the satisfaction of the client. It is therefore imperative for managers in hotel industry to apply the Servqual model for the measurement of service quality in their own hotel company, in order to satisfy the guest's expectations and ensure a position on the growing global tourist market.

The results of the quantitative application of Servqual instrument show that this model can provide managers with useful information for the assessment of expectations and perception of hotel guests, with the aim of learning about gaps in individual service quality dimensions. To sum up, this article tend to clarify the Servqual model as not only provider to the managers with a clear picture of the quality of the provided service, but also helping in discovering the needs, wishes and expectations of the guests. The same is analyzed by determining thecharacteristics of service quality that are most important for guests. We can say that it helps managers in setting the standards for the provision of services in the hospitality industry.

Marketing Strategies in Hotel Industry

Strategic or institutional management is the conduct of drafting, implementing and evaluating cross-functional decisions that will enable an organization to achieve its long-term objectives. It is the process of specifying the organization's mission, vision and objectives, developing policies and plans, often in terms of projects and programs, which are designed to achieve these objectives, and then allocating resources to implement the policies and plans, projects and programs. A balanced scorecard is often used to evaluate the overall performance of the business and its progress towards objectives.

Strategic management is a level of managerial activity under setting goals and over Tactics. Strategic management provides overall direction to the enterprise and is closely related to the field of Organization Studies. In the field of business administration it is useful to talk about "strategic alignment" between the organization and its environment or "strategic consistency". According to Arieu (2007), "there is strategic consistency when the actions of an organization are consistent with the expectations of management, and these in turn are with the market and the context."

"Strategic management is an ongoing process that evaluates and controls the business and the industries in which the company is involved; assesses its competitors and sets goals and strategies to meet all existing and potential competitors; and then reassesses each strategy annually or quarterly [i.e. regularly] to determine how it has been implemented and whether it has succeeded or needs replacement by a new strategy to meet changed circumstances, new technology, new competitors, a new economic environment., or a new social, financial, or political environment."

Strategy Formulation

Strategic formulation is a combination of three main processes which are as follows:

- Performing a situation analysis, self-evaluation and competitor analysis: both internal and external; both micro-environmental and macro-environmental.
- Concurrent with this assessment, objectives are set. These objectives should be parallel to a time-line; some are in the short-term and others on the long-term. This involves crafting vision statements (long term view of a possible

future), mission statements (the role that the organization gives itself in society), overall corporate objectives (both financial and strategic), strategic business unit objectives (both financial and strategic), and tactical objectives.

- These objectives should, in the light of the situation analysis, suggest a strategic plan. The plan provides the details of how to achieve these objectives.

Marketing Action Plan

- Placement and execution of required resources are financial, manpower, operational support, time, technology support
- Operating with a change in methods or with alteration in structure
- Distributing the specific tasks with responsibility or moulding specific jobs to individuals or teams.
- The process should be managed by a responsible team. This is to keep direct watch on result, comparison for betterment and best practices, cultivating the effectiveness of processes, calibrating and reducing the variations and setting the process as required.
- Introducing certain programs involves acquiring the requisition of resources: a necessity for developing the process, training documentation, process testing, and imalgation with (and/or conversion from) difficult processes.

As and when the strategy implementation processes, there have been so many problems arising such as human relations, the employee-communication. Such a time, marketing strategy is the biggest implementation problem usually involves, with emphasis on the appropriate timing of new products. An organization, with an effective management, should try to implement its plans without signaling this fact to its competitors. In order for a policy to work, there must be a level of consistency from every person in an organization, specially management. This is what needs to occur on both the tactical and strategic levels of management.

Strategy Evaluation

- Measuring the effectiveness of the organizational strategy, it's extremely important to conduct a SWOT analysis to figure out the strengths, weaknesses, opportunities and threats (both internal and external) of the entity in question. This may require to take certain precautionary measures or even to change the entire strategy.

In corporate strategy, Johnson and Scholes present a model in which strategic options are evaluated against three key success criteria:

- Suitability (would it work?)
- Feasibility (can it be made to work?)
- Acceptability (will they work it?).

Suitability

Suitability deals with the overall rationale of the strategy. The key point to consider is whether the strategy would address the key strategic issues underlined by the organisation's strategic position.

- Does it make economic sense?
- Would the organization obtain economies of scale, economies of scope or experience economy?
- Would it be suitable in terms of environment and capabilities?

Tools that can be used to evaluate suitability include:

- Ranking strategic options
- Decision trees.

Feasibility

Feasibility is concerned with whether the resources required to implement the strategy are available, can be developed or obtained. Resources include funding, people, time and information.

Tools that can be used to evaluate feasibility include:

- cash flow analysis and forecasting
- break-even analysis
- resource deployment analysis.

Acceptability

Acceptability is concerned with the expectations of the identified stakeholders (mainly shareholders, employees and customers) with the expected performance outcomes, which can be return, risk and stakeholder reactions.

- Return deals with the benefits expected by the stakeholders (financial and non-financial). For example, shareholders would expect the increase of their wealth, employees would expect improvement in their careers and customers would expect better value for money.
- Risk deals with the probability and consequences of failure of a strategy (financial and non-financial).
- Stakeholder reactions deals with anticipating the likely reaction of stakeholders. Shareholders could oppose the issuing of new shares, employees and unions could oppose outsourcing for fear of losing their jobs, customers could have concerns over a merger with regards to quality and support.

Tools that can be used to evaluate acceptability include:

- what-if analysis
- stakeholder mapping.

General Approaches

In general terms, there are two main approaches, which are opposite but complement each other in some ways, to strategic management:

- The Industrial Organizational Approach:
    - o based on economic theory — deals with issues like competitive rivalry, resource allocation, economies of scale
    - o assumptions — rationality, self discipline behaviour, profit maximization.
- The Sociological Approach:
    - o deals primarily with human interactions
    - o assumptions — bounded rationality, satisfying behaviour, profit sub-optimality. An example of a company that currently operates this way is Google.

Strategic management techniques can be viewed as bottom-up, top-down, or collaborative processes. In the bottom-up approach, employees submit proposals to their managers who, in turn, funnel the best ideas further up the organization. This is often accomplished by a capital budgeting process. Proposals are assessed using financial criteria such as return on investment or cost-benefit analysis. Cost underestimation and benefit overestimation are major sources of error. The proposals that are approved form the substance of a new strategy, all of which is done without a grand strategic design or a strategic architect. The top-down approach is the most common by far. In it, the CEO, possibly with the assistance of a strategic planning team, decides on the overall direction the company should take. Some organizations are starting to experiment with collaborative strategic planning techniques that recognize the emergent nature of strategic decisions.

The Strategy Hierarchy

In most (large) corporations there are several levels of management. Strategic management is the highest of these levels in the sense that it is the broadest-applying to all parts of the firm-while also incorporating the longest time horizon. It gives direction to corporate values, corporate culture, corporate goals, and corporate missions. Under this broad corporate strategy there are typically business-level competitive strategies and functional unit strategies. Corporate strategy refers to the overarching strategy of the diversified firm. Such a corporate strategy answers the questions of "which businesses should we be in?" and "how does being in these businesses create synergy and/or add to the competitive advantage of the corporation as a whole?"

Business strategy refers to the aggregated strategies of single business firm or a strategic business unit (SBU) in a diversified corporation. According to Michael Porter, a firm must formulate a business strategy that incorporates either cost leadership, differentiation or focus in order to achieve a sustainable competitive advantage and long-term success in its chosen areas or industries. Alternatively, according to W. Chan Kim and Renée Mauborgne, an organization can achieve high growth and profits by creating a Blue Ocean Strategy that breaks the previous value-cost tradeoff by simultaneously pursuing both differentiation and low cost.

Functional strategies include marketing strategies, new product development strategies, human resource strategies, financial strategies, legal strategies, supply-chain strategies, and information technology management strategies. The emphasis is on short and medium term plans and is limited to the domain of each department's functional responsibility. Each functional department attempts to do its part in meeting overall corporate objectives, and hence to some extent their strategies are derived from broader corporate strategies.

Many companies feel that a functional organizational structure is not an efficient way to organize activities so they have reengineered according to processes or SBUs. A strategic business unit is a semi-autonomous unit that is usually responsible for its own budgeting, new product decisions, hiring decisions, and price setting. An SBU is treated as an internal profit centre by corporate headquarters. A technology strategy, for example, although it is focused on technology as a means of achieving an organization's overall objective(s), may include dimensions that are beyond the scope of a single business unit, engineering organization or IT department.

An additional level of strategy called operational strategy was encouraged by Peter Drucker in his theory of management by objectives (MBO). It is very narrow in focus and deals with day-to-day operational activities such as scheduling criteria. It must operate within a budget but is not at liberty to adjust or create that budget. Operational level strategies are informed by business level strategies which, in turn, are informed by corporate level strategies.

Since the turn of the millennium, some firms have reverted to a simpler strategic structure driven by advances in information technology. It is felt that knowledge management systems should be used to share information and create common goals. Strategic divisions are thought to hamper this process. This notion of strategy has been captured under the rubric of dynamic strategy, popularized by Carpenter and Sanders's textbook. This work builds on that of Brown and Eisenhart as well as Christensen and portrays firm strategy, both business and corporate, as necessarily embracing ongoing strategic change, and the seamless integration of strategy formulation and implementation. Such change and implementation are usually built into the strategy through the staging and pacing facets.

Historical Development of Strategic Management

Birth of Strategic Management

Strategic management as a discipline originated in the 1950s and 60s. Although there were numerous early contributors to the literature, the most influential pioneers were Alfred D. Chandler, Philip Selznick, Igor Ansoff, and Peter Drucker.

Alfred Chandler recognized the importance of coordinating the various aspects of management under one all-encompassing strategy. Prior to this time the various functions of management were separate with little overall coordination or strategy. Interactions between functions or between departments were typically handled by a boundary position, that is, there were one or two managers that relayed information back and forth between two departments. Chandler also stressed the importance of taking a long term perspective when looking to the future. In his 1962 groundbreaking work *Strategy and Structure*, Chandler showed that a long-term coordinated strategy was necessary to give a company structure, direction, and focus. He says it concisely, "structure follows strategy."

In 1957, Philip Selznick introduced the idea of matching the organization's internal factors with external environmental circumstances. This core idea was developed into what we now call SWOT analysis by Learned, Andrews, and others at the Harvard Business School General Management Group. Strengths and weaknesses of the firm are assessed in light of the opportunities and threats from the business environment.

Igor Ansoff built on Chandler's work by adding a range of strategic concepts and inventing a whole new vocabulary. He developed a strategy grid that compared market penetration strategies, product development strategies, market development strategies and horizontal and vertical integration and diversification strategies. He felt that management could use these strategies to systematically prepare for future opportunities and challenges. In his 1965 classic *Corporate Strategy*, he developed the gap analysis still used today in which we must understand the gap between where we are currently and where we would like to be, then develop what he called "gap reducing actions".

Peter Drucker was a prolific strategy theorist, author of dozens of management books, with a career spanning five decades. His contributions to strategic management were many but two are most important. Firstly, he stressed the importance of objectives. An organization without clear objectives is like a ship without a rudder. As early as 1954 he was developing a theory of management based on objectives. This evolved into his theory of management by objectives (MBO). According to Drucker, the procedure of setting objectives and monitoring your progress towards them should permeate the entire organization, top to bottom. His other seminal contribution was in predicting the importance of what today we would call intellectual capital. He predicted the rise of what he called the "knowledge worker" and explained the consequences of this for management. He said that knowledge work is non-hierarchical. Work would be carried out in teams with the person most knowledgeable in the task at hand being the temporary leader.

In 1985, Ellen-Earle Chaffee summarized what she thought were the main elements of strategic management theory by the 1970s:

- Strategic management involves adapting the organization to its business environment.
- Strategic management is fluid and complex. Change creates novel combinations of circumstances requiring unstructured non-repetitive responses.
- Strategic management affects the entire organization by providing direction.
- Strategic management involves both strategy formation (she called it content) and also strategy implementation (she called it process).
- Strategic management is partially planned and partially unplanned.
- Strategic management is done at several levels: overall corporate strategy, and individual business strategies.
- Strategic management involves both conceptual and analytical thought processes.

Growth and Portfolio Theory

In the 1970s much of strategic management dealt with size, growth, and portfolio theory. The PIMS study was a long term study, started in the 1960s and lasted for 19 years, that attempted to understand the Profit Impact of Marketing Strategies (PIMS), particularly the effect of market share. Started at General Electric, moved to Harvard in the early 1970s, and then moved to the Strategic Planning Institute in the late 1970s, it now contains decades of information on the relationship between profitability and strategy. Their initial conclusion was unambiguous: The greater a company's market share, the greater will be their rate of profit. The high market share provides volume and economies of scale. It also provides experience and learning curve advantages. The combined effect is increased profits. The studies conclusions continue to be drawn on by academics and companies today: "PIMS provides compelling quantitative evidence as to which business strategies work and don't work"-Tom Peters.

The benefits of high market share naturally lead to an interest in growth strategies. The relative advantages of horizontal integration, vertical integration, diversification, franchises, mergers and acquisitions, joint ventures, and organic growth were discussed. The most appropriate market dominance strategies were assessed given the competitive and regulatory environment.

There was also research that indicated that a low market share strategy could also be very profitable. Schumacher (1973), Woo and Cooper (1982), Levenson (1984), and later Traverso (2002) showed how smaller niche players obtained very high returns.

By the early 1980s the paradoxical conclusion was that high market share and low market share companies were often very profitable but most of the companies in between were not. This was sometimes called the "hole in the middle" problem. This anomaly would be explained by Michael Porter in the 1980s.

The management of diversified organizations required new techniques and new ways of thinking. The first CEO to address the problem of a multi-divisional company was Alfred Sloan at General Motors. GM was decentralized into semi-autonomous "strategic business units" (SBU's), but with centralized support functions.

One of the most valuable concepts in the strategic management of multi-divisional companies was portfolio theory. In the previous decade Harry Markowitz and other financial theorists developed the theory of portfolio analysis. It was concluded that a broad portfolio of financial assets could reduce specific risk. In the 1970s marketers extended the theory to product portfolio decisions and managerial strategists extended it to operating division portfolios. Each of a company's operating divisions were seen as an element in the corporate portfolio. Each operating division (also called strategic business units) was treated as a semi-independent profit centre with its own revenues, costs, objectives, and strategies. Several techniques were developed to analyse the relationships between elements in a portfolio. B.C.G. Analysis, for example, was developed by the Boston Consulting Group in the early 1970s. This was the theory that gave us the wonderful image of a CEO sitting on a stool milking a cash cow. Shortly after that the G.E. multi factoral model was developed by General Electric. Companies continued to diversify until the 1980s when it was realized that in many cases a portfolio of operating divisions was worth more as separate completely independent companies.

The Marketing Revolution

The 1970s also saw the rise of the marketing oriented firm. From the beginnings of capitalism it was assumed that the key requirement of business success was a product of high technical quality. If you produced a product that worked well and was durable, it was assumed you would have no difficulty selling them at a profit. This was called the production orientation and it was generally true that good products could be sold without effort, encapsulated in the saying "Build a better mousetrap and the world will beat a path to your door." This was largely due to the growing numbers of affluent and middle class people that capitalism had created. But after the untapped demand caused by the second world war was saturated in the 1950s it became obvious that products were not selling as easily as they had been. The answer was to concentrate on selling.

The 1950s and 1960s is known as the sales era and the guiding philosophy of business of the time is today called the sales orientation. In the early 1970s Theodore Levitt and others at Harvard argued that the sales orientation had things backward. They claimed that instead of producing products then trying to sell them to the customer, businesses should start with the customer, find out what they wanted, and then produce it for them. The customer became the driving force behind all strategic business decisions. This marketing orientation, in the decades since its introduction, has been reformulated and repackaged under numerous names including customer orientation, marketing philosophy, customer intimacy, customer focus, customer driven, and market focused.

The Japanese Challenge

By the late 70s, Americans had started to notice how successful Japanese industry had become. In industry after industry, including steel, watches, ship building, cameras, autos, and electronics, the Japanese were surpassing American and European companies. Westerners wanted to know why. Numerous theories purported to explain the Japanese success including:

- Higher employee morale, dedication, and loyalty;
- Lower cost structure, including wages;
- Effective government industrial policy;
- Modernization after WWII leading to high capital intensity and productivity;
- Economies of scale associated with increased exporting;
- Relatively low value of the Yen leading to low interest rates and capital costs, low dividend expectations, and inexpensive exports;
- Superior quality control techniques such as Total Quality Management and other systems introduced by W. Edwards Deming in the 1950s and 60s.

Although there was some truth to all these potential explanations, there was clearly something missing. In fact by 1980 the Japanese cost structure was higher than the American. And post WWII reconstruction was nearly 40 years in the past. The first management theorist to suggest an explanation was Richard Pascale.

In 1981, Richard Pascale and Anthony Athos in *The Art of Japanese Management* claimed that the main reason for Japanese success was their superior management techniques. They divided management into 7 aspects (which are also known as McKinsey 7S Framework): Strategy, Structure, Systems, Skills, Staff, Style, and Supraordinate goals (which we would now call shared values). The first three of the 7 S's were called hard factors and this is where American companies excelled. The remaining four factors (skills, staff, style, and shared values) were called soft factors and were not well understood by American businesses of the time. Americans did not yet place great value on corporate culture, shared values and beliefs, and social cohesion in the workplace. In Japan the task of management was seen as managing the whole complex of human needs, economic, social, psychological, and spiritual. In America work was seen as something that was separate from the rest of one's life. It was quite common for Americans to exhibit a very different personality at work compared to the rest of their lives. Pascale also highlighted the difference between decision making styles; hierarchical in America, and consensus in Japan. He also claimed that American business lacked long term vision, preferring instead to apply management fads and theories in a piecemeal fashion.

One year later, *The Mind of the Strategist* was released in America by Kenichi Ohmae, the head of McKinsey & Co.'s Tokyo office. (It was originally published in Japan in 1975.) He claimed that strategy in America was too analytical. Strategy should be a creative art: It is a frame of mind that requires intuition and intellectual flexibility. He claimed that Americans constrained their strategic options by thinking in terms of analytical techniques, rote formula, and step-by-step processes. He compared the culture of Japan in which vagueness, ambiguity, and tentative decisions were acceptable, to American culture that valued fast decisions.

Also in 1982, Tom Peters and Robert Waterman released a study that would respond to the Japanese challenge head on. Peters and Waterman, who had several years earlier collaborated with Pascale and Athos at McKinsey & Co. asked "What makes an excellent company?". They looked at 62 companies that they thought were fairly successful. Each was subject to six performance criteria. To be classified as an excellent company, it had to be above the 50th percentile in 4 of the 6 performance metrics for 20 consecutive years. Forty-three companies passed the test. They then studied these successful companies and interviewed key executives. They concluded in *In Search of Excellence* that there were 8 keys to excellence that were shared by all 43 firms. They are:

- A bias for action — Do it. Try it. Don't waste time studying it with multiple reports and committees.
- Customer focus — Get close to the customer. Know your customer.
- Entrepreneurship — Even big companies act and think small by giving people the authority to take initiatives.
- Productivity through people — Treat your people with

respect and they will reward you with productivity.

- Value-oriented CEOs—The CEO should actively propagate corporate values throughout the organization.
- Stick to the knitting—Do what you know well.
- Keep things simple and lean—Complexity encourages waste and confusion.
- Simultaneously centralized and decentralized—Have tight centralized control while also allowing maximum individual autonomy.

The basic blueprint on how to compete against the Japanese had been drawn. But as J.E. Rehfeld (1994) explains it is not a straight forward task due to differences in culture. A certain type of alchemy was required to transform knowledge from various cultures into a management style that allows a specific company to compete in a globally diverse world. He says, for example, that Japanese style kaizen (continuous improvement) techniques, although suitable for people socialized in Japanese culture, have not been successful when implemented in the U.S. unless they are modified significantly.

In 2009, industry consultants Mark Blaxill and Ralph Eckardt suggested that much of the Japanese business dominance that began in the mid 1970s was the direct result of competition enforcement efforts by the Federal Trade Commission (FTC) and U.S. Department of Justice (DOJ). In 1975 the FTC reached a settlement with Xerox Corporation in its anti-trust lawsuit. (At the time, the FTC was under the direction of Frederic M. Scherer). The 1975 Xerox consent decree forced the licensing of the company's entire patent portfolio, mainly to Japanese competitors. This action marked the start of an activist approach to managing competition by the FTC and DOJ, which resulted in the compulsory licensing of tens of thousands of patent from some of America's leading companies, including IBM, AT&T, DuPont, Bausch & Lomb, and Eastman Kodak.

Within four years of the consent decree, Xerox's share of the U.S. copier market dropped from nearly 100% to less than 14%. Between 1950 and 1980 Japanese companies consummated more than 35,000 foreign licensing agreements, mostly with U.S. companies, for free or low-cost licenses made possible by the FTC and DOJ. The post-1975 era of anti-trust initiatives by Washington

D.C. economists at the FTC corresponded directly with the rapid, unprecedented rise in Japanese competitiveness and a simultaneous stalling of the U.S. manufacturing economy.

Gaining Competitive Advantage

The Japanese challenge shook the confidence of the western business elite, but detailed comparisons of the two management styles and examinations of successful businesses convinced westerners that they could overcome the challenge. The 1980s and early 1990s saw a plethora of theories explaining exactly how this could be done. They cannot all be detailed here, but some of the more important strategic advances of the decade are explained below.

Gary Hamel and C. K. Prahalad declared that strategy needs to be more active and interactive; less "arm-chair planning" was needed. They introduced terms like strategic intent and strategic architecture. Their most well known advance was the idea of core competency. They showed how important it was to know the one or two key things that your company does better than the competition.

Active strategic management required active information gathering and active problem solving. In the early days of Hewlett-Packard (H-P), Dave Packard and Bill Hewlett devised an active management style that they called *management by walking around* (MBWA). Senior H-P managers were seldom at their desks. They spent most of their days visiting employees, customers, and suppliers. This direct contact with key people provided them with a solid grounding from which viable strategies could be crafted. The MBWA concept was popularized in 1985 by a book by Tom Peters and Nancy Austin. Japanese managers employ a similar system, which originated at Honda, and is sometimes called the 3 G's (Genba, Genbutsu, and Genjitsu, which translate into "actual place", "actual thing", and "actual situation").

Probably the most influential strategist of the decade was Michael Porter. He introduced many new concepts including; 5 forces analysis, generic strategies, the value chain, strategic groups, and clusters. In 5 forces analysis he identifies the forces that shape a firm's strategic environment. It is like a SWOT analysis with structure and purpose. It shows how a firm can use these forces to obtain a sustainable competitive advantage. Porter modifies

Chandler's dictum about structure following strategy by introducing a second level of structure: Organizational structure follows strategy, which in turn follows industry structure. Porter's generic strategies detail the interaction between cost minimization strategies, product differentiation strategies, and market focus strategies. Although he did not introduce these terms, he showed the importance of choosing one of them rather than trying to position your company between them. He also challenged managers to see their industry in terms of a value chain. A firm will be successful only to the extent that it contributes to the industry's value chain. This forced management to look at its operations from the customer's point of view. Every operation should be examined in terms of what value it adds in the eyes of the final customer.

In 1993, John Kay took the idea of the value chain to a financial level claiming " Adding value is the central purpose of business activity", where adding value is defined as the difference between the market value of outputs and the cost of inputs including capital, all divided by the firm's net output. Borrowing from Gary Hamel and Michael Porter, Kay claims that the role of strategic management is to identify your core competencies, and then assemble a collection of assets that will increase value added and provide a competitive advantage. He claims that there are 3 types of capabilities that can do this; innovation, reputation, and organizational structure.

The 1980s also saw the widespread acceptance of positioning theory. Although the theory originated with Jack Trout in 1969, it didn't gain wide acceptance until Al Ries and Jack Trout wrote their classic book "Positioning: The Battle For Your Mind" (1979). The basic premise is that a strategy should not be judged by internal company factors but by the way customers see it relative to the competition. Crafting and implementing a strategy involves creating a position in the mind of the collective consumer. Several techniques were applied to positioning theory, some newly invented but most borrowed from other disciplines. Perceptual mapping for example, creates visual displays of the relationships between positions. Multidimensional scaling, discriminant analysis, factor analysis, and conjoint analysis are mathematical techniques used to determine the most relevant characteristics (called dimensions or factors) upon which positions should be based.

Preference regression can be used to determine vectors of ideal positions and cluster analysis can identify clusters of positions.

Others felt that internal company resources were the key. In 1992, Jay Barney, for example, saw strategy as assembling the optimum mix of resources, including human, technology, and suppliers, and then configure them in unique and sustainable ways.

Michael Hammer and James Champy felt that these resources needed to be restructured. This process, that they labeled reengineering, involved organizing a firm's assets around whole processes rather than tasks. In this way a team of people saw a project through, from inception to completion. This avoided functional silos where isolated departments seldom talked to each other. It also eliminated waste due to functional overlap and interdepartmental communications.

In 1989 Richard Lester and the researchers at the MIT Industrial Performance Centre identified seven best practices and concluded that firms must accelerate the shift away from the mass production of low cost standardized products. The seven areas of best practice were:

- Simultaneous continuous improvement in cost, quality, service, and product innovation
- Breaking down organizational barriers between departments
- Eliminating layers of management creating flatter organizational hierarchies.
- Closer relationships with customers and suppliers
- Intelligent use of new technology
- Global focus
- Improving human resource skills.

The search for "best practices" is also called benchmarking. This involves determining where you need to improve, finding an organization that is exceptional in this area, then studying the company and applying its best practices in your firm.

A large group of theorists felt the area where western business was most lacking was product quality. People like W. Edwards Deming, Joseph M. Juran, A. Kearney, Philip Crosby, and Armand Feignbaum suggested quality improvement techniques like total quality management (TQM), continuous improvement (kaizen), lean manufacturing, Six Sigma, and return on quality (ROQ).

An equally large group of theorists felt that poor customer service was the problem. People like James Heskett (1988), Earl Sasser (1995), William Davidow, Len Schlesinger, A. Paraurgman (1988), Len Berry, Jane Kingman-Brundage, Christopher Hart, and Christopher Lovelock (1994), gave us fishbone diagramming, service charting, Total Customer Service (TCS), the service profit chain, service gaps analysis, the service encounter, strategic service vision, service mapping, and service teams. Their underlying assumption was that there is no better source of competitive advantage than a continuous stream of delighted customers.

Process management uses some of the techniques from product quality management and some of the techniques from customer service management. It looks at an activity as a sequential process. The objective is to find inefficiencies and make the process more effective. Although the procedures have a long history, dating back to Taylorism, the scope of their applicability has been greatly widened, leaving no aspect of the firm free from potential process improvements. Because of the broad applicability of process management techniques, they can be used as a basis for competitive advantage.

Some realized that businesses were spending much more on acquiring new customers than on retaining current ones. Carl Sewell, Frederick F. Reichheld, C. Gronroos, and Earl Sasser showed us how a competitive advantage could be found in ensuring that customers returned again and again.

This has come to be known as the loyalty effect after Reicheld's book of the same name in which he broadens the concept to include employee loyalty, supplier loyalty, distributor loyalty, and shareholder loyalty. They also developed techniques for estimating the lifetime value of a loyal customer, called customer lifetime value (CLV). A significant movement started that attempted to recast selling and marketing techniques into a long term endeavour that created a sustained relationship with customers (called relationship selling, relationship marketing, and customer relationship management). Customer relationship management (CRM) software (and its many variants) became an integral tool that sustained this trend.

James Gilmore and Joseph Pine found competitive advantage in mass customization. Flexible manufacturing techniques allowed businesses to individualize products for each customer without losing economies of scale. This effectively turned the product into a service. They also realized that if a service is mass customized by creating a "performance" for each individual client, that service would be transformed into an "experience". Their book, *The Experience Economy,* along with the work of Bernd Schmitt convinced many to see service provision as a form of theatre. This school of thought is sometimes referred to as customer experience management (CEM).

Like Peters and Waterman a decade earlier, James Collins and Jerry Porras spent years conducting empirical research on what makes great companies. Six years of research uncovered a key underlying principle behind the 19 successful companies that they studied: They all encourage and preserve a core ideology that nurtures the company. Even though strategy and tactics change daily, the companies, nevertheless, were able to maintain a core set of values. These core values encourage employees to build an organization that lasts. In *Built To Last* (1994) they claim that short term profit goals, cost cutting, and restructuring will not stimulate dedicated employees to build a great company that will endure. In 2000 Collins coined the term "built to flip" to describe the prevailing business attitudes in Silicon Valley. It describes a business culture where technological change inhibits a long term focus. He also popularized the concept of the BHAG (Big Hairy Audacious Goal).

Arie de Geus (1997) undertook a similar study and obtained similar results. He identified four key traits of companies that had prospered for 50 years or more. They are:

- Sensitivity to the business environment — the ability to learn and adjust
- Cohesion and identity — the ability to build a community with personality, vision, and purpose
- Tolerance and decentralization — the ability to build relationships
- Conservative financing.

A company with these key characteristics he called a living company because it is able to perpetuate itself. If a company emphasizes knowledge rather than finance, and sees itself as an ongoing community of human beings, it has the potential to become great and endure for decades. Such an organization is an organic entity capable of learning (he called it a "learning organization") and capable of creating its own processes, goals, and persona.

There are numerous ways by which a firm can try to create a competitive advantage-some will work but many will not. In order to help firms avoid a hit and miss approach to the creation of competitive advantage Will Mulcaster suggests that firms engage in a dialogue that centres around the question "Will the proposed competitive advantage create Perceived Differential Value?" The dialogue should raise a series of other pertinent questions, including:-

"Will the proposed competitive advantage create something that is different from the competition?"

"Will the difference add value in the eyes of potential customers?"-This question will entail a discussion of the combined effects of price, product features and consumer perceptions.

"Will the product add value for the firm?"-Answering this question will require an examination of cost effectiveness and the pricing strategy.

The Military Theorists

In the 1980s some business strategists realized that there was a vast knowledge base stretching back thousands of years that they had barely examined. They turned to military strategy for guidance. Military strategy books such as *The Art of War* by Sun Tzu, *On War* by von Clausewitz, and *The Red Book* by Mao Zedong became instant business classics. From Sun Tzu, they learned the tactical side of military strategy and specific tactical prescriptions. From Von Clausewitz, they learned the dynamic and unpredictable nature of military strategy. From Mao Zedong, they learned the principles of guerrilla warfare. The main marketing warfare books were:

- *Business War Games* by Barrie James, 1984
- *Marketing Warfare* by Al Rieš and Jack Trout, 1986
- Leadership Secrets of Attila the Hun by Wess Roberts, 1987

Philip Kotler was a well-known proponent of marketing warfare strategy.

There were generally thought to be four types of business warfare theories. They are:

- Offensive marketing warfare strategies
- Defensive marketing warfare strategies
- Flanking marketing warfare strategies
- Guerrilla marketing warfare strategies.

The marketing warfare literature also examined leadership and motivation, intelligence gathering, types of marketing weapons, logistics, and communications.

By the turn of the century marketing warfare strategies had gone out of favour. It was felt that they were limiting. There were many situations in which non-confrontational approaches were more appropriate. In 1989, Dudley Lynch and Paul L. Kordis published *Strategy of the Dolphin: Scoring a Win in a Chaotic World.* "The Strategy of the Dolphin" was developed to give guidance as to when to use aggressive strategies and when to use passive strategies. A varicty of aggressiveness stralegies were developed.

In 1993, J. Moore used a similar metaphor. Instead of using military terms, he created an ecological theory of predators and prey, a sort of Darwinian management strategy in which market interactions mimic long term ecological stability.

Strategic Change

In 1970, Alvin Toffler in *Future Shock* described a trend towards accelerating rates of changc. Hc illustrated how social and technological norms had shorter lifespans with each generation, and he questioned society's ability to cope with the resulting turmoil and anxiety. In past generations periods of change were always punctuated with times of stability. This allowed society to assimilate the change and deal with it before the next change arrived. But these periods of stability are getting shorter and by the late 20th century had all but disappeared. In 1980 in *The Third Wave,* Toffler characterized this shift to relentless change as the defining feature of the third phase of civilization (the first two phases being the agricultural and industrial waves). He claimed that the dawn of this new phase will cause great anxiety for those that grew up in the previous phases, and will cause much conflict and opportunity in the business world. Hundreds of authors, particularly since the early 1990s, have attempted to explain what this means for business strategy. In 1997, Watts Wacker and Jim Taylor called this upheaval a "500 year delta." They claimed these major upheavals occur every 5 centuries. They said we are currently making the transition from the "Age of Reason" to a new chaotic Age of Access. Jeremy Rifkin (2000) popularized and expanded this term, "age of access" three years later in his book of the same name.

In 1968, Peter Drucker (1969) coined the phrase Age of Discontinuity to describe the way change forces disruptions into the continuity of our lives. In an age of continuity attempts to predict the future by extrapolating from the past can be somewhat accurate. But according to Drucker, we are now in an age of discontinuity and extrapolating from the past is hopelessly ineffective. We cannot assume that trends that exist today will continue into the future. He identifies four sources of discontinuity: new technologies, globalization, cultural pluralism, and knowledge capital.

In 2000, Gary Hamel discussed strategic decay, the notion that the value of all strategies, no matter how brilliant, decays over time.

In 1978, Dereck Abell (Abell, D. 1978) described strategic windows and stressed the importance of the timing (both entrance and exit) of any given strategy. This has led some strategic planners to build planned obsolescence into their strategies.

In 1989, Charles Handy identified two types of change. Strategic drift is a gradual change that occurs so subtly that it is not noticed until it is too late. By contrast, transformational change is sudden and radical. It is typically caused by discontinuities (or exogenous shocks) in the business environment. The point where a new trend is initiated is called a strategic inflection point by Andy Grove. Inflection points can be subtle or radical.

In 2000, Malcolm Gladwell discussed the importance of the tipping point, that point where a trend or fad acquires critical mass and takes off.

In 1983, Noel Tichy wrote that because we are all beings of habit we tend to repeat what we are comfortable with. He wrote that this is a trap that constrains our creativity, prevents us from exploring new ideas, and hampers our dealing with the full complexity of new issues. He developed a systematic method of dealing with change that involved looking at any new issue from three angles: technical and production, political and resource allocation, and corporate culture.

In 1990, Richard Pascale (Pascale, R. 1990) wrote that relentless change requires that businesses continuously reinvent themselves. His famous maxim is "Nothing fails like success" by which he means that what was a strength yesterday becomes the root of weakness today, We tend to depend on what worked yesterday and refuse to let go of what worked so well for us in the past. Prevailing strategies become self-confirming. In order to avoid this trap, businesses must stimulate a spirit of inquiry and healthy debate. They must encourage a creative process of self renewal based on constructive conflict.

In 1996, Art Kleiner (1996) claimed that to foster a corporate culture that embraces change, you have to hire the right people; heretics, heroes, outlaws, and visionaries. The conservative bureaucrat that made such a good middle manager in yesterday's hierarchical organizations is of little use today. A decade earlier Peters and Austin (1985) had stressed the importance of nurturing champions and heroes. They said we have a tendency to dismiss new ideas, so to overcome this, we should support those few people in the organization that have the courage to put their career and reputation on the line for an unproven idea.

In 1996, Adrian Slywotzky showed how changes in the business environment are reflected in value migrations between industries, between companies, and within companies. He claimed that recognizing the patterns behind these value migrations is necessary if we wish to understand the world of chaotic change. In "Profit Patterns" (1999) he described businesses as being in a state of strategic anticipation as they try to spot emerging patterns. Slywotsky and his team identified 30 patterns that have transformed industry after industry.

In 1997, Clayton Christensen (1997) took the position that great companies can fail precisely because they do everything right since the capabilities of the organization also defines its disabilities. Christensen's thesis is that outstanding companies lose their market leadership when confronted with disruptive technology. He called the approach to discovering the emerging markets for disruptive technologies agnostic marketing, i.e., marketing under the implicit assumption that no one-not the company, not the customers-can know how or in what quantities a disruptive product can or will be used before they have experience using it.

A number of strategists use scenario planning techniques to deal with change. Kees van der Heijden (1996), for example, says that change and uncertainty make "optimum strategy" determination impossible. We have neither the time nor the information required for such a calculation. The best we can hope for is what he calls "the most skillful process". The way Peter Schwartz put it in 1991 is that strategic outcomes cannot be known in advance so the sources of competitive advantage cannot be predetermined.

The fast changing business environment is too uncertain for us to find sustainable value in formulas of excellence or competitive advantage. Instead, scenario planning is a technique in which multiple outcomes can be developed, their implications assessed, and their likeliness of occurrence evaluated. According to Pierre Wack, scenario planning is about insight, complexity, and subtlety, not about formal analysis and numbers.

In 1988, Henry Mintzberg looked at the changing world around him and decided it was time to reexamine how strategic management was done. He examined the strategic process and concluded it was much more fluid and unpredictable than people had thought. Because of this, he could not point to one process that could be called strategic planning. Instead he concludes that there are five types of strategies. They are:

- Strategy as plan-a direction, guide, course of action-intention rather than actual
- Strategy as ploy-a maneuver intended to outwit a competitor
- Strategy as pattern-a consistent pattern of past behaviour-realized rather than intended
- Strategy as position-locating of brands, products, or companies within the conceptual framework of consumers or other stakeholders-strategy determined primarily by factors outside the firm
- Strategy as perspective-strategy determined primarily by a master strategist

In 1998, Mintzberg developed these five types of management strategy into 10 "schools of thought". These 10 schools are grouped into three categories. The first group is prescriptive or normative. It consists of the informal design and conception school, the formal planning school, and the analytical positioning school. The second group, consisting of six schools, is more concerned with how strategic management is actually done, rather than prescribing optimal plans or positions. The six schools are the entrepreneurial, visionary, or great leader school, the cognitive or mental process school, the learning, adaptive, or emergent process school, the power or negotiation school, the corporate culture or collective process school, and the business environment or reactive school. The third and final group consists of one school, the configuration or transformation school, an hybrid of the other schools organized into stages, organizational life cycles, or "episodes".

In 1999, Constantinos Markides also wanted to reexamine the nature of strategic planning itself. He describes strategy formation and implementation as an on-going, never-ending, integrated process requiring continuous reassessment and reformation. Strategic management is planned and emergent, dynamic, and interactive. J. Moncrieff (1999) also stresses strategy dynamics. He recognized that strategy is partially deliberate and partially unplanned. The unplanned element comes from two sources: emergent strategies (result from the emergence of opportunities and threats in the environment) and Strategies in action (ad hoc actions by many people from all parts of the organization).

Some business planners are starting to use a complexity theory approach to strategy. Complexity can be thought of as chaos with a dash of order. Chaos theory deals with turbulent systems that rapidly become disordered. Complexity is not quite so unpredictable. It involves multiple agents interacting in such a way that a glimpse of structure may appear. Axelrod, R., Holland, J., and Kelly, S. and Allison, M.A., call these systems of multiple actions and reactions complex adaptive systems. Axelrod asserts that rather than fear complexity, business should harness it. He says this can best be done when "there are many participants, numerous interactions, much trial and error learning, and abundant attempts to imitate each others' successes". In 2000, E. Dudik wrote that an organization must develop a mechanism for understanding the source and level of complexity it will face in the future and then transform itself into a complex adaptive system in order to deal with it.

Information-and Technology-driven Strategy

Peter Drucker had theorized the rise of the "knowledge worker" back in the 1950s. He described how fewer workers would be doing physical labour, and more would be applying their minds. In 1984, John Nesbitt theorized that the future would be driven largely by information: companies that managed information well could obtain an advantage, however the profitability of what he calls the "information float" (information that the company had and others desired) would all but disappear as inexpensive computers made information more accessible.

Daniel Bell (1985) examined the sociological consequences of information technology, while Gloria Schuck and Shoshana Zuboff looked at psychological factors. Zuboff, in her five year study of eight pioneering corporations made the important distinction between "automating technologies" and "infomating technologies". She studied the effect that both had on individual workers, managers, and organizational structures.

She largely confirmed Peter Drucker's predictions three decades earlier, about the importance of flexible decentralized structure, work teams, knowledge sharing, and the central role of the knowledge worker. Zuboff also detected a new basis for managerial authority, based not on position or hierarchy, but on knowledge (also predicted by Drucker) which she called "participative management".

In 1990, Peter Senge, who had collaborated with Arie de Geus at Dutch Shell, borrowed de Geus' notion of the learning organization, expanded it, and popularized it. The underlying theory is that a company's ability to gather, analyse, and use information is a necessary requirement for business success in the information age. In order to do this, Senge claimed that an organization would need to be structured such that:

- People can continuously expand their capacity to learn and be productive,
- New patterns of thinking are nurtured,
- Collective aspirations are encouraged, and
- People are encouraged to see the "whole picture" together.

Senge identified five disciplines of a learning organization. They are:

- Personal responsibility, self reliance, and mastery — We accept that we are the masters of our own destiny. We make decisions and live with the consequences of them. When a problem needs to be fixed, or an opportunity exploited, we take the initiative to learn the required skills to get it done.
- Mental models — We need to explore our personal mental models to understand the subtle effect they have on our behaviour.
- Shared vision — The vision of where we want to be in the future is discussed and communicated to all. It provides guidance and energy for the journey ahead.
- Team learning — We learn together in teams. This involves a shift from "a spirit of advocacy to a spirit of enquiry".
- Systems thinking — We look at the whole rather than the parts. This is what Senge calls the "Fifth discipline". It is the glue that integrates the other four into a coherent strategy. For an alternative approach to the "learning organization".

Since 1990 many theorists have written on the strategic importance of information, including J.B. Quinn, J. Carlos Jarillo, D.L. Barton, Manuel Castells, J.P. Lieleskin, Thomas Stewart, K.E. Sveiby, Gilbert J. Probst, and Shapiro and Varian to name just a few.

Thomas A. Stewart, for example, uses the term intellectual capital to describe the investment an organization makes in knowledge. It is composed of human capital (the knowledge inside the heads of employees), customer capital (the knowledge inside the heads of customers that decide to buy from you), and structural capital (the knowledge that resides in the company itself).

Manuel Castells, describes a network society characterized by: globalization, organizations structured as a network, instability of employment, and a social divide between those with access to information technology and those without.

Geoffrey Moore (1991) and R. Frank and P. Cook also detected a shift in the nature of competition. In industries with high technology content, technical standards become established and this gives the dominant firm a near monopoly. The same is true of networked industries in which interoperability requires compatibility between users. An example is word processor documents. Once a product has gained market dominance, other products, even far superior products, cannot compete. Moore showed how firms could attain this enviable position by using E.M. Rogers five stage adoption process and focusing on one group of customers at a time, using each group as a base for marketing to the next group. The most difficult step is making the transition between visionaries and pragmatists. If successful a firm can create a bandwagon effect in which the momentum builds and your product becomes a de facto standard.

Evans and Wurster describe how industries with a high information component are being transformed. They cite Encarta's demolition of the Encyclopedia Britannica (whose sales have plummeted 80% since their peak of $650 million in 1990). Encarta's reign was speculated to be short-lived, eclipsed by collaborative encyclopedias like Wikipedia that can operate at very low marginal costs. Encarta's service was subsequently turned into an on-line service and dropped at the end of 2009. Evans also mentions the music industry which is desperately looking for a new business model. The upstart information savvy firms, unburdened by cumbersome physical assets, are changing the competitive landscape, redefining market segments, and disintermediating some channels. One manifestation of this is personalized marketing. Information technology allows marketers to treat each individual as its own market, a market of one. Traditional ideas of market segments will no longer be relevant if personalized marketing is successful.

The technology sector has provided some strategies directly. For example, from the software development industry agile software development provides a model for shared development processes.

Access to information systems have allowed senior managers to take a much more comprehensive view of strategic management than ever before. The most notable of the comprehensive systems is the balanced scorecard approach developed in the early 1990s by Drs. Robert S. Kaplan (Harvard Business School) and David Norton (Kaplan, R. and Norton, D. 1992). It measures several factors financial, marketing, production, organizational development, and new product development in order to achieve a 'balanced' perspective.

Knowledge-driven Strategy

Most current approaches to business "strategy" focus on the mechanics of management — e.g., Drucker's operational "strategies" — and as such are not true business strategy. In a post-industrial world these operationally focused business strategies hinge on conventional sources of advantage have essentially been eliminated:

- Scale used to be very important. But now, with access to capital and a global marketplace, scale is achievable by multiple organizations simultaneously. In many cases, it can literally be rented.
- Process improvement or "best practices" were once a favoured source of advantage, but they were at best temporary, as they could be copied and adapted by competitors.
- Owning the customer had always been thought of as an important form of competitive advantage. Now, however, customer loyalty is far less important and difficult to maintain as new brands and products emerge all the time.

In such a world, differentiation, as elicudated by Michael Porter, Botten and McManus is the only way to maintain economic or market superiority (i.e., comparative advantage) over competitors. A company must OWN the thing that differentiates it from competitors. Without IP ownership and protection, any product, process or scale advantage can be compromised or entirely lost. Competitors can copy them without fear of economic or legal consequences, thereby eliminating the advantage.

Strategic Decision Making Processes

Will Mulcaster argues that whilst much research and creative thought has been devoted to generating alternative strategies, too little work has been done on what influences the quality of strategic decision making and the effectiveness with which strategies are implemented. For instance, in retrospect it can be seen that the financial crisis of 2008/9 could have been avoided if the banks had paid more attention to the risks associated with their investments, but how should banks change the way in which they make decisions in order to improve the quality of their decisions in the future? Mulcaster's Managing Forces framework addresses this issue by identifying 11 forces that should be incorporated into the processes of decision making and strategic implementation. The 11 forces are:-Time; Opposing forces; Politics; Perception; Holistic effects; Adding value; Incentives; Learning capabilities; Opportunity cost; Risk; Style. The mnemonic "TOPHAILORS" is used to assist in the memory of these forces.

The Psychology of Strategic Management

Several psychologists have conducted studies to determine the psychological patterns involved in strategic management. Typically senior managers have been asked how they go about making strategic decisions. A 1938 treatise by Chester Barnard, that was based on his own experience as a business executive, sees the process as informal, intuitive, non-routinized, and involving primarily oral, 2-way communications. Bernard says "The process is the sensing of the organization as a whole and the total situation relevant to it. It transcends the capacity of merely intellectual methods, and the techniques of discriminating the factors of the situation. The terms pertinent to it are "feeling", "judgement", "sense", "proportion", "balance", "appropriateness". It is a matter of art rather than science." In 1973, Henry Mintzberg found that senior managers typically deal with unpredictable situations so they strategize in *ad hoc*, flexible, dynamic, and implicit ways.. He says, "The job breeds adaptive information-manipulators who prefer the live concrete situation. The manager works in an environment of stimulous-response, and he develops in his work a clear preference for live action."

In 1982, John Kotter studied the daily activities of 15 executives and concluded that they spent most of their time developing and working a network of relationships from which they gained general insights and specific details to be used in making strategic decisions. They tended to use "mental road maps" rather than systematic planning techniques.

Daniel Isenberg's 1984 study of senior managers found that their decisions were highly intuitive. Executives often sensed what they were going to do before they could explain why. He claimed in 1986 that one of the reasons for this is the complexity of strategic decisions and the resultant information uncertainty.

Shoshana Zuboff (1988) claims that information technology is widening the divide between senior managers (who typically make strategic decisions) and operational level managers (who typically make routine decisions). She claims that prior to the widespread use of computer systems, managers, even at the most senior level, engaged in both strategic decisions and routine administration, but as computers facilitated (She called it "deskilled") routine processes, these activities were moved further down the hierarchy, leaving senior management free for strategic decions making.

In 1977, Abraham Zaleznik identified a difference between leaders and managers. He describes leadershipleaders as visionaries who inspire. They care about substance. Whereas managers are claimed to care about process, plans, and form. He also claimed in 1989 that the rise of the manager was the main factor that caused the decline of American business in the 1970s and 80s.The main difference between leader and manager is that, leader has followers and manager has subordinates. In capitalistic society leaders make decisions and manager usually follow or execute. Lack of leadership is most damaging at thc level of strategic management where it can paralyze an entire organization.

According to Corner, Kinichi, and Keats, strategic decision making in organizations occurs at two levels: individual and aggregate. They have developed a model of parallel strategic decision making. The model identifies two parallel processes both of which involve getting attention, encoding information, storage and retrieval of information, strategic choice, strategic outcome, and feedback. The individual and organizational processes are not independent however. They interact at each stage of the process.

Reasons why strategic plans fail

There are many reasons why strategic plans fail, especially:

- Failure to execute by overcoming the four key organizational hurdles:
  - o Cognitive hurdle
  - o Motivational hurdle
  - o Resource hurdle
  - o Political hurdle.
- Failure to understand the customer:
  - o Why do they buy

- o Is there a real need for the product
- o inadequate or incorrect marketing research.

- Inability to predict environmental reaction:
  - o What will competitors do:
    - Fighting brands
    - Price wars.
  - o Will government intervene.
- Over-estimation of resource competence:
  - o Can the staff, equipment, and processes handle the new strategy
  - o Failure to develop new employee and management skills.
- Failure to coordinate:
  - o Reporting and control relationships not adequate
  - o Organizational structure not flexible enough.
- Failure to obtain senior management commitment:
  - o Failure to get management involved right from the start
  - o Failure to obtain sufficient company resources to accomplish task.
- Failure to obtain employee commitment:
  - o New strategy not well explained to employees
  - o No incentives given to workers to embrace the new strategy.
- Under-estimation of time requirements:
  - o No critical path analysis done.
- Failure to follow the plan:
  - o No follow through after initial planning
  - o No tracking of progress against plan
  - o No consequences for above.
- Failure to manage change:
  - o Inadequate understanding of the internal resistance to change
  - o Lack of vision on the relationships between processes, technology and organization.

- Poor communications:
  - o Insufficient information sharing among stakeholders
  - o Exclusion of stakeholders and delegates.

Limitations of Strategic Management

Although a sense of direction is important, it can also stifle creativity, especially if it is rigidly enforced. In an uncertain and ambiguous world, fluidity can be more important than a finely tuned strategic compass. When a strategy becomes internalized into a corporate culture, it can lead to group think. It can also cause an organization to define itself too narrowly. An example of this is marketing myopia.

Many theories of strategic management tend to undergo only brief periods of popularity. A summary of these theories thus inevitably exhibits survivorship bias (itself an area of research in strategic management). Many theories tend either to be too narrow in focus to build a complete corporate strategy on, or too general and abstract to be applicable to specific situations. Populism or faddishness can have an impact on a particular theory's life cycle and may see application in inappropriate circumstances.

In 2000, Gary Hamel coined the term strategic convergence to explain the limited scope of the strategies being used by rivals in greatly differing circumstances. He lamented that strategies converge more than they should, because the more successful ones are imitated by firms that do not understand that the strategic process involves designing a custom strategy for the specifics of each situation.

Ram Charan, aligning with a popular marketing tagline, believes that strategic planning must not dominate action. "Just do it!", while not quite what he meant, is a phrase that nevertheless comes to mind when combatting analysis paralysis.

The Linearity Trap

It is tempting to think that the elements of strategic management – (i) reaching consensus on corporate objectives; (ii) developing a plan for achieving the objectives; and (iii) marshalling and allocating the resources required to implement the plan – can be approached sequentially. It would be convenient, in other words, if one could deal first with the noble question of ends, and then address the mundane question of means.

But in the world in which strategies have to be implemented, the three elements are interdependent. Means are as likely to determine ends as ends are to determine means. The objectives that an organization might wish to pursue are limited by the range of feasible approaches to implementation. (There will usually be only a small number of approaches that will not only be technically and administratively possible, but also satisfactory to the full range of organizational stakeholders.) In turn, the range of feasible implementation approaches is determined by the availability of resources.

And so, although participants in a typical "strategy session" may be asked to do "blue sky" thinking where they pretend that the usual constraints – resources, acceptability to stakeholders, administrative feasibility – have been lifted, the fact is that it rarely makes sense to divorce oneself from the environment in which a strategy will have to be implemented. It's probably impossible to think in any meaningful way about strategy in an unconstrained environment. Our brains can't process "boundless possibilities", and the very idea of strategy only has meaning in the context of challenges or obstacles to be overcome. It's at least as plausible to argue that acute awareness of constraints is the very thing that stimulates creativity by forcing us to constantly reassess both means and ends in light of circumstances.

The key question, then, is, "How can individuals, organizations and societies cope as well as possible with... issues too complex to be fully understood, given the fact that actions initiated on the basis of inadequate understanding may lead to significant regret?"

The answer is that the process of developing organizational strategy must be iterative. It involves toggling back and forth between questions about objectives, implementation planning and resources. An initial idea about corporate objectives may have to be altered if there is no feasible implementation plan that will meet with a sufficient level of acceptance among the full range of stakeholders, or because the necessary resources are not available, or both.

Even the most talented manager would no doubt agree that "comprehensive analysis is impossible" for complex problems. Formulation and implementation of strategy must thus occur side-by-side rather than sequentially, because strategies are built on assumptions which, in the absence of perfect knowledge, will never be perfectly correct. Strategic management is necessarily a "repetitive learning cycle [rather than] a linear progression towards a clearly defined final destination." While assumptions can and should be tested in advance, the ultimate test is implementation. You will inevitably need to adjust corporate objectives and/or your approach to pursuing outcomes and/or assumptions about required resources. Thus a strategy will get remade during implementation because "humans rarely can proceed satisfactorily except by learning from experience; and modest probes, serially modified on the basis of feedback, usually are the best method for such learning."

It serves little purpose (other than to provide a false aura of certainty sometimes demanded by corporate strategists and planners) to pretend to anticipate every possible consequence of a corporate decision, every possible constraining or enabling factor, and every possible point of view. At the end of the day, what matters for the purposes of strategic management is having a clear view – based on the best available evidence and on defensible assumptions – of what it seems possible to accomplish within the constraints of a given set of circumstances. As the situation changes, some opportunities for pursuing objectives will disappear and others arise. Some implementation approaches will become impossible, while others, previously impossible or unimagined, will become viable.

The essence of being "strategic" thus lies in a capacity for "intelligent trial-and error" rather than linear adherence to finally honed and detailed strategic plans. Strategic management will add little value — indeed, it may well do harm — if organizational strategies are designed to be used as a detailed blueprints for managers. Strategy should be seen, rather, as laying out the general path-but not the precise steps-by which an organization intends to create value.

Strategic management is a question of interpreting, and continuously reinterpreting, the possibilities presented by shifting circumstances for advancing an organization's objectives. Doing so requires strategists to think *simultaneously* about desired objectives, the best approach for achieving them, and the resources implied by the chosen approach. It requires a frame of mind that admits of no boundary between means and ends.

Marketing Mix

The term "marketing mix" was first used in 1953 when Neil Borden, in his American Marketing Association presidential address, took the recipe idea one step further and coined the term "marketing-mix". A prominent marketer, E. Jerome McCarthy, proposed a 4 P classification in 1960, which has seen wide use. The four Ps concept is explained in most marketing textbooks and classes.

Four Ps

Elements of the marketing mix are often referred to as 'the four Ps':

- *Product*-A tangible object or an intangible service that is mass produced or manufactured on a large scale with a specific volume of units. Intangible products are service based like the tourism industry & the hotel industry or codes-based products like cellphone load and credits. Typical examples of a mass produced tangible object are the motor car and the disposable razor. A less obvious but ubiquitous mass produced service is a computer operating system.
- *Price* – The price is the amount a customer pays for the product. It is determined by a number of factors including market share, competition, material costs, product identity and the customer's perceived value of the product. The business may increase or decrease the price of product if other stores have the same product.
- *Place* – Place represents the location where a product can be purchased. It is often referred to as the distribution channel. It can include any physical store as well as virtual stores on the Internet.
- *Promotion* represents all of the communications that a marketer may use in the marketplace. Promotion has four distinct elements: advertising, public relations, word of mouth and point of sale. A certain amount of crossover occurs when promotion uses the four principal elements together, which is common in film promotion. Advertising covers any communication that is paid for, from cinema commercials, radio and Internet adverts through print

media and billboards. Public relations are where the communication is not directly paid for and includes press releases, sponsorship deals, exhibitions, conferences, seminars or trade fairs and events. Word of mouth is any apparently informal communication about the product by ordinary individuals, satisfied customers or people specifically engaged to create word of mouth momentum. Sales staff often plays an important role in word of mouth and Public Relations.

Broadly defined, optimizing the marketing mix is the primary responsibility of marketing. By offering the product with the right combination of the four Ps marketers can improve their results and marketing effectiveness. Making small changes in the marketing mix is typically considered to be a tactical change. Parm Bains says making large changes in any of the four Ps can be considered strategic. For example, a large change in the price, say from $19.00 to $39.00 would be considered a strategic change in the position of the product. However a change of $130 to $129.99 would be considered a tactical change, potentially related to a promotional offer.

The term 'marketing mix' however, does not imply that the 4P elements represent options. They are not trade-offs but are fundamental marketing issues that always need to be addressed. They are the fundamental actions that marketing requires whether determined explicitly or by default.

Four Cs

A formal approach to this customer-focused marketing mix is known as Four Cs (Commodity, Cost, Channel, Communication). Koichi Shimizu proposed a four Cs classification in 1973.

The four elements are:

1. Commodity (Original meaning of Latin: Commodus= convenient) : the product for the consumers or citizens. Not product out.
2. Cost (Original meaning of Latin: Constare= It makes sacrifices) : producing cost, selling cost, purchasing cost and social cost.
3. Channel (Original meaning is a Canal) : Flow of commodity : marketing channels.

4. Communication (Original meaning of Latin:Communio= sharing of meaning) : marketing communication : It doesn't promote the sales.

The Four Cs can be compared to the Four Ps. This system is basically the four Ps renamed and reworded to provide a customer focus. The four Cs Model provides a demand/customer centric version alternative to the well-known four Ps supply side model (product, price, place, promotion) of marketing management.

The Four Cs model is more consumer-oriented and attempts to better fit the movement from mass marketing to niche marketing. The Product part of the Four Ps model is replaced by Consumer or Consumer Models, shifting the focus to satisfying the consumer needs. Another C replacement for Product is Capable. By defining offerings as individual capabilities that when combined and focused to a specific industry, creates a custom solution rather than pigeon-holing a customer into a product. Pricing is replaced by Cost reflecting the total cost of ownership. Many factors affect Cost, including but not limited to the customer's cost to change or implement the new product or service and the customer's cost for not selecting a competitor's product or service. Placement is replaced by Convenience. With the rise of internet and hybrid models of purchasing, Place is becoming less relevant. Convenience takes into account the ease of buying the product, finding the product, finding information about the product, and several other factors. Finally, the Promotions feature is replaced by Communication which represents a broader focus than simply Promotions. Communications can include advertising, public relations, personal selling, viral advertising, and any form of communication between the firm and the consumer.

The Four Cs model has been criticized for simply being nothing more than the Four Ps with different points of emphasis. In particular, the Four Cs inclusion of customers in the marketing mix is criticized, since customers are a *target* of marketing, while the other elements of the marketing mix are *tactics*. The Four Cs also exclude numerous strategies for product development, distribution, and pricing, while assuming that consumers want two-way communications with companies.

3

Challenges and Strategies of Hospitality Industry

Competitiveness refers to-*the ability and willingness to compete* and two most important underlying criteria of competitiveness are-'Profitability' and 'Productivity', that is, increased competitiveness is reflected in sustained growth in productivity and profitability.

Since 'productivity' and 'profitability' are vital for all organizations, industries, sectors and nations, it indicates that the concept of competitiveness is equally applicable to each of these entities, so it is a must that they appreciate the conceptual framework of competitiveness and the various forms that it takes, (commercial competitiveness, market competitiveness etc.) along with the fact that it is a complex ongoing process affected by a range of factors/inputs.

Although, 'competitiveness' in parlance of business (and industries) is not a new phenomenon and is usually discussed in terms of – the decisions it makes, the resources it has, and the environmental factors which surrounds the business, but lately, the trend of categorizing and evaluating nations on basis of their competitiveness has become a norm among economists, policy makers, business executives and investors.

Liberalization, Privatization and Globalization (LPG) have worked together for reducing protection and creating a rapidly changing competitive environment resulting in fierce international competition 'in' and 'for' the world-market. With this, there has been a growing realization that avoiding the rigors of competition is not possible and developing strategies for enhancing sustainable competitiveness has emerged as a 'must do' exercise for all. However, the context of 'competitiveness' might vary for business, industries and nations, depending on their-objectives, form, nature and functions – that is-from completely social to hardcore commercial.

Competitiveness of Nations and the Service Sector-Most of the (developing) economies are in rapid transit towards becoming 'service economies" and therefore 'competitiveness of service sector' is emerging as a crucial factor influencing the overall competitiveness of a country, and India is no exception to this, where the share of services is increasingly getting higher in the total GDP, and also the growth rate of India's 'service exports' is higher then the world average, hence for India, out of the three pillars of competitiveness, one is certainly it's service sector (agriculture and manufacturing are the remaining two.)

Variables of Competitiveness at country, industry and firm level-The paper deals with the issue of competitiveness at all the three levels (country, industry and firm) taking-'India' as the variable for 'country' and 'Indian Tourism and Hospitality Industry' as the variable for 'industry', and at the firm level, the paper identifies cases from many different organizations, rather then taking a particular organization as a variable, because a broader canvas is required to capture the diversity of businesses operating in this domain, and any one organization cannot symbolize the complete tourism and hospitality industry because this industry is formed by a combination of very different businesses. (Only infrastructure business, or only hotel business or only aviation business can not represent this industry alone, but all these businesses jointly do so).

Competitiveness Challenges of Indian Tourism and Hospitality Industry – as mentioned above, different diverse businesses jointly form this industry *(transportation, hotels, infrastructure, aviation etc.)*, and a balanced development of all these different businesses and high coordination amongst all the participants is a prerequisite for enhancing competitiveness of this industry and creating this 'fine blend' of such 'polar elements' is a tough challenge in itself.

This industry can be called as the "industry of big paradoxes", first, on one hand it has almost unbeatable competitive advantages, huge potential and high growth rates *(in terms of-generating foreign exchange, growth rates, & employment generation),* and on the other hand, inspite of above mentioned positives, Indian Tourism and Hospitality Industry is still way behind even from its small neighbours in South-East Asia, not to mention the large counterparts like China.

Second paradox is that, on one hand, in order to be competitive, this industry needs the cooperation of both public and private sector players as both play a vital role in it, and on the other hand, cut throat competition also exists between the two in this industry itself.

Finally, the 'offering' of this industry is also paradoxical. For India, where 'history' is an important attraction for tourists, this industry has to offer 'history', but it can not loose sight of modernization either, in other words, Indian Tourism and Hospitality Industry has to be a 'historian' and a 'futurist' simultaneously.

Thus, in order to find a sustainable solution to the competitiveness issue of this industry, the paper suggest that it is important to identify the reasons behind its lack of competitiveness and then to search for 'breakthrough solutions' to face the unique challenges it offers, by undertaking a study of the innovative and best practices developed and adopted by players of this industry in the global arena which are applicable in Indian conditions and finally, redefining the role of government and private players to create a more competitive landscape might also be an effective part of the overall solution.

Case Study: Hongkong

The tourism industry has been a major source of revenue for Hong Kong. Along with the boom of tourism is the increase investment in hotel industry. Indeed, these two sectors have been indispensable that the subsequent decline in tourism following the economic crisis has impacted hotel operations significantly. The tourism and hotel industry in Hong Kong has been suffered major decline although it has manifested recovery during the previous years.

The factors contributing to the decline include high rates due to the high cost of living, the outbreak of SARS, deteriorating image of Hong Kong as shopper's paradise and the development of tourist attractions in other countries in the region. The following section will review the development of the tourism industry from its subsequent decline and its way to recovery.

Part A

Macro Analysis

The business environment is generally successful and attractive. The gross domestic product has grown consistently and became the envy of developed and developing systems. The unemployment rate has always been in a low rate while the demand for the employment remains to be buoyant. With this, there appeared to be an increase in the standard of living explaining the social stability in the country. The government policy on the other hand has adopted a policy of positive non interventionism. In general, the business environment of the country is favourable for investors.

Hotel Industry

Hong Kong's hotel industry is a popular channel of investment along with the booming of the tourism industry. Tourism is a major revenue earner in Hong Kong. It has become the second largest source of foreign exchange. Hong Kong serves as the travel gateway for the vast majority of business and recreational travels to China and as the primary travel hub for South East Asia. The hotel industry was geared to the tourist trade especially at the upper end (Gerzenberg, 1994).

In the years prior to the hand back to China, hotel room rates rose to high levels. Room rates may have been slashed and two for one flight promotions run but the image of Hong Kong as expensive destination has been fixed in the minds of potential tourist travellers.

Tourism and hotel industry has slumped badly during the Asian financial crisis. Despite the major rebound in the number of tourists coming during 1999-2000, the actual revenue received has declined. Explanations for the decline in revenue from tourists differed but include the high costs of living compare to other locations in the region. In addition to this, HK is no longer seen as a shopper's paradise. It has been characterized by the lack of initiatives to provide tourist attractions and above all the high level of pollution affects the territory.

In 1999, hotel prices in Asia rose again as the region recovered from the economic crisis of 1997-1998. Room rates in South Korea,

Japan and Taiwan rose by 32%, 38% and 30% in euros. However, China and Hong Kong experienced continued fall in room rates by 31.5% though it stabilized slightly in 1999 and towards the end of that year. Yet the reality remains that hotels are property and properties are major investments and assets in Hong Kong. By 2000, room rates and occupancy are again at high levels (Joseph, 2005). One of the bright spot for Hong Kong hoteliers is the climbing of tourism.

By the end of last year, there were about 612 hotels and tourist guest houses in Hong Kong with 52, 512 rooms. The average occupancy rates in all hotel categories were 87% for the whole of 2006. This marked a one-percentage-growth as compared to 2005 regardless of the 7.4% increase in room supplies between December 2005 and December 2006. During 2006, about 62.75 of all visitors stayed one night and longer, a trend which reflects the importance of Hong Kong as a regional transport hub.

Today, the Hong Kong tourism and hotel industry is gambling its future as a tourist destination for Disneyland. The industry is expecting a boost from the increased number of tourists especially those coming from mainland China.

In 2003, Beijing has eased the travel rules for mainland tourist to Hong Kong which allowed people for Chinese cities to travel individually rather than in organized groups. It has also doubled the currency allowed for mainland tourists to take with them when traveling abroad. These new polices are part of the series of measures to help stimulate Hong Kong's' flagging tourism, lift property and share prices (Bezlova, 2004). As a result, China has become the major source of tourist arrivals in Hong Kong.

Competitor Analysis

The erosion of Hong Kong's price competitiveness resulting from regional currency turmoil and depreciation has made other destinations such as Thailand, Malaysia and Singapore to become more competitive. Thus, the industry must try harder to attract the foreign market by providing competitive packages, attractive tourism products and high quality services and satisfactory experiences. The need for such initiatives has been illustrated by the decreasing rate of hotel occupancy despite increase of visitor arrivals.

There are increasing worries that the current tourism boom may fade in the years to come as wealthy mainland travellers set their destinations to Paris and London. Hong Kong is also competing with the nearby Macau.

For the next decade, it plans to create 60,000 new hotel rooms (Joseph, 2005). Macau is also planning to penetrate the untapped market of China by investing in the monopolized gaming industry. It is next to Hong Kong which is likely to benefit from the ease of travel rules from China. As Chinese people enjoy more and longer holidays, the urban rich are traveling in great numbers to Macau for gaming activities. The influx of mainland Chinese has already uplifted the economic growth of Macau which is highly dependent on tourism (Bezlova, 2004).

The local competition in the hotel industry is intense. The choices are vast and there are so many competitors. Few cities offer large numbers of first rate hotels and few places competes with the services that made the Hong Kong hotel industry legendary.

Most of the hotels and guest houses are situated on Hong Kong Island and in Kowloon but there are also selections in the New Territories (including the outlying islands). The keen competition and the laws of supply and demand have ensured that these hotels maintain the highest standards.

Pestle Analysis

This analysis audits the impact on the market of large and usually long terms factors: political, economic, social, technological, legal and environmental changes going around the industry. These factors have dramatic impact on the working dynamics of the marketplace.

Political factors such as government intervention distort the marketplace. Economic factors include the cycles of growth and decline that impact business. For instance, the increase or decrease in consumer spending impact the host of businesses from consumer goods. Social factors such as the increasing number of double income families impact the standard of living which may increase the purchasing power of consumers.

Technological factors are changes in technology which created the need for people to upgrade their skills to remain employable and for businesses to engage in new technologies so that they are not left behind by their competitors. Legal factors involve general legislations that affect all organizations such as employment laws and other industry specific regulations. Lastly are the environmental factors such as pollution control and the spread of diseases such as SARS that has affected businesses in the Asian region.

Political Factors

- Government Policy of non Interventionism on Businesses
- Autonomy from People's Republic of China.

Economic Factors

- High Gross Domestic Product
- High Purchasing Power
- Low unemployment rate
- High Operating Costs.

Social Factors

- Social Stability
- Increase in the Standard of Living
- Lack of Skilled workers.

Technological Factors

- Use of Information and Communication Technology in the Hotel industry
- Technology transfer arrangements with foreign investors The use of Information Technology in various aspects of the industry.

Legal Factors

- Ease of Travel Rules from Mainland China
- Accommodations are subject for 3 percent government tax.

Environmental Factors

- High Levels of Pollution
- Fear of SARS outbreak.

Five Forces Analysis

This analysis discusses five competitive forces governing the tourism and hotel industry.

Force	*Strength*	*Trend*	*Comments*
Entry	High	Changing	Developers are seeing new hotel prospects at the South side of Hong Kong. This would mean new entrants in the industry. Also, 37 percent increase in hotel development is expected until 2008.
Suppliers	Low	Changing	Suppliers can negotiate prices and agreements based on the quantity of goods supplied.
Buyers	High	Increasing	The high purchasing power and increase in disposable income would mean that tourists are likely to spend more in exchange for satisfaction and best experience. This would require the hotels to improve their service standards if they are to remain competitive. Conversely, this may cause tourist to go other destinations such as Paris and London.
Substitutes	Low	Not Changing	Hotels are not the only means for lodging. Hotels may also compete with lodging services such as tourists' guest houses and resorts.

Rivalry	High	Increasing	The competition for tourist with neighbouring countries is likely to increase. The development of tourist attractions such as casinos in Macau is likely to affect arrivals in Hong Kong. Also, the competitiveness of Thailand, Malaysia and Singapore in terms quality and price competitiveness is likely to impact the industry

Mobility Barriers

Ownership

Hostels and Guesthouses have minimal capital investment and are traditionally small hotels owned by an individual or family. The dependence of small hotels on individual and the type of security available for loan are among the factors that mitigates against the availability of external finance from lending institutions. While independently owned hotels may till be dominant in the industry, the growth of the industry has been greatly associated with the emergence of hotel groups. The increase in the size of hotel has resulted from these firms building or acquiring hotels in various locations under a central management. These hotels may be grouped in a restricted geographical area or distributed within the country or between countries. International hotels have essentially national companies with a head office in a particular country and engage to a greater extent of hotel operations in the country and other countries.

Marketing and Distribution Systems

Hostels and Guesthouses rely on personal recommendation and repeated visits rather than systematic promotion. On the other hand hotel groups have the marketing capability to promote its services. The international hotels are more advantageous in this aspect due to broad scope of the marketing activities in different countries. These last two groups have larger market and can formulate operations to meet market needs through employing promotion on a wider scale.

Another barrier is in terms of the suppliers. Hotel groups has economies of buying because it can buy bulk and negotiate with advantageous prices and terms with suppliers of a wide range of goods. This is something which small hotels could not afford.

Part B

Future Scenarios for the Industry

Hotels in Hong Kong can be described as being capable of providing high levels of services and facilities. More than 20 million tourists are expected to visit the city every year mainly from mainland China. Developers are building up to nine new hotels in the remote industrial sectors on the south side of Hong Kong. Overall, the numbers of hotel rooms are expected to increase by 37 percent by mid 2008 to 56,816 rooms. Occupancy rates among the highest worldwide has already declined to 86 percent in 2005 from 88 percent in the previous year.

The introduction of the seven day free visa in 1993 and the five day work week in China had positive impacts in its outbound travel to Hong Kong. This implied that positive policies such as simplified visa application and extended visa-free status play an important role in attracting international tourists to Hong Kong. HK tourism authorities emphasized the importance of positive policies for the China outbound travel market and the top agenda is to make visas easier for Chinese tour groups. Further, the relaxation on the issue of travel document formalities boosts travel numbers.

The tourism industry of Hong Kong has lobbied the Chinese government to increase daily quotas and this allowed additional 358 tourists into Hong Kong each day. With the increasing standard of living and further relaxation of the outbound travel, mainland Chinese travellers will continue to be the most important tourist market for Hong Kong in the future. Tourism related industry such as Hotels must strive to ensure that they provide the best experience and satisfaction possible. With the political and economic condition in China, outbound vacation travel will continue to expand and Hong Kong will be the first to benefit from this growing trend. In order to maximize and get fast return, Hong Kong must shift its emphasis to the China Market and design appropriate marketing strategies.

Conclusion

The tourism and hotel industry has been characterized by significant development, subsequent decline and recovery. This industry has been considered to be one of the major sources of revenues for the country. However, it has declined greatly following the economic crisis and the outbreak of epidemic in the country. This can also be attributed to the high cost of living and the lack of tourist attractions that will entice tourist to visit the country. The condition was even worsen by the intense competition with other international destinations such as Malaysia, Thailand and Singapore. All of which are offering relatively low prices with the quality services.

To date, the industry is recovering by developing attractions such as the Disneyland. While this will boost the industry, competition will also strengthen as other countries are developing their tourist attractions such as casinos in Macau. Indeed, the hotel industry must improve its competitive position by enhancing the experience of guests through quality services, innovation and affordable prices.

Recommendations

- Enhance Hong Kong's image as Asia's world city by leveraging endorsements in a wide audience reach. This would entail making use of traditional channels to communicate the essence of unique Hong Kong experiences to the targeted market segments.
- Introduce and develop major tourism attractions that will boost tourist's stay in Hong Kong. The construction of Disneyland has helped in promoting the country as a tourist destination. Also, Macau's concept of casino and gaming activities is a good example of tourist attraction.
- The importance of offering high quality experiences meaningful to the hotel guests is unquestionable. They should maximize the arrivals of visitors, length of stay, repeat visits and satisfaction through initiatives that will

enhance visitor's experiences. Chinese mainland tourists are expected to be the most important market of the industry and hotels must ensure that they offer the best experience through quality service and modern facilities.

- Hoteliers must find a way of offering competitive prices that will suit the budget of travellers. The high costs of living has always been the problem of Hong Kong and this has led to the lost of potential tourist to other competitive locations in Asia.
- Offer promotional packages. A great example of this was the cooperation of HKTB and 53 Hong Kong Hotels in 2004 to offer discounted room rates to bona fide employees of airlines, tour operators, travel agents and tourist offices outside Hong Kong. The promotion showed the range of experiences Hong Kong offers so that these key influencers could in turn motivate and inform their customers about the city.
- Develop e-business. This will help hoteliers to better serve e-consumers by improving the quality of their online offers, expanding the quality of services and developing more competitive e-distribution channels.

The Importance of the Small Hotel

Boutique Hotel

Boutique hotel is a term popularised in North America and the United Kingdom to describe intimate, usually luxurious or quirky hotel environments. Boutique hotels differentiate themselves from larger chain/branded hotels and motels by providing personalized accommodation and services/facilities. Sometimes known as "design hotels" or "lifestyle hotels", boutique hotels began appearing in the 1980s in major cities like London, New York, and San Francisco. Typically boutique hotels are furnished in a themed, stylish and/or aspirational manner. They usually are considerably smaller than mainstream hotels, often ranging from 3 to 50 guest rooms.

Boutique hotels are always individual and are therefore extremely unlikely to be found amongst the homogeneity of large chain hotel groups. Guest rooms and suites may be fitted with telephony and Wi-Fi Internet, air-conditioning, honesty bars and often cable/pay TV, but equally may have none of these, focusing on quiet and comfort rather than gadgetry. Guest services are often attended to by 24-hour hotel staff. Many boutique hotels have on-site dining facilities, and the majority offer bars and lounges that may also be open to the general public.

Despite this definition, the popularity of the boutique term and concept has led to some confusion about the term. Boutique hotels have typically been unique properties operated by individuals or companies with a small collection. However, their successes have prompted multi-national hotel companies to try to establish their own brands in order to capture a market share. The most notable example is Starwood Hotels and Resorts Worldwide's W Hotels, ranging from large boutique hotels, such as the W Union Square NY, to the W 'boutique resorts' in the Maldives, to true luxury boutique hotel collections, such as the Bulgari collection, Kimpton Hotels & Restaurants, SLS Hotels, Thompson Hotels, Joie De Vie hotels, The Keating Hotel, and O Hotel, among many others.

There is some overlap between the concept of a small boutique hotel and a bed and breakfast.

In the United States, New York remains the centre of the boutique hotel phenomenon, as the original Schrager-era boutique hotels remain relevant and are joined by scores of independent and small-chain competitors, mainly clustered about Midtown and downtown Manhattan. The French Quarter and Garden District, New Orleans have several dozen boutique hotels, most of which are located in old homes or inns. These usually provide an ambience based on 19th-century antiques, artwork with New Orleans themes, vintage or reproduction furniture and decor and/or interesting historical associations. Miami and Miami Beach also have several boutique hotels, found mostly along the beachfront streets Ocean Drive and Collins Drive. Most of these are in buildings from the heyday of the Art Deco period. Their attractions include the Art Deco ambiance, beach access, nouvelle and Latin cuisines, and tropical-themed interior decor.

The concept of boutique or design hotels has spread throughout the world. Including European countries like Spain, and East Asian countries such as Thailand, where many boutique or design hotels are sprouting, especially in resort locations, such as Phuket and Hua Hin. Other Far Eastern cities in which boutique and design hotels are becoming increasingly popular include Bangkok, Singapore, and Hong Kong. Boutique hotels are even appearing in such places as Indonesia, mainland China, Iceland, Peru, and Turkey, demonstrating that the concept has penetrated beyond the typical design capitals of the world and is entering new markets.

Hotels and Other Accommodations

Significant Points

- Service occupations account for almost two-thirds of the industry's employment—by far the largest occupational group.
- Hotels employ many young workers and first-time job holders in part-time and seasonal jobs.
- Job opportunities should be good as low entry requirements for many jobs lead to high turnover and replacement needs.

Nature of the Industry

People travel for a variety of reasons, including for vacations, business, and visits to friends and relatives. For many of these travellers, hotels and other accommodations will be where they stay while out of town. For others, hotels may be more than just a place to stay; they are destinations in themselves. Resort hotels and casino hotels, for example, offer a variety of activities to keep travellers and families occupied for much of their stay.

Goods and services. Hotels and other accommodations are as different as the many family and business travellers they accommodate. The industry includes all types of lodging, from luxurious five-star hotels to youth hostels and RV (recreational vehicle) parks. While many provide simply a place to spend the night, others cater to longer stays by providing food service, recreational activities, and meeting rooms. In 2008, 64,300 establishments provided accommodations to suit many different needs and budgets.

Hotels and motels comprise the majority of establishments in this industry and are generally classified as offering either full-service or limited service. Full-service properties offer a variety of services for their guests, but they almost always include at least one or more restaurant and beverage service options other than self-service—from coffee bars and lunch counters to cocktail lounges and formal restaurants. They also usually provide room service. Larger full-service properties usually have a variety of retail shops on the premises, such as gift boutiques, newsstands, and drug and cosmetics counters, some of which may be geared to an exclusive clientele. Additionally, a number of full-service hotels offer guests access to laundry and valet services, swimming pools, beauty salons, and fitness centres or health spas. A small—but growing—number of luxury hotel chains also manage condominium units in combination with their transient rooms, providing both hotel guests and condominium owners with access to the same services and amenities.

The largest hotels often have banquet rooms, exhibit halls, and spacious ballrooms to accommodate conventions, business meetings, wedding receptions, and other social gatherings. Conventions and business meetings are major sources of revenue for these properties. Some commercial hotels are known as conference hotels—fully self-contained entities specifically designed for large-scale meetings. They provide physical fitness and recreational facilities for meeting attendees, in addition to state-of-the-art audiovisual and technical equipment, a business centre, and banquet services.

Limited-service hotels are free-standing properties that do not have on-site restaurants or most other amenities that must be provided by a staff other than the front desk or housekeeping. They usually offer continental breakfasts, vending machines or small packaged items, Internet access, and sometimes unattended game rooms or swimming pools in addition to daily housekeeping services. The numbers of limited-service properties have been growing. These properties are not as costly to build and maintain. They appeal to budget-conscious family vacationers and travellers who are willing to sacrifice amenities for lower room prices.

Hotels can also be categorized based on a distinguishing feature or service provided by the hotel. *Conference hotels* provide meeting and banquet rooms, and usually food service, to large groups of people. *Resort hotels* offer luxurious surroundings with a variety of recreational facilities, such as swimming pools, golf courses, tennis courts, game rooms, and health spas, as well as planned social activities and entertainment. Resorts typically are located in vacation destinations or near natural settings, such as mountains, seashores, theme parks, or other attractions. As a result, the business of many resorts fluctuates with the season. Some resort hotels and motels provide additional convention and conference facilities to encourage customers to combine business with pleasure. During the off season, many of these establishments solicit conventions, sales meetings, and incentive tours to fill their otherwise empty rooms; some resorts even close for the off-season.

Extended-stay hotels typically provide rooms or suites with fully equipped kitchens, entertainment systems, office space with computer and telephone lines, fitness centres, and other amenities. Typically, guests use these hotels for a minimum of 5 consecutive nights, often while on an extended work assignment or lengthy vacation or family visit. *All-suite hotels* offer a living room or sitting room in addition to a bedroom.

Casino hotels combine both lodging and legalized gaming on the same premises. Along with the typical services provided by most full-service hotels, casino hotels also contain casinos where patrons can wager at table games, play slot machines, and make other bets. Some casino hotels also contain conference and convention facilities.

In addition to hotels, *bed-and-breakfast inns, RV parks, campgrounds,* and *rooming and boarding houses* provide lodging for overnight guests and are included in this industry. *Bed-and-breakfast inns* provide short-term lodging in private homes or small buildings converted for this purpose and are characterized by highly personalized service and inclusion of breakfast in the room rate. Their appeal is quaintness; they typically provide unusual service and unique decor.

RV parks and campgrounds cater to people who enjoy recreational camping at moderate prices. Some parks and campgrounds provide service stations, general stores, shower and toilet facilities, and coin-operated laundries. While some are designed for overnight travellers only, others are for vacationers who stay longer. Some camps provide accommodations, such as cabins and fixed campsites, and other amenities, such as food services, recreational facilities and equipment, and organized recreational activities. Examples of these overnight camps include children's camps, family vacation camps, hunting and fishing camps, and outdoor adventure retreats that offer trail riding, white-water rafting, hiking, fishing, game hunting, and similar activities.

Other short-term lodging facilities in this industry include *guesthouses,* or small cottages located on the same property as a main residence, and *youth hostels*—dormitory-style hotels with few frills, occupied mainly by students traveling on limited budgets. Also included are *rooming and boarding houses,* such as fraternity houses, sorority houses, off-campus dormitories, and workers' camps. These establishments provide temporary or longer term accommodations that may serve as a principal residence for the period of occupancy. These establishments also may provide services such as housekeeping, meals, and laundry services.

Industry organization. In recent years, the hotel industry has been dominated by a few large national hotel chains. To the traveller, familiar chain establishments represent dependability and quality at predictable rates. Many chains recognize the importance of brand loyalty to guests and have expanded the range of lodging options offered under one corporate name to include a full range of hotels from limited-service, economy-type hotels to luxury inns. While these national corporations own some of the hotels, many properties are independently owned but affiliated with a chain through a franchise agreement or management contract. Increasingly, hotel chains are moving away from owning properties to managing them. As part of a chain, individual hotels can participate in the company's national reservations service or incentive program, thereby appearing to belong to a larger enterprise.

For those who prefer more personalized service and a unique experience, *boutique hotels* are becoming more popular. These smaller hotels are generally found in urban locations and provide patrons good service and more distinctive decor and food selection.

Although there are nationwide RV parks and campgrounds, most small lodging establishments are individually owned and operated by a single owner, who may employ a small staff to help operate the business.

Recent developments. The lodging industry is moving towards more limited-service properties mostly in suburban, residential, or commercial neighborhoods, often locating hotels near popular restaurants. Many full-service properties are limiting or quitting the food service business altogether, choosing to contract out their food service operations to third party restaurateurs, including long-term arrangements with chain restaurant operators. Urban business and entertainment districts are providing a greater mix of lodging options to appeal to a wider range of travellers.

Increased competition among establishments in this industry has spurred many independently owned and operated hotels and other lodging places to join national or international reservation systems. This allows travellers to make multiple reservations for lodging, airlines, and car rentals with one telephone call or Internet search. Nearly all hotel chains and many independent lodging facilities operate online reservation systems through the Internet or maintain Web sites that allow individuals to book rooms. Online marketing of properties is so popular with guests that many hotels promote themselves with elaborate Web sites and allow people to investigate availability and rates.

Working Conditions

Hours. Because hotels are open around the clock, employees frequently work varying shifts or variable schedules. Employees who work the late shift generally receive additional compensation. Many employees enjoy the opportunity to work part-time, nights or evenings, or other schedules that fit their availability for work and the hotel's needs. Hotel managers and many department supervisors may work regularly assigned schedules, but they also routinely work longer hours than scheduled, especially during peak travel times or when multiple events are scheduled. Also, they may be called in to work on short notice in the event of an emergency or to cover a position. Those who are self-employed, often owner-operators of small inns, camp sites, or RV parks, tend to work long hours and often live at the establishment or nearby.

Office and administrative support workers generally work scheduled hours in an office setting, meeting with guests, clients, and hotel staff. Their work can become hectic—processing orders and invoices, dealing with demanding guests, or servicing requests that require a quick turnaround. Job hazards typically are limited to muscle and eye strain common to working with computers and office equipment.

Computer specialists, information technology technicians, and audiovisual technicians who are employed mostly by larger convention hotels typically maintain standard hours servicing the property's Web sites and computer and communications networks. However, they often work long hours setting up and testing equipment for events that require their services. Work environment. Work in hotels and other accommodations can be demanding and hectic. Hotel staffs provide a variety of services to guests and must do so efficiently, courteously, and accurately. They must maintain a pleasant demeanor even during times of stress or when dealing with an impatient or irate guest. Alternately, work at slower times, such as the off-season or overnight periods, can seem slow and tiresome. Still, hotel workers must be ready to provide guests and visitors with gracious customer service at any hour.

Food preparation and food service workers in hotels must withstand the strain of working during busy periods and being on their feet for many hours. Kitchen workers lift heavy pots and kettles and work near hot ovens and grills. Job hazards include slips and falls, cuts, and burns, but injuries are seldom serious. Food service workers often carry heavy trays of food, dishes, and glassware. Many of these workers work part time, including evenings, weekends, and holidays.

Employment

Hotels and other accommodations provided 1.9 million wage and salary jobs in 2008. Employment is concentrated in cities and resort areas. Compared with establishments in other industries, hotels and other accommodations tend to be small. About 74 percent employed fewer than 20 workers and 54 percent employed fewer than 10. As a result, lodging establishments offer opportunities for those who are interested in owning or running their own business. Although establishments tend to be small, the majority of jobs are in larger hotels—those with more than 100 employees.

Hotels and other lodging places often provide first jobs to many new entrants to the labour force. In 2008, about 19 percent of the workers were younger than age 25, compared with about 13 percent across all industries.

Occupations in the Industry

The vast majority of workers in this industry—83 percent in 2008—were employed in service and office and administrative support occupations. Workers in these occupations usually learn their skills on the job. Postsecondary education is not required for most entry-level positions; however, college training may be helpful for advancement in some of the occupations. For those in administrative support—mainly hotel desk clerks—and service occupations, positive personality traits and a customer-service orientation may be more important than formal schooling. The most important traits for success in the hotels and other accommodations industry are good communication skills; the ability to get along with people in stressful situations; a neat, clean appearance; and a pleasant manner.

Service occupations. Service workers are by far the largest occupational group in the industry, accounting for 65 percent of the industry's employment. Most service jobs are in housekeeping occupations, including *maids and housekeeping cleaners* and *janitors and cleaners*, and in food preparation and serving jobs, including *waiters and waitresses, bartenders, fast food and counter workers*, and various other kitchen and dining room workers. The industry also employs many *baggage porters and bellhops, gaming services workers*, and *grounds maintenance workers*.

Workers in cleaning and housekeeping occupations ensure that the lodging facility is clean and in good condition for the comfort and safety of guests. *Maids and housekeeping cleaners* clean lobbies, halls, guestrooms, and bathrooms. They make sure that guests not only have clean rooms, but have all the necessary furnishings and supplies. They change sheets and towels, vacuum carpets, dust furniture, empty wastebaskets, and mop bathroom floors. In larger hotels, the housekeeping staff may include assistant housekeepers, floor supervisors, housekeepers, and executive housekeepers. *Janitors* help with the cleaning of the public areas of the facility, empty trash, and perform minor maintenance work.

Workers in the various *food preparation and serving* occupations deal with customers in the dining room or at a service counter. *Waiters and waitresses* take customers' orders, serve meals, and prepare checks. In smaller establishments, they often set tables, escort guests to their seats, accept payment, and clear tables. In larger restaurants, some of these tasks are assigned to other workers.

Bartenders fill beverage orders for customers seated at the bar or from waiters and waitresses who serve patrons at tables. *Dining room and cafeteria attendants* and *bartender helpers* assist waiters, waitresses, and bartenders by clearing, cleaning, and setting up tables, replenishing supplies at the bar, and keeping the serving areas stocked with linens, tableware, and other supplies. *Fast food and counter workers* take orders and serve food at fast-food counters and in coffee shops; they also may operate the cash register.

A variety of food preparation workers prepare food in the kitchen. Larger hotels employ *chefs and head cooks* who create menus, develop recipes, and oversee food preparation operations and personnel. *Food preparation and serving supervisors* direct workers and supervise specific tasks, such as overseeing banquet cooks or bartenders and servers at a private function, while the chef tends to other activities. *Restaurant cooks* specialize in the preparation of many different kinds of foods and menu items, generally cooking from scratch and typically only when ordered by diners. They may have titles such as salad chef, grill chef, or pastry chef. Individual chefs may oversee the day-to-day operations of different kitchens in a hotel, such as a full-service restaurant that specializes in fine-dining, a casual or counter-service establishment, or banquet operations. Chef positions generally are attained after years of experience and, sometimes, formal training, including apprenticeships. Larger establishments also employ *executive chefs* and *food and beverage directors* who plan menus, purchase food, and supervise kitchen personnel for all of the kitchens in the property. *Food preparation workers* shred lettuce for salads, cut up food for cooking, and perform simple cooking steps under the direction of the chef or head cook. Beginners may advance to more skilled food preparation jobs with experience or specialized culinary training.

Many full-service hotels employ a uniformed staff to assist arriving and departing guests. *Baggage porters and bellhops* carry bags and escort guests to their rooms. *Concierges* arrange special or personal services for guests. They may take messages, arrange for babysitting, make restaurant reservations, provide directions, arrange for or give advice on entertainment and local attractions, and monitor requests for housekeeping and maintenance. *Doorkeepers* help guests into and out of their cars, summon taxis, and carry baggage into the hotel lobby.

Hotels also employ the largest percentage of *gaming services* workers because a large share of gaming takes place in casino hotels. Some gaming services positions are associated with oversight and direction—supervision, surveillance, and investigation—while others involve working with the games or patrons themselves, by tending the slot machines, handling money, writing and running tickets, dealing cards, and performing related duties.

The industry also employs a large number of *recreation and fitness workers*. At resort hotels and at vacation and recreational camps, recreation workers organize and conduct recreation activities for guests and campers. *Camp counselors* lead and instruct children and teenagers in outdoor-oriented forms of recreation, such as swimming, hiking, horseback riding, and camping. In addition, counselors at vacation and resident camps also provide guidance and supervise daily living and general socialization. Other types of campgrounds may employ trail guides for activities such as hiking, hunting, and fishing.

Office and administrative support occupations. These positions accounted for 19 percent of the jobs in hotels and other accommodations in 2008. Hotel desk clerks, bookkeeping and accounting clerks, and switchboard operators ensure that the front office operates smoothly. *Hotel, motel, and resort desk clerks* process reservations and guests' registrations and checkouts, monitor arrivals and departures, handle complaints, and receive and forward mail. The duties of hotel desk clerks depend on the size of the facility. In smaller lodging places, one clerk or a manager may do everything. In larger hotels, a larger staff divides the duties among several types of clerks.

Management, business, and financial operations occupations. Hotels and other lodging places employ many different types of managers to direct and coordinate the activities of the front office, kitchen, dining room, and other departments, such as housekeeping, accounting, personnel, purchasing, publicity, sales, security, and maintenance. *Lodging managers*, typically the general manager and assistant managers, make decisions that affect the general operations of the hotel, including setting room rates, establishing credit policy, and having ultimate responsibility for resolving problems. In smaller establishments, lodging managers also may perform many of the front-office administrative tasks. In the smallest establishments, the owners—sometimes a family team—do all the work necessary to operate the business.

Other managers are responsible for different phases of hotel operations. For example, *food and beverage managers* oversee restaurants, lounges, and catering or banquet operations. *Rooms managers* look after reservations and occupancy levels to ensure proper room assignments and authorize discounts, special rates, or promotions. Large hotels, especially those with conference centres, use an executive committee structure to better facilitate departmental communications and coordinate activities. Other managers who may serve on a hotel's executive committee include *public relations* or *sales managers, human resource directors, executive housekeepers,* and *heads of hotel security.*

Other occupations. Hotels and other accommodations employ a variety of workers found in many other industries. *General maintenance and repair workers* fix leaky faucets, do some painting and carpentry, make sure that heating and air-conditioning equipment works properly, mow lawns, and exterminate pests. The industry also employs cashiers, accountants, personnel workers, and entertainers. As properties acquire and use more sophisticated computer systems, they employ more *computer specialists* to help maintain these systems as well as the hotel's Web site, and computer connections for guests. Also, many additional workers inside a hotel may work for other companies under contract to the hotel or may provide personal or retail services directly to hotel guests from space rented by the hotel. This group includes guards and security officers, barbers and cosmetologists, fitness trainers and aerobics instructors, valets, gardeners, and parking attendants.

Training and Advancement

Most large hotel properties employ persons in occupations that require a wide range of skills and experience. Most entry level jobs require little or no previous training; basic tasks usually can be learned in a short time. Lodging managers and many department heads usually require some formal training, or years of hospitality industry experience, or both. All positions in this industry require employees to maintain a customer-service orientation. Almost all workers in the hotel and other accommodations industry undergo some on-the-job training provided under the supervision of an experienced employee or manager to acclimate new employees to any unique characteristics of the property or the local area.

Hotel managers and owners recognize the importance of personal service and attention to guests, so they look for persons with positive personality traits and good communication skills when filling many guest services positions, such as desk clerk and host and hostess positions. Many hotel managers place a greater emphasis on customer service skills while providing specialized training in other skill areas, such as computer technology and software. Vocational courses and apprenticeship programs in food preparation, catering, and hotel and restaurant management, offered through restaurant and lodging associations and trade unions, provide training opportunities. Programs range in length from a few months to several years.

Service workers. Most service workers need only a high school diploma or equivalent to get hired, but some can be hired with even less. Some entry-level jobs are filled by students looking for part-time or seasonal work. Most hotels, particularly the chain hotels, have some formal training sessions for new employees that may include video or online training. Advancement opportunities for service workers in the hotel industry vary widely. Some workers, such as housekeepers and janitors, generally have few opportunities for advancement. In large properties, some may advance to supervisory positions. Advancement opportunities for chefs and cooks are better than those for most other service occupations. Cooks often advance to chef or to supervisory and management positions, such as executive chef, restaurant manager, or food service manager. Hotel desk clerks sometimes advance to supervisory or managerial front-office positions.

Promotional opportunities often are greatest for those who are willing to take on a new assignment in a different department. Advancement for those who excel at customer service and demonstrate a willingness to learn front-office jobs can serve as a steppingstone to jobs in public relations, advertising, sales, and management.

Management, business, and financial operations occupations. Many hotels fill first-level manager positions by promoting staff from within—particularly those with good communication skills, a solid educational background, tact, loyalty, and a capacity to endure hard work and long hours. People with these qualities still advance to manager jobs, but, more recently, lodging chains have primarily been hiring persons with 4-year college degrees in the liberal arts or other fields and starting them in assistant manager or management trainee positions. Bachelor's and Master's degree programs in hotel, restaurant, and hospitality management provide the strongest background for a career as a hotel manager, with nearly 150 colleges and universities offering such programs. Graduates of these programs are highly sought by employers in this industry because of their familiarity with technical issues and their ability to learn related skills quickly. Eventually, they may advance to a top management position in a hotel or a corporate management position in a large chain operation.

Upper management positions, such as general manager, food service manager, or sales manager, generally require considerable formal training and job experience. Some department managers, executive housekeepers, and executive chefs, generally require some specialized training and extensive on-the-job experience. To advance to positions with more responsibilities, lodging managers frequently change employers or relocate within a chain to a property in another area.

Office and administrative support occupations. For office and administrative support workers, advancement opportunities in the hotel industry vary widely. These occupations offer excellent entry-level job prospects and can serve as a steppingstone to jobs in hospitality, public relations, advertising, sales, and management.

Outlook

The hotels and other accommodations industry is expected grow by 5 percent over the 2008-18 period. The industry employs large numbers of part-time and younger workers who typically do not stay in these jobs for very long. The need to replace these workers will create job opportunities in an array of occupations and localities.

Employment change. Wage and salary employment in hotels and other accommodations is expected to increase by 5 percent between 2008 and 2018, compared with 11 percent growth projected for all industries combined. Travel and tourism typically grows during expansion periods in the economy, which results in a greater need for transient rooms. The hotel market is expected to see increases in the number of rooms, but the greatest number of rooms is expected to open in limited service hotels that do not provide food service. Many of these newer hotels are being built in the suburbs where a growing population is increasingly based and a foundation of business establishments is being developed.

Employment outlook varies somewhat by service class of hotel and occupation. Growth of full-service hotels, casino hotels, and the smaller luxury hotel market that specializes in personal service will cause employment of lodging managers to grow more slowly than the average. The accelerating trend among chain-affiliated hotels to establish regional management and staffing teams among several properties and across service classes should provide current assistant managers or department managers with opportunities to demonstrate their readiness for advancement, but may also limit the prospects for new manager positions. Opportunities should be more limited for self-employed managers or owners of small lodging places, such as bed-and-breakfast inns, because of the competition from long-established chains as they move into untapped markets that were once friendly to the quainter properties. Job opportunities at outdoor recreation and RV parks should grow as RVs and driving vacations gain popularity in the United States. Also, gaming services and gaming manager occupations should grow as more casino hotels are built.

Employment of hotel, motel, and resort desk clerks is expected to grow faster than some other occupations in the industry in part because the growing numbers of limited-service hotels still require desk clerks. However, employment of dishwashers will decline within the industry—reflecting the increasing number of hotels and other accommodations that either do not offer full-service restaurants or contract them out to other food service establishments.

Job prospects. Although most of the hotels opening over the next decade will be limited-service hotels, most of the job openings will arise in full-service hotels, including convention, casino, and resort hotels, because they employ the most workers. Limited-service properties do not operate restaurants or lounges; therefore, these establishments offer a narrower range of employment opportunities. The streamlined organizational structure, however, offers a faster route to the general manager level for those more interested in running or owning their own hotel. Job opportunities will be concentrated in the largest hotel occupations, such as building cleaning workers and hotel, motel, and resort desk clerks. These workers are found in all types of hotels and accommodations, from the limited-service economy hotels to posh casino hotels. They also are important to the luxury hotel segment that emphasizes personal service. Some occupations in this industry have relatively high numbers of workers who leave their jobs and must be replaced. Many young people, and those looking only for seasonal or part-time work, take food service and administrative jobs that require little or no previous training. To attract and retain workers, the hotel and other accommodations industry is placing greater emphasis on training and retaining employees. Job opportunities in this industry should be good for first-time jobseekers, people with limited experience, and those interested in making a career in the lodging industry.

Earnings

Industry earnings. Earnings in hotels and other accommodations generally are much lower than the average for all industries. In 2008, average earnings for all nonsupervisory workers in this industry were $402 a week, compared with $608 a week for workers throughout private industry. Some workers in this industry earn the Federal minimum wage, which was $7.25 per hour as of July 2009. Some States have laws that establish a higher minimum wage.

Food and beverage service workers, as well as hosts and hostesses, maids and housekeeping cleaners, concierges, and baggage porters and bellhops, derive their earnings from a combination of hourly wages and customer tips. Waiters and waitresses often derive the majority of their earnings from tips, which vary greatly depending on menu prices and the volume of customers served. Many employers also provide free meals and furnish uniforms. Food service personnel may receive extra pay for working at banquets and on other special occasions.

The Chain Hotel Concept

Prior to examining the concept and the idea behind hotel chains and what exactly they are, it's important to have a peek at the interesting aspects of what a hotel is, what its mission supposed to be and how its operations are being carried out. With such an understanding, it's easier to see the value, purpose and the excitement behind hotel chains as opposed to a hotel.

As we all know, a hotel is regarded as an institution and or a service provider's establishment to offer paid lodging facilities to customers on limited time or short term basis. These facilities provided include, accommodation consisting of a room with a bed and other furniture (limited to the product bought), meals on room and board basis, attached bathrooms, air conditioning and climate control facilities, as well as, telephone facilities, cable television, internet connectivity and access plus the desirable mini bar. These are only some of the items included in a hotel room.

Apart from the facilities provided in the rooms of these hotels to the guests, there are many other additions and assortments available for a person staying in these hotels. They come in the form of, multi cuisine restaurants, swimming pools, fitness training centres, spas, conference and banquet halls and many others.

Another aspect that anyone comes across with hotels is the classification. As a result of the tourism industry worldwide expanding at a rapid rate during recent decades, for purposes of comparability and standards, rating systems have been introduced. This rating system takes the form of one to five stars classification where the most stars bearing hotels provide the best product and the lower star hotels provide a mediocre or average product to their guests. 'Some consider this disadvantageous to smaller hotels whose quality of accommodation could fall into one class but the lack of an item such as an elevator would prevent it from reaching a higher categorization. In some countries, there is an official body with standard criteria for classifying hotels, but in many others there is none. There have been attempts at unifying the classification system so that it becomes an internationally recognized and reliable standard but large differences exist in the quality of the accommodation and the food within one category of hotel, sometimes even in the same country.

With a proper understanding of the concept, idea and the purpose behind a hotel, it is helpful now to look at the term hotel chain. The term hotel chain traits back its origins to the 1920s where a great trend began which shifted individual ownership of hotels to corporate ownership as a result of increasing costs of building and operating hotels.

As the corporate world took over the hotel business, they didn't believe in a single hotel at a single location but a chain of hotels at different locations with the same name but not necessarily with the same capacity and product range. Chain operations of 'hotels allows for efficient management through the use of mass purchasing, central reservations and billings, and extensive advertising and promotion campaigns. Today about 30 percent of all American hotels and motels are affiliated with chains or franchised groups.

Going International

In general, to be called a hotel, an establishment must have a minimum of six letting bedrooms, at least three of which must have attached (ensuite) private bathroom facilities. Although hotels are classified into 'Star' categories (1-Star to 5-Star), there is no standard method of assigning these ratings, and compliance with customary requirements is voluntary. A US hotel with a certain rating, for example, is may look very different from a European or Asian hotel with the same rating, and would provide a different level of amenities, range of facilities, and quality of service. Whereas hotel chains assure uniform standards throughout, non-chain hotels (even within the same country) may not agree on the same standards.

In Germany, for example, only about 30 percent of the hotels chcose to comply with the provisions of the rules established by the German Hotels & Restaurants association. Although both WTO and ISO have been trying to persuade hotels to agree on some minimum requirements as worldwide norms, the entire membership of the Paris-based International Hotel & Restaurant (IH&RA) opposes any such move. According to IH&RA, to harmonize hotel classification based on a single grading (which is uniform across national boundaries) would be an undesirable and impossible task.

As a rough guide: A 1-Star hotel provides a limited range of amenities and services, but adheres to a high standard of facility-wide cleanliness. A 2-Star hotel provides good accommodation and better equipped bedrooms, each with a telephone and attached private bathroom. A 3-Star hotel has more spacious rooms and adds high-class decorations and furnishings and colour TV. It also offers one or more bars or lounges. A 4-Star hotel is much more comfortable and larger, and provides excellent cuisine, room service, and other amenities.

A 5-Star hotel offers most luxurious premises, widest range of guest services, as well as swimming pool and sport and exercise facilities. The Official Hotel Guide (published in the US, and followed world wide) has its own classification scheme that ranks hotels in nine categories as (1) Moderate Tourist Class, (2) Tourist Class, (3) Superior Tourist Class, (4) Moderate First Class, (5) Limited Service First Class, (6) First Class, (7) Moderate Deluxe, (8) Deluxe, and (9) Superior Deluxe.

Marriott International

Marriott International, Inc. (NYSE: MAR) is a worldwide operator and franchisor of a broad portfolio of hotels and related lodging facilities. Founded by J. Willard Marriott, the company is now led by son J.W. (Bill) Marriott, Jr. Today, Marriott International has about 3,150 lodging properties located in the United States and 67 other countries and territories.

Marriott's operations are grouped into the following five business segments:

- Full-service lodging-65%
- Select-service lodging-11%
- Extended-stay lodging-5%
- Timeshare-15%
- Synthetic fuel-4% (primarily a tax shelter).

History

Marriott was founded by J. Willard Marriott 1927 when he and his wife opened a root beer stand in Washington D.C.. As a missionary in the sweltering, humid summers in Washington, Marriott was convinced that what the city needed was a such a place to get a cool drink. They later expanded their enterprises into a chain of restaurants and hotels.

The Key Bridge Marriott in Arlington, Virginia is Marriott International's longest operating hotel, and celebrated its 50th anniversary in 2009. Their son and current Chairman and Chief Executve Officer, J.W. (Bill) Marriott, Jr. has led the company to spectacular worldwide growth. Today, Marriott International has about 3,150 lodging properties located in the United States and 67 other countries and territories.

Marriott International was formed in 1992 when Marriott Corporation split into two companies, Marriott International and Host Marriott Corporation.

In 2002 Marriott International began a major restructuring by spinning off many Senior Living Services Communities (which is now part of Sunrise Senior Living) and Marriott Distribution Services, so that it could focus on hotel ownership and management. The changes were completed in 2003.

In April 1995, Marriott International acquired a 49% interest in the Ritz-Carlton Hotel Company LLC. Marriott International believed that it could increase sales and profit margins at the Ritz, a troubled chain with a significant number of properties either losing money or barely breaking even. The cost of Marriott's initial investment was estimated to be about $200 million in cash and assumed debt. The next year, Marriott spent $331 million to take over the Ritz-Carlton Atlanta and buy a majority interest in two properties owned by William Johnson, a real estate developer who had purchased the Boston Ritz Carlton in 1983 and expanded his Ritz holdings over the next twenty years.

The Ritz began expansion into the lucrative timeshare market among other new initiatives made financially possible by the deep pockets of Marriott, which also lent its own in-house expertise in certain areas. There were other benefits for Ritz-Carlton flowing from its relationship with Marriott, such as being able to take advantage of the parent company's reservation system and buying power. The partnership was solidified in 1998 when Marriott boosted its interest in Ritz-Carlton to 99 percent. By 1999 revenues from the 35 hotels it operated around the world totaled about $1.4 billion. Marriott International owned Ramada International Hotels & Resorts until its sale on September 15, 2004 to Cendant. It is the first hotel chain to serve food that is completely free of trans fats at all of its North American properties.

In 2005, Marriott International and Marriott Vacation Club International comprised two of the 53 entities that contributed the maximum of $250,000 to the second inauguration of President George W. Bush.

On July 19, 2006, Marriott announced that all lodging buildings they operate in the United States and Canada would become non-smoking beginning September 2006. "The new policy includes all guest rooms, restaurants, lounges, meeting rooms, public space and employee work areas."

Terrorist Attacks

Several Marriott hotels around the world have been the target of bombings.

- 2001 Marriott world trade centre 9/11 atacks
- 2003 Marriott Hotel bombing
- 2008 Islamabad Marriott bombing
- 2009 Jakarta bombings.

Great America Parks

Marriott also developed three and ultimately opened two theme parks entitled Marriott's Great America from 1976 until 1984. The parks were located in Gurnee, Illinois, Santa Clara, California and a proposed but never-built location in the Washington, DC area, and were themed celebrating American history. The American-themed areas under Marriott's tenure of ownership included "Carousel Plaza" (the first section beyond the main gates); small-town-themed "Hometown Square"; "The Great Midwest Livestock Exposition At County Fair" with a Turn of the Century rural-fair theme; "Yankee Harbor", inspired by a 19th century New England port; "Yukon Territory," resembling a Canadian/Alaskan logging camp; and the French Quarter-modeled "Orleans Place". At opening, both parks were laid out nearly identically.

In 1984, Marriott disposed of its theme park division; both parks were sold and today are associated with national theme park chains. The Gurnee location was sold to Six Flags Theme Parks where it operates today as Six Flags Great America. The Santa Clara location was sold to the City of Santa Clara, who retained the underlying property and sold the park to Kings Entertainment Company, renamed Paramount Parks in 1993. From 1993 to 2006, the Santa Clara location was known as Paramount's Great America. In 2006, Paramount Parks was acquired by Cedar Fair Entertainment Company; the Santa Clara park operates today as California's Great America. In the years after their sale, the layouts of the parks have diverged substantially.

Marriott Brands

Full Service Lodging

- Marriott Hotels & Resorts
- JW Marriott Hotels & Resorts
- Renaissance Hotels & Resorts
- Marriott Conference Centres

- Ritz-Carlton Hotels & Resorts
- BVLGARI Hotels & Resorts
- Edition Hotels & Resorts
- Autograph Collection Hotels & Resots.

Select Service Lodging

- Courtyard by Marriott
- Fairfield Inn by Marriott
- SpringHill Suites by Marriott.

Extended Stay Lodging

- Residence Inn by Marriott
- TownePlace Suites by Marriott
- Marriott ExecuStay
- Marriott Executive Apartments.

Timeshare

- Marriott Vacation Club International (MVCI)
- Marriott Grand Residence Club
- The Ritz-Carlton Club
- The Ritz-Carlton Destination Club.

Marriott Rewards

Marriott International also offers Marriott Rewards, a loyalty ("rewards") program that allows members to earn points or airline miles for their stays at participating Marriott brand hotels, in addition to other membership benefits.

20 Largest Hotels in the World

Las Vegas is famous for many items! Besides gambling, wedding, conventions, destination resorts, Las Vegas is famous for the size of the hotels.

Below we have listed the 20 largest hotels in the world, 15 of the 20 are located within a two-mile radius within Las Vegas. Also, 21 of the top 28 hotels are located within the same two-mile radius.

Ranked number one, the First World Hotel has topped the list. It is not located in Las Vegas, but in Malaysia. Pictured on the right, this multicolor structure is a real eye catcher.

The MGM Grand is also pictured to the right, it reigned as the number one largest hotel for years, now taking the number two seat.

Size	*Hotel*	*Location*	*Rooms*
1.	First World Hotel	Malaysia	6,118
2.	MGM Grand	Las Vegas	5,690
3.	Luxor	Las Vegas	4,408
4.	Mandalay Bay (Inc. The Hotel) 3,223 & 1118	Las Vegas	4,341
5.	The Venetian	Las Vegas	4,027
6.	Excalibur	Las Vegas	4,008
7.	Bellagio	Las Vegas	3,993
8.	Circus Circus	Las Vegas	3,774
9.	Planet Hollywood	Las Vegas	3,697
10.	Shinagawa Prince Hotel Tokyo	Tokyo	3,680
11.	Ambassador City Jomtien	Thailand	3,610
12.	Flamingo Las Vegas	Las Vegas	3,565
13.	Palazzo	Las Vegas	3,443
14.	Hilton Hawaiian Village	Honolulu	3,386
15.	Caesar's Palace	Las Vegas	3,349
16.	Mirage	Las Vegas	3,044
17.	Monte Carlo	Las Vegas	3,002
18.	The Venetian Macao	Macau	3,000
19.	Las Vegas Hilton	Las Vegas	2,956
20.	Paris Las Vegas	Las Vegas	2,916
Honorable Mention			
21.	Treasure Island	Las Vegas	2,895
22.	Gaylord Opryland	Nashville	2,883
23.	Disney's Pop Century	Orlando	2,880
24.	Bally's	Las Vegas	2,814
25.	Wynn Las Vegas	Las Vegas	2,716
26.	Imperial Palace	Las Vegas	2,635
27.	Harrah's Las Vegas	Las Vegas	2,576
28.	Stratosphere	Las Vegas	2,444

Largest Hotel

The largest hotel in the world is the First World Hotel in Genting Highlands, Malaysia. This biggest hotel took the title from the MGM Grand Las Vegas in Las Vegas, Nevada. The First World Hotel hass 6,118 rooms with prices starting as low as $60.00 USD/night.

IHG (InterContinental Hotels Group)

Is the worlds largest and most global hotel chain. IHG's brands include: InterContinental Hotels, Crowne Plaza, Hotel Indigo, Holiday Inn, Holiday Inn Express, Staybridge Suites, and Candlewood Suites.

As of March 2009 they had over 4,200 hotels in their portfolio representing over 621,000 Rooms.

Best Western uses the tag line "The Worlds Largest Hotel Chain"; however with a portfolio of just under 4,000 hotels representing 303,000 rooms. They come in number 7 behind IHG, Wyndham, Marriott, Hilton, Accor, and Choice Hotels.

Revenue Management Techniques in Hospitality Industry – A comparison with Reference to Star and Economy Hotels

The hospitality industry is part of a larger enterprise known as the travel and tourism industry. It is one of the oldest industries in the world. In early days, traders, explorers, missionaries and pilgrims needed a break in their journeys requiring food, shelter and rest.

People opened their homes and kitchens to these weary travellers, and an industry was born. Although accommodation today is varied and their services have changed and expanded over the ages, one thing about the hospitality industry has remained the same, guests are always welcome! From a friendly greeting at the door, room service, breakfast, to a host of facilities' the hospitality industry offers travellers a home away from home.

Hospitality is defined as "the friendly reception and treatment of strangers". For most people, hospitality means entertaining guests with courtesy and warmth. Hospitality is also an industry made up of businesses that provide lodging, food and other services to travellers. The main components of this industry are hotels, motels, inns, resorts and Restaurants.

In a broad sense, the hospitality industry might refer to any group engaged in tourism, entertainment, transportation or lodging including cruise lines, airlines, railways, car rental companies and tour operators.

However the two main segments are the lodging industry also called the hotel industry, and the food and beverage industry, also called the restaurant industry. The lodging industry is made up of businesses providing temporary housing, and such a business is called a lodging establishment and the people who stay in it are called guests or clients.

What is Revenue Management?

Revenue Management is a technique to optimize the revenue earned from a fixed, perishable resource. The challenge is to sell the right resources to the right customer at the right time.

Revenue Management implements the basic principles of supply and demand economics in a tactical way to generate incremental revenues. There are three essential conditions for revenue management to be applicable:

- That there is a fixed amount of resources available for sale.
- That the resources sold are perishable. This means that there is a time limit to selling the resources, after which they cease to be of value.
- That different customers are willing to pay a different price for using the same amount of resources.

Revenue Management is of especially high relevance in cases where the constant costs are relatively high compared to the variable costs. The less variable costs there are, the more the additional revenue earned will contribute to the overall profit.

To illustate this, we can take the example of the luxury hotel which charges different prices for different customers. In India it is generally practiced in star hotels to maximise the revenues. The customer who is price sensitive and time conscious generally pays lesser tariffs than a customer who is willing to pay more and books the room one or two days before the stay.

Revenue Management in other words tries to maximise revenues by managing the tradeoff between a low occupancy and higher room rate senario (business customers) versus a high occupancy and lower room rate (vacation customers).

Demand forecasting: Pricing and demand are inter-related and need to be coordinated. In the hospitality industry, demand for a room is cyclic in nature and follows a trend. Revenue management models help pinpoint demand by minimising uncertainity and producing the best possible forecast.

Allocation: the revenue management also puts light on the allocation of inventory (hotel rooms) among different segments. For example, if a hotel has two price categories of rooms, say Rs.4500 and Rs. 6000.

Since the pricing is different for the two rooms, these rooms are each targeted at a different customer set.

Based on the historical preference pattern of customers in each segment, it would be possible to estimate the number of customers who would be willing to pabuy these rooms at a given price with a reasonable variance. For example, an average 50 customers may be willing to pay Rs. 6000 for some rooms, but it could also mean that the actual number of customers who turn up for Rs. 6000 could be 60 or even 40 with some probability, or 80 or 30 with a lesser probability.

Overbooking: Overbooking is a practice of intentionally selling more rooms than available in order to offset the effect of cancellations. For example, suppose in the hotel industry, there are 180 rooms available, there is no certainity that all the rooms would be booed at a point of time. In the same way, during the season, there is a possibility of over booking.

Therefore if the booking is done 181 customers instead of 180, the hotel may end up with only 173 or less than 180 customers, since the probability of exactly 181 customers turning up is low, the revenue from that aditional customer generally compensates more than the expected cost.

Classification of Hotels

Hotels are classified into five main types:

- Economy/limited-service hotels
- Mid-market hotels
- All-suite hotels
- First class or executive hotels
- Luxury or deluxe hotels.

For the purpose of our research, Economy and Executive hotels are selected.

Normally hotels have four rate categories: (1) Rack rates, (2) Group and tour rates, (3) Special and promotional rates and (4) package rates.

(1) Rack rates are normal room rates. It is based on the category of the room, type of bedding and occupancy. Unless specified, guests are quoted the rack rates and are charged for the same.

(2) Group and Tour rates are a discounted room rate for an organisation, which has blocked a large number of rooms. Most hotels have group rates that are lower than the rack rates. This rate is generally extended to a trade association or fraternal organisation that has scheduled a meeting, seminar or conference at the hotel. Discounts are also offered to a tour operator, in return for a commitment to purchase a minimum number of rooms over a given period of time.

(3) Special and promotional rates are offered to corporate travellers, traveling sales representatives, military personnel, airlines staff or other regular clients. Some times special rates are also offered along with an advertising campaign or to promote the hotel during lean periods.

(4) Package rates are offered to the public along with other services such as banquet or a ball, or recreational facilities or a special event. Such a package normally includes accommodation, tickets to the concerned event and transportation from hotel to the venue and back. Other popular packages offered by hotels are honeymoon, weekend, Christmas, New Year or any other sports activity. The package rate is normally lower than the combined component or rack rate.

A Case Study on Bentleys Hotel (Economy) and Hotel Godwin Hotel Bentleys, Colaba (Economy Hotel)

Bentley's is one of Mumbai's (formerly known as Bombay, India) best budget tourist hotels. It is highly rated in most Tourist/ Traveller's Guides, including The Lonely Planet.

Ideally situated in South Mumbai, it is in the heart of the downtown area, close to the business, entertainment and shopping areas. The hotel has a clean, quiet, comfortable and homely atmosphere.

Victorian Ambiance

The hotel gets 95% of its customers as foreign tourists. The occupancy rate in this hostel is 110%. The rooms are occupied for the 365 days in this year. Demand is more than

Supply in this hotel. The customers are not provided with any food in this hotel. The hotel does not practice differential pricing for its customers. It charges single price for all of its customers irrespective of different nationality. Tourists generally would like to stay in this hotel for the wonderful service provided by the hotel. Generally the hotel gets repeated customers and the customer loyalty is very good over here.

Marketing Strategies adopted by the hotel to attract more tourists:

- Reservation is done directly without the help of middleman like travel agents.
- Hotel provides prompt service to the enquiries of the customers mails. Usually the queries are answered within an hour.
- The services provided by the housekeepers are also very good. They are excellent in communication and they meet the customer demand promptly.
- Generally in this hotel, 80% of the customers are repeated which means there is customer loyalty to the maximum extent.
- Usually the hotels provide one room to one customer in a day. But Bentleys uses its perishable capacity 3 times a day for the purpose of maximizing the revenue.

Hotel Godwin, Colaba (Three Star Hotel)

The hotel has been accredited as a 3 star hotel and is situated in colaba. They find most of their customers from Gulf. Hotel Godwin, a 3 Star Hotel with 52 rooms has been serving the travellers and business community for well over 30 years and from the testimonials of its patrons, both Indian and Foreign, it is considered a real home away from home. hotel godwin occupies an ideal location from the point of view of businessmen and tourists. Adjacent to Colaba Causeway, the fashionable shopping centre in South Mumbai, it is close to the tourists attractions like the Gateway of India; Museum, the business centres of Flora

Fountain, Churchgate Reclamation and Nariman Point, Offices of National & International Airlines, and headquarters of both the main Railway line close by. Prominent Clubs, Cinemas & Restaurants are near by.

- They get the customers through travel agents in Mumbai and the other parts of India.
- The average occupancy rate is 60%
- Most of the customers are tourists.
- They charge different tariff to different customers.
- Usually they get repeated customers.
- They do overbook the rooms to maximize the revenues.
- There are 65 employees in the hotel.

Revenue Management Strategies Adopted by the Hotels Findings

- It is believed that the hotels, which are functioning at the large scale, are good in revenue management and they apply most advanced techniques to manage their revenues. But through this research on star and economy hotels, it can be said that the star hotels provide the state of the art facilities and services to the customers and very hygiene food to the customers. But when it comes to the occupancy rates measure in terms of foreign tourists, the economy hotels are exceedingly doing well.
- Economy Hotels give importance to the cultural values of the country.
- The concept of overbooking is followed in both kinds of hotels.
- The market segmentation is not there in case of economy hotels. But it is practiced in star hotels.
- Rooms are booked directly through internet by the customers in case of economy hotels and indirectly through the travel agents in case of star hotels.
- Economy hotels do not practice revenue management techniques neither through its differential pricing nor through market segmentation. They just manage their revenues by applying the concept of logical booking.

4

Beverage and Food Service

Kitchen work and chefs The heart of the hotel is the kitchen. Guests who patronize these hotels would visit them for various reasons, for locality, comfort, pricing and even for the food that is served and presented to them. Also there are some who visit these hotels for the purpose of having a meal or snack. Whatever the case maybe, the kitchen plays an important role for the existence and sustenance of the hotel.

Working in a hotel kitchen could be interesting, tiring, challenging and even exciting. With all the modern technology and gadgetry, these kitchens have turned out be somewhat high tech and more convenient. Some kitchens in luxurious hotels are so well equipped and maintained, with freezer rooms, to separate kitchens for the preparation of cakes, bread and pastry. With all the novel stoves, ovens and microwaves it is indeed a fantastic place to work in and a wonderful experience. Depending on size and class of the hotel, the kitchen staff may vary. Most of the top hotels have an Executive Chef and working under him there are different categories of chefs.

They are Chef de Cuisine, Chef de Partie, Demi Chef, Commis Chef, Sous Chef etc. The duties of these chefs will vary from one to another. The Executive Chef or the Head Chef generally will oversee and supervise the department, and will instruct them accordingly as to what the duties for the day are. They are also responsible in all matters pertaining to the department, such as leave, attending to personal issues, attending board meetings and scheduling the work to each staff member. They are expected to work on shift basis as a hotel function 24-7.

Not only preparation, the presentation of the food is also equally important. An expected attribute of a chef is creativity and novelty. They are responsible from the start of the preparation of the food to the final presentation. They are expected to present the food to the guest in a manner that is appealing. Most of the elite hotels are continuously trying to improvise ways and means to allure guest to their hotels by having food fares and promotions. This has been a successful way earning revenue and is patronized by many guests for food experiences. Being creative could help a chef to present a meal in the most appetizing way, thus winning the heart of the customer.

Good communication skills are important to be successful in your mission. While constant training of the staff is done by the Executive Chefs, they are also expected at times to speak to guests and attend to some special need. Cleanliness and good hygiene is maintained at all times, it is said that the standard of the hotel could be judged by its kitchen.

Food and Beverage Services

Food and beverage services are among the most visible locations at ski areas, and a ski area's environmental commitment is often judged by the environmental practices within these establishments. Pollution prevention (P2) opportunities for restaurants address a broad range of operations, including solid waste management, grounds and facility maintenance, and restaurant supply purchasing.

A restaurant's pre-tax profit is typically only 3 to 9 percent of its total revenue; therefore, money saved through reductions in operating costs (that is, through reduced energy consumption and water use) can significantly increase the profit margin.

While some restaurants have already taken advantage of the many P2 opportunities available to them, a survey by the National Restaurant Association shows that for some of the most common P2 techniques and best practices, there is still room for improvement across the industry.

Numerous programs exist for the food and beverage service industry that help restaurants and their customers minimize environmental impacts. This chapter uses the Green Restaurant Association's approach as an outline to present the environmental practices a restaurant should consider.

Green Restaurant Association

Involvement in environmental programs is a good way for a restaurant to learn more about environmental best practice opportunities. An environmental resource for the food service industry is the Green Restaurant Association (GRA), which helps member restaurants reduce environmental impacts with twelve "eco-steps". The GRA's primary operational components are research, environmental consulting, education, public relations and marketing, and community organizing and consumer activism.

To become a member of the GRA, a restaurant must sign a statement of its commitment to making environmental improvements based on the 12 "eco-steps" listed below.

After a member restaurant has made positive environmental changes, the GRA will include the restaurant in the "Green Restaurant Guide," which serves as a directory for environmentally conscious restaurants. The GRA also offers fee-based consulting services to member restaurants and initiates public relations and marketing initiatives, such as having restaurants featured on CNN, to increase restaurant exposure and consumer awareness.

GRA's 12 eco-steps are outlined below and discussed further in Sections 9.2 through 9.13.

1. Elimination of Polystyrene Foam (commonly known as styrofoam). Replace all polystyrene foam products with environmentally friendly alternatives: paper, bamboo or sugarcane paper, recyclable plastic, biodegradable plastic, and so on. *This is the minimum environmental standard for becoming a member of the GRA.*
2. Comprehensive Recycling. Initiate or improve recycling programs for glass, plastic, bimetal, cardboard, and mixed paper.
3. Waste Reduction and Reuse. Increase bulk purchasing and reduce excessive packaging for food, condiments, and so on. Replace disposable products with reusable alternatives: eating ware, aprons, tea strainers, cups, and so on.
4. Biodegradable Plastic. Transition to corn-based "plastic" products that are biodegradable and petroleum-free: cups, utensils, garbage bags, and straws.

5. Recycled Products. Transition to recycled products with the highest postconsumer content available and non-tree-fiber paper products: napkins, paper towels, toilet paper, office paper, take-out containers, coffee jackets, plates, and bowls.
6. Non-Chlorine-Bleached Paper Products. Transition to non-bleached or non-chlorinebleached paper products: cups, wax paper, plates, take-out containers, bags, pastry bags and grabbers, napkins, paper towels, coffee filters, and office paper.
7. Nontoxic Cleaners, Landscaping and Pest Management. Replace hazardous chemical products with biodegradable and nontoxic alternatives; dish detergent, germicides, disinfectants, toilet bowl cleaners, drain cleaner, floor wash, floor polish, glass cleaners, degreasers, and laundry detergent. For landscaping, switch to nontoxic, nonsynthetic, and organic fertilizers, pesticides, or herbicides. For pest control, use nontoxic products or services.
8. Energy Efficiency. Improve the energy efficiency of lighting, refrigeration, air conditioning, gas appliances, and so on. Obtain assistance with using government and private rebate programs. Make connections with energy consultants to learn about more extensive programs.
9. Water Efficiency. Improve the water efficiency of toilets, faucets, laundry, sprinkler systems, and so on.
10. Composting. Divert food waste from landfills and create nutrient-rich soil for gardening and landscaping.
11. "Green" Electricity. Change to an energy provider that uses solar, wind, small-scale hydroelectric, geothermal, or methane-based power that is renewable and less polluting to ecosystems.
12. Employee Education Program. Train all employees, managers, and owners. Topics covered should include
    - An environmental profile of the restaurant industry
    - A history of environmental issues relevant to food service: landfills, water pollution, air pollution, clear-cutting, and global warming

- Data describing the restaurant impacts (positive and negative) on the environment.

Elimination of Polystyrene Foam

Polystyrene foam (Styrofoam) is widely used in restaurants in insulated cups for hot beverages and take-out containers. Production of polystyrene involves use of known (benzene) and suspected (styrene and 1,3-butadiene) human carcinogenic substances (styrene and 1,3-butadiene). Styrene is also known to be toxic to the reproductive system. Polystyrene can be recycled; however, its recycling rates are low. Styrofoam is light in weight, but bulky in size, so hauling Styrofoam to the nearest available recycling facility is often not economically feasible. The value of a load of Styrofoam may not even cover the cost of shipping. To reduce environmental impacts, restaurants should consider switching from Styrofoam to non-bleached paper wraps, cardboard containers, or other sustainable food packaging.

According to a report published by the Environmental Defence Waste Reduction Task Force, McDonalds has completed the switch from polystyrene foam "clamshells" to paper-based wraps for packaging its sandwich items. The wraps provide a 70 to 90 percent reduction in packaging volume, resulting in significantly less space being consumed in landfills. Compared to the polystyrene foam boxes they replaced, the new sandwich wraps also offer a substantial savings in energy used and substantial reductions in pollutant releases measured over the full life-cycle of the packaging. McDonalds is also testing Earth Shell packaging products in 300 of its restaurants throughout the U.S.. These sustainable containers are made from potato starch, natural limestone, 100 percent postconsumer recycled fiber, biodegradable polymer and wax coatings, and water.

Comprehensive Recycling

The "Recycling Guidebook for the Hospitality and Restaurant Industry" provides a general overview of developing and implementing a comprehensive recycling program. The first step mentioned in this resource is to conduct a waste audit in order to evaluate the waste stream, enabling a restaurant to better target the commodities that should be included in a recycling program. Materials that are commonly recycled in restaurants include;

- *Paper,* including cardboard, computer paper, register tape, and telephone books
- *Metals,* including aluminum, tin, and steel cans
- *Green, brown, and clear glass*
- *#1 Polyethylene* (PET) and *#2 high-density polyethylene (HDPE)* plastics
- *Printer cartridges.*

Convenience is the key to a successful recycling program. An EPA Waste Wise tip sheet notes that a convenient collection system will encourage both customers and employees to carefully sort recyclables by material type and to eliminate contaminants. Collecting uncontaminated recyclables (commodities that are properly sorted and free of excess food and beverage waste) will save time otherwise spent in sorting out contaminants.

Further, uncontaminated recyclables have higher value if they are sold. Presented below are other restaurant recycling tips listed in the "Recycling Guidebook for the Hospitality and Restaurant Industry."

- Recycling and trash bins should look different from each other and be clearly marked. Both types of bins should be conveniently located in the kitchen and bar areas so that employees will use them.
- Self-serve establishments should post signs to inform customers about the recycling program and provide specific instructions. Either strategically places bins for collection of recyclable commodities, or have customers leave such commodities on a designated counter for collection by staff.
- If lack of space is a problem, specially designed equipment such as can, glass, and plastic crushers are available to reduce the volume of recyclable materials.
- Recyclable collection bins in public areas should be well-marked. Choose bins with specialized openings, such as a hole for cans or a slot for newspapers, for these areas.
- Set up a logbook or a receipt system to record the volume of recyclables leaving the premises in order to facilitate tracking and compensation.

Waste Reduction and Reuse

Waste reduction and material reuse should be the first step in minimizing the waste that a restaurant produces because it is more efficient to reduce waste at the source or reuse material than it is to recycle. As mentioned in audit is an effective way to evaluate a restaurant's waste streams. Doing so enables staff to identify wastes that are nonessential to operations, such as excess packaging material. This process can also identify disposable products that can be replaced with durable, reusable ones. For example, disposable plastic tableware and silverware should be replaced with washable or compostable utensils.

EPA's Waste Wise program is a free, 3-year, goal-oriented program that assists businesses in assessing and reducing their waste streams.11 EPA designed Waste Wise to be a flexible program, in which the participant determines how much time and money to invest. Key aspects of successful Waste Wise programs include;

- Waste assessments
- Employee education
- Measurement and reporting
- Program maintenance.

The above aspects are fundamental in assessing, developing, implementing, and maintaining a viable waste reduction and reuse program. Waste assessments provide a full understanding of waste streams and provide a basis for targeting specific waste reduction goals. However, these goals will only be reached with the full support of the restaurant – from managers and servers to cooks and food preparation staff. Therefore, employee education is critical to the success of the program.

It is also important that program efforts be measured regularly. Tracking and documenting the costs, savings, and effects of a waste reduction and reuse program are the only ways to determine the environmental and economic impacts of implementing the program. Program data can also provide insight into the effectiveness of employee education programs. Lastly, program maintenance is imperative to realize long-term benefits from a waste reduction and reuse program. A successful program is not a result of one-time changes but a cumulative result of permanent procedural and behavioural changes.

Several other guidance documents provide specific waste reduction and reuse ideas for the restaurant industry. Presented below are some examples of common waste reduction techniques that are discussed in "Food for Thought: Restaurant Guide to Waste Reduction and Recycling."

- Purchase and serve beverages in bulk rather than in bottles, cans, or individual packets.
- Buy bar mixes, juices, and coffee in bulk.
- Use health department-approved, refillable condiment containers.
- Purchase cleaning supplies in concentrated form.
- Use cloth towels and reusable table linens and tableware.
- Use vendors that take back packaging material and pallets.

Another way that restaurants can minimize their waste and overall environmental impact is purchasing products through local food supply vendors and grocers. Local sourcing is of particular benefit to the tourism sector, where visitors appreciate locally distinctive food, drink, and other products. For example, several Aspen Skiing Company-owned restaurants purchase natural, chemical-free beef and hamburger from local ranchers to support the ranching community and thus preserve open space, as well as to provide guests with healthy food. The pilot program began in winter 1998 and expanded significantly in 2000. The beef costs twice as much per pound, however

Aspen Skiing Company absorbs the additional cost. By purchasing local produce and supplies, restaurants minimize the affects of excessive transportation and shipping. Such efforts should be accounted for when evaluating the environmental impact and overall performance of a restaurant.

Biodegradable Plastic

As long as customers wish to take their food "to go," restaurants will need to stock disposable goods such as food containers and silverware. According to Biocorp, a manufacturer of biodegradable plastic tableware and silverware, nearly 113 billion disposable cups, 39 billion disposable eating utensils, and 29 billion disposable plates are used in the U.S. every year, and half these items are made of plastic. Because restaurants cannot control what happens to these items once they are in customers' hands, the most effective way to minimize their environmental impacts is to purchase biodegradable products.

Biodegradable products are typically made of corn, starch, or paper with an easily biodegradable coating. The Earth Shell is one example of a biodegradable food service product. Biocorp also manufactures biodegradable composting bags, silverware, plates, and beverage containers. "Scientists Perfecting Planet-Friendly Plastics," an article published by the Environmental News Network, explains that the starch used to create these biodegradable plastics– typically wheat gluten – costs about 15 cents per pound, whereas the least costly commercial plastics cost about $1 per pound. Thus, when this starch-based plastic becomes widely available to manufacturers, it could be the cheapest plastic available.

Currently, however, most manufactured environment-friendly plastics cost about $2.50 per pound, although recent projects have brought their costs down to approximately $1.50 per pound. Because biodegradable plastics are more expensive than regular plastic, the biodegradable plastic industry has a challenge in breaking into a very competitive market.

Recycled Products

Restaurants use several types of products that can be replaced with items made from recycled materials. Most of the products with recycled content that can easily be purchased are paper products such as napkins, toilet paper, tissues, paper towels, paper tablecloths, take-out containers, register tape, and office paper. Since 1998, EPA has required federal facilities to purchase products with recycledcontent material. The resulting increased demand for recycled content paper has driven down its cost to the point that recycled-content products are the same price or less expensive than virgin material products.

Non-chlorine-bleached Paper Products

Restaurants should avoid purchasing bleached paper products. Seventh Generation, a vendor of environmentally friendly, nontoxic consumer products, explains that chlorine is used by the paper industry for two purposes: to dissolve lignin, a natural material that holds a tree's cellulous fibers together, and to whiten the final paper product. However, chlorine reacts with the virgin natural substances of trees and recycled paper material to form both dioxins and organochlorines. As these substances are discharged and accumulate in the environment, they can have profound long- and short-term health effects on exposed humans and wildlife. One concern regarding dioxins is that they are known carcinogens, or cancer-causing substances. Short-term reactions to overexposure to chlorine may also occur, including airway inflammation and bronchial hyperresponsiveness. Organochlorines are of concern because they are suspected to be endocrine modifiers, which act as hormones in the body and can disrupt the human immune system.

Nontoxic Cleaners, Landscaping, and Pest Management

Restaurant personnel use a wide variety of chemicals to clean kitchen, dishwashing, and restroom facilities. Some cleaning products used include toilet and tile cleaner, glass cleaner, carpet cleaner, spot remover, disinfectant, and oven cleaner. Many of these products contain chemicals that are harmful to human health and the environment, which is a concern for both restaurant staff and customers. Vendors offer environmentally preferable cleaning supplies with equal or better cleaning performance at equal or less cost.

Many restaurants have outdoor areas with landscaping. There are several relatively simple steps that a restaurant manager can take to minimize the environmental impact of maintaining these areas, including water conservation and selection of climate-appropriate indigenous plants. Some "green" practices for landscape management include

- Watering vegetation using "deficit" irrigation, or frequent light watering
- Selecting plants based on watering needs (Typically, indigenous plants are most efficient in using water.)
- Watering grounds during the coolest hours of the day (typically at night) Finally, pest management can also be an issue for restaurants.

Energy Efficiency

Most restaurant operations, such as cooking and cleaning, are energy-intensive. EPA's EnergyStar® Program. estimates that reducing energy consumption by 20 percent can increase a restaurant's profit by one-third, a good economic incentive to make energy efficiency investments. Making this sort of reduction is feasible when restaurants implement strategic energy conservation measures. The EnergyStar® Program analysis of restaurant energy use shows that over 60 percent of a restaurant's energy is used for cooking, heating water, and heating the establishment.

The National Restaurant Association also published tips for reducing energy costs for restaurants.

Turn on and Off

- Preheat equipment in accordance with manufacturer specifications; post preheating times near equipment.
- Turn off appliances when not in use.
- Install occupancy sensors in walk-in refrigerators and freezers.

Cooking Efficiency – Lower it/Fill it up

- Cook using equipment at full capacity when possible.
- Cook at lowest temperatures first.
- Turn off equipment during downtime.
- Use lids to minimize heat loss.

Watch Thermostats – Stay Cool and Save Money

- Set thermostats to manufacturer-recommended temperatures.
- Apply new-generation "clear" coatings to reduce solar gain from large, south-and west-facing windows.
- Use the "unoccupied" and "night setback" thermostat options.
- Ensure tamper-proof temperature settings by using locking covers on thermostats.

Keep It Clean for Energy Efficiency

- Clean condenser and evaporator coils on air conditioning and refrigeration equipment.
- Change all filters regularly.
- Preventively maintain equipment.

Dishwashing Equipment

- Heat water only to the temperature required for specific tasks.

- Install equipment of proper size.
- Fully load the machine for each cycle.

As restaurants undergo renovation or technology upgrades, managers should evaluate the energy efficiency of new equipment. Green Seal is an independent, nonprofit organization dedicated to protecting the environment by promoting the manufacture and sale of environmentally responsible consumer products. Green Seal sets environmental standards and awards a "Green Seal of Approva" to products that cause less harm to the environment than other, similar products. Commercial consumers can use Green Seal's web site to search for resourceefficient Products

Water Efficiency

Restaurants use water in almost every aspect of their operations, including food preparation and cooking, cleaning, in restroom facilities, and as a beverage for customers. For each of these aspects, there are technologies or best management practices (BMP) that conserve water. In a collaborative effort, Agricultural and Biological Engineering, EPA, and Purdue University created an environmental enrichment toolkit for the lodging industry. Included in this document is a section that outlines the following water conservation tactics for restaurants:

- Wash food products in buckets, bowls, or other containers.
- Only run dishwashers with full loads.
- Regularly inspect dishwasher pumps for water leaks.
- Defrost or thaw frozen foods in the refrigerator instead of water.
- Install low-flow taps in kitchens and restrooms.
- Use low-flow toilets in restrooms.
- Immediately fix any leaking or dripping faucet.
- Install infrared-activated faucets and toilets in restrooms.
- Purchase and use water-saving kitchen equipment.
- Track water consumption by regularly monitoring utility bills.
- Establish an effective employee training program on water conservation.

Composting

EPA estimates that food wastes comprise 6.7 percent by weight of the total U.S. municipal solid waste stream. One option for diverting food wastes from landfills is composting. Businesses with well-established composting programs divert 50 to 100 percent of their food scraps and reduce their overall solid waste by 33 to 85 percent.

Composting can be done both on and off site; however, for restaurants where space is limited, the most feasible option is to collect food scraps for an off-site composting program. This option also transfers the responsibility of monitoring the chemical balance of the compost from the restaurant owner to the local composting operation. However, technologies are available that enable restaurants to manage their compost on site.

Case Study: Composting At Keystone Ranch

Keystone Ranch, a horse ranch resort in Keystone, Colorado, implemented a composting program that combines horse manure with vegetable and meat scraps from the Ranch Restaurant. The ranch rents a 30-cubic yard container from a local hauler that holds almost 20 tons of material. Biodegradable cornstarch-based bags are placed at four stations to collect food waste during food preparation and uneaten food from customers. Keystone Ranch estimates that between 10 and 15 percent of the contents of the full 30-cubic yard container is food waste. The rest of the compost mixture is manure collected from the stalls of 15 to 80 horses. The hauler transports the container to the Twin Landfill Corporation in a nearby town, where the compost is further processed, screened, and then sold to landscapers and farmers. As a result of the composting program, which complements an established glass, aluminum, tin, cardboard, and paper recycling program, the Ranch Restaurant is "rapidly approaching a zero-waste status." Because the tipping fee for compostable material is 30 percent less than that for solid waste, the program sustains itself financially and has diverted 450 tons of organic waste from the local landfill.

Green Electricity

In addition to efforts to minimize their energy use, restaurants can minimize the environmental impacts of the energy they do use by purchasing renewable electricity. By using a renewable source of energy, a restaurant decreases its dependency on nonrenewable fossil fuels and eliminates greenhouse gas emissions associated with its electricity use. Renewable energy sources include wind, solar, geothermal, and biomass.

The availability of green electricity varies from region to region, so restaurants interested in purchasing energy from a renewable source should contact their city or state government agencies or local electric utility. Non-profit green energy certification programs, such as Green-e and Cleaner and Greener, may also be able to help direct restaurant owners to local green energy providers.

Employee Education Program

The development of an employee education program is critical to maintaining an environmentally responsible restaurant. An environmental education program should teach both the "how" and "why" of each aspect of the program. An understanding of why an employee should ensure that certain environmental procedures are followed adds meaning to the task. Because of high turnover in many restaurants, environmental education should be a regular, multimedia program, and should include both written and verbal instruction in all languages of the employees. Environmental awareness expectations should be outlined during new-hire training and reinforced throughout the period of employment.

Restaurant managers should consider acknowledging employees who demonstrate superior dedication to minimizing environmental impacts. For example, employees may be offered a percentage of the cost savings resulting from environmental projects implemented at their suggestion. Such recognition would not only reward the employees, but would send a message to customers that the restaurant is actively pursuing "greener" practices. Once the expectation of excellent environmental performance is established, maintaining the program will require less effort.

Finally, restaurant managers should encourage employees to provide feedback regarding areas for improvement. Many employees will have ideas of how to improve the environment they work in, and with a forum to voice ideas, innovations can be made.

Food and Beverage Serving and Related Workers

Significant Points

- Most jobs are part time and have few educational requirements, attracting many young people to the occupation—21 percent of these workers were 16 to 19 years old in 2008, about six times the proportion for all workers.

- Job openings are expected to be abundant through 2018, which will create excellent opportunities for jobseekers.
- Tips comprise a major portion of earnings for servers, so keen competition is expected for jobs in fine dining and more popular restaurants where potential tips are greatest.

Nature of the Work

Food and beverage serving and related workers are the front line of customer service in full-service restaurants, casual dining eateries, and other food service establishments. These workers greet customers, escort them to seats and hand them menus, take food and drink orders, and serve food and beverages. They also answer questions, explain menu items and specials, and keep tables and dining areas clean and set for new diners. Most work as part of a team, helping coworkers to improve workflow and customer service.

Waiters and waitresses, also called *servers*, are the largest group of these workers. They take customers' orders, serve food and beverages, prepare itemized checks, and sometimes accept payment. Their specific duties vary considerably, depending on the establishment. In casual-dining restaurants serving routine, straightforward fare, such as salads, soups, and sandwiches, servers are expected to provide fast, efficient, and courteous service. In fine dining restaurants, where more complicated meals are prepared and often served over several courses, waiters and waitresses provide more formal service emphasizing personal, attentive treatment at a more leisurely pace.

Waiters and waitresses may meet with managers and chefs before each shift to discuss the menu and any new items or specials, review ingredients for potential food allergies, or talk about any food safety concerns.

They also discuss coordination between the kitchen and the dining room and any customer service issues from the previous day or shift. In addition, waiters and waitresses usually check the identification of patrons to ensure they meet the minimum age requirement for the purchase of alcohol and tobacco products wherever those items are sold.

Waiters and waitresses sometimes perform the duties of other food and beverage service workers, including escorting guests to tables, serving customers seated at counters, clearing and setting up tables, or operating a cash register. However, full-service restaurants frequently hire other staff, such as hosts and hostesses, cashiers, or dining room attendants, to perform these duties.

Bartenders fill drink orders either taken directly from patrons at the bar or through waiters and waitresses who place drink orders for dining room customers. Bartenders check the identification of customers seated at the bar to ensure they meet the minimum age requirement for the purchase of alcohol and tobacco products. They prepare mixed drinks, serve bottled or draught beer, and pour wine or other beverages. Bartenders must know a wide range of drink recipes and be able to mix drinks accurately, quickly, and without waste. Some establishments, especially those with higher volume, use equipment that automatically measures, pours, and mixes drinks at the push of a button. Bartenders who use this equipment, however, still must work quickly to handle a large volume of drink orders and be familiar with the ingredients for special drink requests. Much of a bartender's work still must be done by hand.

Besides mixing and serving drinks, bartenders stock and prepare garnishes for drinks; maintain an adequate supply of ice, glasses, and other bar supplies; and keep the bar area clean for customers. They also may collect payment, operate the cash register, wash glassware and utensils, and serve food to customers who dine at the bar. Bartenders usually are responsible for ordering and maintaining an inventory of liquor, mixers, and other bar supplies.

Hosts and hostesses welcome guests and maintain reservation and waiting lists. They may direct patrons to coatrooms, restrooms, or to a place to wait until their table is ready. Hosts and hostesses assign guests to tables suitable for the size of their group, escort patrons to their seats, and provide menus. They also enter reservations, arrange parties, and assist with other special requests. In some restaurants, they act as cashiers.

Dining room and cafeteria attendants and bartender helpers—sometimes referred to collectively as the bus staff—assist waiters, waitresses, and bartenders by cleaning and setting tables, removing dirty dishes, and keeping serving areas stocked with supplies. They may also assist waiters and waitresses by bringing meals out of the kitchen, distributing dishes to individual diners, filling water glasses, and delivering condiments. They may carry trays to dining tables for patrons. *Bartender helpers* keep bar equipment clean and glasses washed. *Dishwashers* clean dishes, cutlery, and kitchen utensils and equipment.

Food also is prepared and served in limited-service eateries, which don't employ servers and specialize in simpler preparations that often are made in advance. Two occupations with large numbers of workers are common in these types of establishments: *combined food preparation and serving workers, including fast food;* and *counter attendants, cafeteria, food concession, and coffee shop*. Combined food preparation and serving workers are employed primarily by fast food restaurants. They take food and beverage orders, retrieve items when ready, fill drink cups, and accept payment. They also may heat food items and assemble salads and sandwiches, which constitutes food preparation. Counter attendants take orders and serve food in snack bars, cafeterias, movie theatres, and coffee shops over a counter or steam table. They may fill cups with coffee, soda, and other beverages and may prepare fountain specialties, such as milkshakes and ice cream sundaes. Counter attendants take carryout orders from diners and wrap or place items in containers. They clean counters, write itemized bills, and sometimes accept payment. Other workers, referred to as *foodservers, nonrestaurant,* serve food to patrons outside of a restaurant environment. They might deliver room service meals in hotels or meals to hospital rooms or act as carhops, bringing orders to parked cars.

Work environment. Food and beverage service workers are on their feet most of the time and often carry heavy trays of food, dishes, and glassware. During busy dining periods, they are under pressure to serve customers quickly and efficiently. The work is relatively safe, but injuries from slips, cuts, and burns often result from hurrying or mishandling sharp tools. Three occupations—food servers, nonrestaurant; dining room and cafeteria attendants and bartender helpers; and dishwashers—reported higher incident rates than many occupations throughout the economy.

Part-time work is more common among food and beverage serving and related workers than among workers in almost any other occupation. In 2008, those on part-time schedules included half of all waiters and waitresses and almost three-fourths of all hosts and hostesses.

Food service and drinking establishments typically maintain long dining hours and offer flexible and varied work opportunities. Many food and beverage serving and related workers work evenings, weekends, and holidays. The long business hours allow for more flexible schedules that appeal to many teenagers who can gain valuable work experience. More than one-fifth of all food and beverage serving and related workers were 16 to 19 years old in 2008—about six times the proportion for all workers.

Training, other Qualifications, and Advancement

Most food and beverage service jobs are entry level and require a high school diploma or less. Generally, training is received on the job; however, those who wish to work at more upscale restaurants, where income from tips is greater and service standards are higher, may need previous experience or vocational training.

Education and training. There are no specific educational requirements for most food and beverage service jobs. Many employers prefer to hire high school graduates for waiter and waitress, bartender, and host and hostess positions, but completion of high school usually is not required for fast-food workers, counter attendants, dishwashers, and dining room attendants and bartender helpers. Many entrants to these jobs are in their late teens or early twenties and have a high school education or less. Usually, they have little or no work experience. Food and beverage service jobs are a major source of part-time employment for high school and college students, multiple job holders, and those seeking supplemental incomes.

All new employees receive some training from their employer. They learn safe food handling procedures and sanitation practices, for example. Some employers, particularly those in fast-food restaurants, teach new workers using self-study programs, on-line programs, audiovisual presentations, and instructional booklets that explain food preparation and service skills. But most food and beverage serving and related workers pick up their skills by observing and working with more experienced workers. Some full-service restaurants also provide new dining room employees with some form of classroom training that alternates with periods of on-the-job work experience. These training programs communicate the operating philosophy of the restaurant, help establish a personal rapport with other staff, teach formal serving techniques, and instill a desire to work as a team. They also provide an opportunity to discuss customer service situations and the proper ways to handle unpleasant circumstances or unruly patrons.

Some food serving workers can acquire more skills by attending relevant classes offered by public or private vocational schools, restaurant associations, or large restaurant chains. Some bartenders acquire their skills through formal vocational training either by attending a school for bartending or a vocational and technical school where bartending classes are taught. These programs often include instruction on State and local laws and regulations, cocktail recipes, proper attire and conduct, and stocking a bar. Some of these schools help their graduates find jobs. Although few employers require any minimum level of educational attainment, some specialized training is usually needed in food handling and legal issues surrounding serving alcoholic beverages. Employers are more likely to hire and promote employees based on people skills and personal qualities than education.

Other qualifications. Restaurants rely on good food and customer service to retain loyal customers and succeed in a competitive industry. Food and beverage serving and related workers who exhibit excellent personal qualities—such as a neat appearance, an ability to work as part of a team, and a natural rapport with customers—will be highly sought after. Most States require workers who serve alcoholic beverages to be at least 18 years of age, but some States require servers to be older. For bartender jobs, many employers prefer to hire people who are 25 or older. All servers that serve alcohol need to be familiar with State and local laws concerning the sale of alcoholic beverages.

Waiters and waitresses need a good memory to avoid confusing customers' orders and to recall faces, names, and preferences of frequent patrons. Knowledge of a foreign language can be helpful to communicate with a diverse clientele and staff. Restaurants and hotels that have rigid table service standards often offer higher wages and have greater income potential from tips, but they may also have stiffer employment requirements, such as prior table service experience or higher education attainment than other establishments.

Advancement. Due to the relatively small size of most food-serving establishments, opportunities for promotion are limited. After gaining experience, some dining room and cafeteria attendants and bartender helpers advance to waiter, waitress, or bartender jobs. For waiters, waitresses, and bartenders, advancement usually is limited to finding a job in a busier or more expensive restaurant or bar where prospects for tip earnings are better. Some bartenders, hosts and hostesses, and waiters and waitresses advance to supervisory jobs, such as dining room supervisor, maitre d', assistant manager, or restaurant general manager. A few bartenders open their own businesses. In larger restaurant chains, food and beverage service workers who excel often are invited to enter the company's formal management training program.

Employment

Food and beverage serving and related workers held 7.7 million jobs in 2008. The distribution of jobs among the various food and beverage serving occupations was as follows:

Combined food preparation and serving workers, including fast food	2,701,700
Waiters and waitresses	2,381,600
Counter attendants, cafeteria, food concession, and coffee shop	525,400
Dishwashers	522,900
Bartenders	508,700
Dining room and cafeteria attendants and bartender helpers	420,700
Hosts and hostesses, restaurant, lounge, and coffee shop	350,700
Food servers, nonrestaurant	189,800
All other food preparation and serving related workers	50,900

The overwhelming majority of jobs for food and beverage serving and related workers were found in food services and drinking places, such as restaurants, fast food outlets, bars, and catering or contract food service operations. Other jobs were in hotels, motels, and other traveller accommodation establishments; amusement, gambling, and recreation establishments; educational services; nursing care facilities; and civic and social organizations.

Jobs are located throughout the country but are more plentiful in larger cities and tourist areas. Vacation resorts offer seasonal employment.

Job Outlook

Average employment growth is expected, and job opportunities should be excellent for food and beverage serving and related workers as turnover is generally very high among these workers, but job competition is often keen for jobs at upscale restaurants.

Employment change. Overall employment of these workers is expected to increase by 10 percent over the 2008-18 decade, which is about as fast as the average for all occupations. Food and beverage serving and related workers are projected to have one of the largest numbers of new jobs arise, about 761,000, over this period. The growth in jobs is expected to increase as the population continues to expand. However, employment will grow more slowly than in the past as people change their dining habits. The growing popularity of take-out food and the growing number and variety of places that offer carryout options, including at many full-service restaurants, will slow the growth of waiters and waitresses and other serving workers.

Projected employment growth will vary by job type. Employment of combined food preparation and serving workers, which includes fast-food workers, is expected to increase faster than the average for all occupations. The limited service segment of the food services and drinking places industry has a low price advantage, fast service, and has been adding healthier foods. Slower than average employment growth is expected for waiters and waitresses, hosts and hostesses, and dining room and cafeteria attendants and bartender helpers, as more people use take-out service. Employment of bartenders, dishwashers, and counter attendants, cafeteria, food concession, and coffee shop will grow about as fast as average. Nonrestaurant servers, such as those who deliver food trays in hotels, hospitals, residential care facilities, or catered events, are expected to have average employment growth.

Job prospects. Job opportunities at most eating and drinking places will be excellent because many people in these occupations change jobs frequently, which creates a large number of openings. Keen competition is expected, however, for jobs in popular restaurants and fine dining establishments, where potential earnings from tips are greatest.

Other Customer Services

Customer satisfaction Studies have shown that the overall satisfaction of the guest in a particular hotel determines the likelihood of the client returning to same. The study identifies that the likely influences of the guest or customer satisfaction being room quality and comfort, staff services, security and amenities topping the priority list.

Customer satisfaction is very important for a hotel to survive. It is important to give prompt attention to the needs of the customer without delay. This could where a reservation or booking is concerned or even a room in a particular floor and facilities required, giving proper feed back and seeing that it is done at the time the guest checks in is very important. It could be very annoying for the guest to find out that his/her needs have not been met, and the guest could be put off about the hotel even before he enters. As such, delivering what you have promised, will gain the confidence of the customer.

An important factor in the hospitality industry, but sometimes goes unheeded is being friendly and approachable. The customer should be made comfortable, and they should be treated as if he is the most important guest in the hotel. A friendly and courteous approach will make the customer feel welcomed. As such at all times remaining polite is very important in the hospitality industry.

Maintaining customer service policies are priority. Do not treat one guest different to the other. In case, there are issues have clear rules, where the guest is not sent from pillar to post to sort out issue. Intervene, take the matter upon yourself and resolve so that the customer is aware that no matter what, the hotel will find a solution.

Customers feel important and recognized, when the hotel goes out that extra mile to attend to detail. Sending out personalized letter, rather than the normal standard hotel leaflets is a sure way to satisfy the customer. Make note of birthdays and anniversaries and other important events during their stay with you. If you had paid attention to detail, you would have these facts with you, or even at the time the reservation is made, the guest would have mentioned it to you. Complimentary notes, flowers or chocolates to the guest could ensure satisfaction. Anticipate your clients need, let it be a book, software, CD or even a requirement, making note of same and supplying it free of charge to the guest, will make the guest feel happy and content.

Some of these will be time consuming but cost effective, some will require just commitment. The existence of the hotel depends on the staff and the management and their approach to the needs and the wants of the guest. As such, taking note and making sure that the guest is satisfied at all cost, will in return bring success and revenue to the hotel.

Make note that one satisfied customer is adequate to promote the hotel to another.

Cashiers

Supermarkets, department stores, gasoline service stations, movie theaters, restaurants, and many other businesses employ cashiers to register the sale of their goods and services. Although specific job duties vary by employer, cashiers usually are assigned to a register at the beginning of their shifts and are given a drawer containing a specific amount of money with which to start—their "till." They must count their till to ensure that it contains the correct amount of money and adequate supplies of change. Some cashiers also handle returns and exchanges. When they do, they must ensure that returned merchandise is in good condition, and determine where and when it was purchased and what type of payment was used.

After entering charges for all items and subtracting the value of any coupons or special discounts, cashiers total the customer's bill and take payment. Forms of payment include cash, personal checks, and gift, credit, and debit cards. Cashiers must know the store's policies and procedures for each type of payment the store accepts. For checks and credit and debit card charges, they may request additional identification from the customer or call in for an authorization. They must verify the age of customers purchasing alcohol or tobacco. When the sale is complete, cashiers issue a receipt to the customer and return the appropriate change. They may also wrap or bag the purchase.

At the end of their shifts, cashiers once again count the drawers' contents and compare the totals with sales data. An occasional shortage of small amounts may be overlooked but, in many establishments, repeated shortages are grounds for dismissal. In addition to counting the contents of their drawers at the end of their shifts, cashiers usually separate and total charge forms, return slips, coupons, and any other noncash items.

Most cashiers use scanners and computers, but some establishments still require price and product information to be entered manually. In a store with scanners, a cashier passes a product's Universal Product Code over the scanning device, which transmits the code number to a computer. The computer identifies the item and its price. In other establishments, cashiers manually enter codes into computers and then descriptions of the items and their prices appear on the screen.

Depending on the type of establishment, cashiers may have other duties as well. In many supermarkets, for example, cashiers weigh produce and bulk food, as well as return unwanted items to the shelves. In convenience stores, cashiers may be required to know how to use a variety of machines other than cash registers, and how to furnish money orders and sell lottery tickets. Operating ticket-dispensing machines and answering customers' questions are common duties for cashiers who work at movie theaters and ticket agencies.

Work environment. Most cashiers work indoors, usually standing in booths or behind counters. Often, they are not allowed to leave their workstations without supervisory approval because they are responsible for large sums of money. The work of cashiers can be very repetitious, but improvements in workstation design in many stores are alleviating problems caused by repetitive motion. In addition, the work can sometimes be dangerous; the risk from robberies and homicides is much higher for cashiers than for other workers, although more safety precautions are being taken to help deter robbers.

About 47 percent of all cashiers worked part time in 2008. Hours of work often vary depending on the needs of the employer. Generally, cashiers are expected to work weekends, evenings, and holidays to accommodate customers' needs. However, many employers offer flexible schedules. Because the holiday season is the busiest time for most retailers, many employers restrict the use of vacation time from Thanksgiving through the beginning of January.

Training, other Qualifications, and Advancement

Cashier jobs usually are entry-level positions requiring little or no previous work experience. They require good customer service skills.

Education and training. Although there are no specific educational requirements, employers filling full-time jobs often prefer applicants with high school diplomas.

Nearly all cashiers are trained on the job. In small businesses, an experienced worker often trains beginners. The trainee spends the first day observing the operation and becoming familiar with the store's equipment, policies, and procedures. After this, trainees are assigned to a register—frequently under the supervision of an experienced worker. In larger businesses, trainees spend several days in classes before being placed at cash registers. Topics typically covered in class include a description of the industry and the company, store policies and procedures, equipment operation, and security.

Training for experienced workers is not common, except when new equipment is introduced or when procedures change. In these cases, the employer or a representative of the equipment manufacturer trains workers on the job.

Other qualifications. People who want to become cashiers should be able to do repetitious work accurately. They also need basic mathematics skills and good manual dexterity. Because cashiers deal constantly with the public, they should be neat in appearance and able to deal tactfully and pleasantly with customers. In addition, some businesses prefer to hire workers who can operate specialized equipment or who have business experience, such as typing, selling, or handling money.

Advancement. Advancement opportunities for cashiers vary. For those working part time, promotion may be to a full-time position. Others advance to head cashier or cash-office clerk. In addition, this job offers a good opportunity to learn about an employer's business and can serve as a steppingstone to a more responsible position.

Employment

Cashiers held about 3.55 million jobs in 2008. Although cashiers are employed in almost every industry, 24 percent of all jobs were in grocery stores. Gasoline stations, department stores, and other retail establishments also employed large numbers of these workers. Outside of retail establishments, many cashiers worked in food services and drinking places.

Job Outlook

Cashiers are expected to grow more slowly than the average for all occupations. Opportunities for full-time and part-time jobs are expected to be good because of the need to replace the large number of workers who leave this occupation.

Employment change. Employment of cashiers is expected to grow by 4 percent between 2008 and 2018 which is slower than the average for all occupations. Continued growth in retail sales is expected, but the rising popularity of purchasing goods online will limit the employment growth of cashiers, although many customers still prefer the traditional method of purchasing goods at stores. Also, the growing use of self-service checkout systems in retail trade, especially at grocery stores, should have an adverse effect on employment of cashiers. These self-checkout systems may outnumber checkouts with cashiers in the future in many establishments. The impact on job growth for cashiers will largely depend on the public's acceptance of this self-service technology.

Job prospects. Opportunities for full-time and part-time cashier jobs should continue to be good because of the need to replace the large number of workers who transfer to other occupations or leave the labour force. There is substantial movement into and out of the occupation because education and training requirements are minimal and the predominance of part-time jobs is attractive to people seeking a short-term source of income rather than a full-time career. Historically, workers under the age of 25 have filled many of the openings in this occupation. In 2008, about 47 percent of all cashiers were 24 years of age or younger.

Because cashiers are needed in businesses and organizations of all types and sizes, job opportunities are found throughout the country. However, job opportunities may vary from year to year because the strength of the economy affects demand for cashiers. Companies tend to hire more cashiers when the economy is strong.

Seasonal demand for cashiers also causes fluctuations in employment.

Chefs, Head Cooks, and Food Preparation and Serving Supervisors

Chefs, head cooks, and food preparation and serving supervisors oversee the daily food service operation of a restaurant or other food service establishment. *Chefs and head cooks* are usually responsible for directing cooks in the kitchen, dealing with food-related concerns, and providing leadership. They are also the most skilled cooks in the kitchen and use their creativity and knowledge of food to develop and prepare recipes.

Food preparation and serving supervisors oversee the kitchen and non-kitchen staff in a restaurant or food service facility. They may also oversee food preparation workers in fast food, cafeteria, or casual dining restaurants, where the menu is fairly standard from day to day, or in more formal restaurants, where a chef provides specific guidelines and exacting standards on how to prepare each item.

All of these workers—chefs, head cooks, and food preparation and serving supervisors—hire, train, and supervise staff, prepare cost estimates for food and supplies, set work schedules, order supplies, and ensure that the food service establishment runs efficiently and profitably. Additionally, these workers ensure that sanitation and safety standards are observed and comply with local regulations. Fresh food must be stored and cooked properly, work surfaces and dishes clean and sanitary, and staff and customers safe from illness or injury to avoid being closed by the health department or law enforcement.

While all chefs have a role in preparing the food, developing recipes, determining serving sizes, planning menus, ordering food supplies, and overseeing kitchen operations to ensure uniform quality and presentation of meals, different types of chefs may have unique roles to perform or specialize in certain aspects of the job. *Executive chefs, head cooks, and chefs de cuisine,* are primarily responsible for coordinating the work of the cooks and directing the preparation of meals. Executive chefs are in charge of all food service operations and also may supervise several kitchens of a hotel, restaurant or corporate dining operation. A *sous chef*, or sub chef, is the second-in-command and runs the kitchen in the absence of the chef. Many chefs earn fame both for themselves and for their kitchens because of the quality and distinctive nature of the food they serve.

As a greater variety of establishments prepare and serve food, chefs and head cooks and first-line supervisors of food preparation and serving workers can be found in a greater variety of places. Grocery and specialty food stores employ these workers to develop recipes and prepare meals for customers to carry out. They increasingly work in residential care facilities, such as nursing homes, and in schools and hospitals. Some chefs and head cooks work for individuals rather than for restaurants, cafeterias, or food manufacturers. *Personal chefs* and *private household cooks* plan and prepare meals in private homes according to the client's tastes or dietary needs. They order groceries and supplies, clean the kitchen, and wash dishes and utensils. They also may serve meals. Personal chefs usually prepare a week's worth of meals in the client's home for the client to heat and serve according to directions. They may be self-employed or work as part of a team of personal chefs and employed by a company that provides this service. Private household cooks typically work full time for one client, such as corporate executives, university presidents, or diplomats, who regularly entertain as a part of their official duties.

While the work of chefs and head cooks is concentrated in the kitchen or in providing overall guidance, food preparation and serving supervisors oversee specific areas of operation in food service establishments or the kitchen and counter areas of quick service restaurants. In fast food and casual dining restaurants, they may share many of the same functions with food service managers. They are responsible for dealing with customer complaints, balancing the books at the end of the day, scheduling workers, and ordering supplies. They also supervise and train kitchen and food preparation staff and ensure that these workers know how to gather food supplies, operate equipment, and assemble orders.

Work environment. Restaurants and other food service facilities where these workers are employed are required to be clean and sanitary. Although the seating areas of eating places are often attractive, kitchens can be crowded and hot and filled with potential dangers, such as hot ovens and slippery floors. Job hazards for those working in kitchens include slips and falls, cuts, and burns, but these injuries are seldom serious. Chefs, head cooks, and supervisors are under constant pressure to get meals prepared quickly, while ensuring quality is maintained and safety and sanitation guidelines are observed. Because the pace can be hectic during peak dining times, workers must be able to communicate clearly so that food orders and service are done correctly.

Work hours in restaurants may include early mornings, late evenings, holidays, and weekends. Schedules for those working in offices, factories and school cafeterias may be more regular. In fine-dining restaurants, work schedules tend to be longer because of the time required to prepare ingredients in advance. Many executive chefs regularly work 12-hour days because they oversee the delivery of foodstuffs early in the day, plan the menu, and prepare those menu items that require the most skill. Depending upon the days of operation, some chefs or other supervisors may take less busy days off to offset the longer hours on other days.

Training, other Qualifications, and Advancement

Most workers in these occupations have prior experience in the food service or hospitality industries. Most start as food preparation workers or line cooks in a full-service restaurant and work their way up to positions with more responsibility. Some attend cooking school or take vocational training classes and participate in internships or apprenticeship programs to acquire the additional skills needed to create menus and run a business.

Education and training. While most chefs, head cooks, and food preparation and serving supervisors have some postsecondary training, many experienced workers with less education can still be promoted. Formal training may take place at a community college, technical school, culinary arts school, or a 2-year or 4-year college with a degree in hospitality. A growing number of chefs participate in training programs sponsored by independent cooking schools, professional culinary institutes, 2-year or 4-year colleges with a hospitality or culinary arts department, or in the armed forces. Some large hotels and restaurants also operate their own training and job-placement programs for chefs and head cooks. Executive chefs, head cooks, and sous chefs who work in fine-dining restaurants require many years of training and experience.

For students in culinary training programs, most of their time is spent in kitchens learning to prepare meals by practicing cooking skills. They learn knife techniques and proper use and care of kitchen equipment. Training programs also include courses in nutrition, menu planning, portion control, purchasing and inventory methods, proper food storage procedures, and use of leftover food to minimize waste. Students also learn sanitation and public health rules for handling food. Training in food service management, computer accounting and inventory software, and banquet service are featured in some training programs. Most formal training programs also require students to get experience in a commercial kitchen through an internship, apprenticeship, or out-placement program.

Although formal training is an important way to enter the profession, many chefs are trained on the job, receiving real work experience and training from chef-mentors in the restaurants where they work. Others enter the profession through formal apprenticeship programs sponsored by professional culinary institutes, industry associations, and trade unions in coordination with the U.S. Department of Labour. The American Culinary Federation accredits more than 200 formal academic training programs and sponsors apprenticeship programs around the country. Typical apprenticeships last 2 years and combine classroom training and work experience. Accreditation is an indication that a culinary program meets recognized standards regarding course content, facilities, and quality of instruction.

Other qualifications. Chefs, head cooks, and food preparation and serving supervisors must demonstrate strong leadership and communication skills and have the ability to motivate others. Chefs and head cooks also must have an intense desire to cook, be creative, and have a keen sense of taste and smell. Personal cleanliness is essential because most States require health certificates indicating that workers are free from communicable diseases. Knowledge of a foreign language can be an asset because it may improve communication with other restaurant staff, vendors, and the restaurant's clientele.

Certification and advancement. The American Culinary Federation certifies pastry professionals, personal chefs, and culinary educators in addition to various levels of chefs. Certification standards are based primarily on experience and formal training. Although certification is not required, it can help to prove accomplishment and lead to advancement and higher-paying positions. Advancement opportunities for chefs, head cooks, and food preparation and serving supervisors depend on their training, work experience, ability to perform more responsible and sophisticated tasks, and their leadership abilities.

Food preparation and serving supervisors may advance to become food service managers while some chefs and head cooks may go into business as caterers or personal chefs or open their own restaurant. Others may become instructors in culinary training programs, consultants on kitchen design, or food product or equipment sales representatives. A number of chefs and head cooks advance to executive chef positions or food service management positions. When staying in the restaurant business, advancement usually involves moving to a better, busier, or bigger restaurant or working at the corporate level overseeing several restaurants or food service facilities or testing new recipe, menu, or design concepts.

Employment

Chefs, head cooks, and food preparation and serving supervisors held 941,600 jobs in 2008. Food preparation and serving supervisors held 88 percent of these jobs and chefs and head cooks held the remaining 12 percent. Nearly half of chefs and head cooks were employed at full-service restaurants. About nine percent each were employed by hotels and the special food services industry that includes caterers and food service contractors. Eight percent were self-employed.

Forty-three percent of food preparation and serving supervisors were employed by limited-service eating places, made up mostly of cafeterias and fast food restaurants and other places that offer simple carry-out food items. Another 25 percent were employed by full-service restaurants. Supervisors are also found in schools, the special food services industry, and a wide variety of other places that serve food.

Job Outlook

Job opportunities are expected to be good, despite slower than average employment growth, due to the large numbers of workers who leave the occupation and need to be replaced. However, keen competition is expected for jobs at upscale restaurants that generally pay more.

Employment change. Employment of chefs, head cooks, and food preparation and serving supervisors is expected to increase by 6 percent over the 2008-18 decade, which is more slowly than the average for all occupations. Growth will be generated by increases in population, a growing variety of dining venues, and continued demand for convenience. As more people opt for the time-saving ease of letting others do the cooking, the need for workers to oversee food preparation and serving will increase. Also, there is a growing consumer desire for healthier, made-from-scratch meals that chefs and head cooks can better prepare.

Job prospects. Job openings for chefs, head cooks, and food preparation and serving supervisors are expected to be good through 2018; however, competition should be keen for jobs at the more upscale restaurants that tend to pay more. Workers with a good business sense will have better job prospects, especially at restaurant chains where attention to costs is very important. Although job growth will create many new positions, the majority of job openings will stem from the need to replace workers who leave the occupation. The tast pace, long hours, and high energy levels required for these jobs often lead to high turnover.

Flight attendants

- Competition for positions is expected to remain keen because the opportunity for travel attracts more applicants than there are jobs.
- Job duties are learned through formal on-the-job training at a flight training centre.
- A high school diploma is the minimum educational requirement, but airlines prefer applicants with a college degree and with experience in dealing with the public.

Nature of the Work

Major airlines are required by law to provide *flight attendants* for the safety and security of the traveling public. Although the primary job of the flight attendants is to ensure that security and safety regulations are followed, attendants also try to make flights comfortable and enjoyable for passengers.

At least 1 hour before takeoff, attendants are briefed by the captain—the pilot in command—on such things as emergency evacuation procedures, coordination of the crew, the length of the flight, expected weather conditions, and any special issues having to do with passengers. Flight attendants make sure that first-aid kits and other emergency equipment are aboard and in working order and that the passenger cabin is in order, with adequate supplies of food, beverages, and any other amenities. As passengers board the plane, flight attendants greet them, check their tickets, and tell them where to store carry-on items.

Before the plane takes off, flight attendants instruct all passengers in the use of emergency equipment and check to see that seatbelts are fastened, seat backs are in upright positions, and all carry-on items are properly stowed. In the air, helping passengers in the event of an emergency is the most important responsibility of a flight attendant. Safety-related actions range from reassuring passengers during rough weather to directing passengers who must evacuate a plane following an emergency landing. Flight attendants also answer questions about the flight, and help small children, elderly or disabled persons, and any others needing assistance. Flight attendants may administer first aid to passengers who become ill. Flight attendants generally serve beverages and on many flights sell precooked meals or snacks. Prior to landing, flight attendants take inventory of headsets, alcoholic beverages, and moneys collected. They also report any medical problems passengers may have had, the condition of cabin equipment, and any lost-and-found articles.

Lead, or first, flight attendants, sometimes known as *pursers*, oversee the work of the other attendants aboard the aircraft, while performing most of the same duties.

Work environment. Because airlines operate around the clock and year round, flight attendants can work nights, holidays, and weekends. In most cases, agreements between the airline and the employees' union determine the total daily and monthly working time. Scheduled on-duty time usually is limited to 12 hours per day, however flight attendants can be scheduled up to 14 hours per day, with somewhat greater maximums for international flying. The Federal Aviation Administration (FAA) requires that flight attendants receive 9 consecutive hours of rest following any duty period.

Attendants usually fly 65 to 90 hours a month and generally spend another 50 hours a month on the ground preparing planes for flights, writing reports following completed flights, and waiting for planes to arrive. Most airlines guarantee a minimum of 65 to 85 flight hours per month, with the option to work additional hours. Flight attendants receive extra compensation for additional hours.

Flight attendants may be away from their home base at least one-third of the time. During this period, the airlines provide hotel accommodations and an allowance for meal expenses.

Flight attendants must be flexible and willing to relocate. However, many flight attendants elect to live in one place and commute to their assigned home base. Home bases and routes worked are bid for and awarded on a seniority basis, so the longer the flight attendant has been employed, the more likely he or she is to work on their preferred flights. Almost all flight attendants start out working on reserve status, or on call. Flight attendants on reserve status usually live near their home base, because they are required to be able to report to their home base on short notice. On small corporate airlines, flight attendants often work on an as-needed basis and must adapt to varying environments and passengers.

The combination of free time and free or discounted airfares provides flight attendants the opportunity to travel. However, the work can be strenuous and trying. Flight attendants stand during much of the flight and must remain pleasant and efficient, regardless of how tired they are or how demanding passengers may be. Occasionally, flight attendants must deal with turbulent flights which can cause difficulties regarding service and cause anxiety among passengers that flight attendants must address.

Working in a moving aircraft leaves flight attendants susceptible to injuries. According to BLS data, full-time flight attendants experienced a much higher than average work-related injury and illness rate. Various physical injuries can occur when opening overhead compartments or while pushing heavy service carts. In addition, medical problems can arise from irregular sleeping and eating patterns, dealing with stressful passengers, working in a pressurized environment, and breathing recycled air.

Training, other Qualifications, and Advancement

Flight attendants must be certified by the FAA. A high school diploma or its equivalent is the minimum educational requirement, but airlines increasingly prefer applicants who have a college degree. Experience in dealing with the public is important, because flight attendants must be able to interact comfortably with strangers and remain calm under duress.

Education and training. A high school diploma or its equivalent is the minimum educational requirement. However, airlines increasingly prefer applicants with a college degree. Applicants who attend schools or colleges that offer flight attendant training may have an advantage over other applicants. Highly desirable areas of concentration include people-oriented disciplines, such as communications, psychology, nursing, travel and tourism, hospitality, and education. Flight attendants for international airlines generally must speak a foreign language fluently. For their international flights, some of the major airlines prefer candidates who can speak two major foreign languages.

Once hired, all candidates must undergo a period of formal training. The length of training, ranging from 3 to 6 weeks, depends on the size and type of carrier and takes place at the airline's flight training centre. Airlines that do not operate training centres generally send new employees to the centre of another airline. Some airlines may provide transportation to the training centres and an allowance for room, board, and school supplies, while other airlines charge individuals for training. New trainees are not considered employees of the airline until they successfully complete the training program. Trainees learn emergency procedures, such as evacuating an airplane, operating emergency systems and equipment, administering first aid, and surviving in the water. In addition, trainees are taught how to deal with disruptive passengers and with hijacking and terrorist situations. New hires learn flight regulations and duties, gain knowledge of company operations and policies, and receive instruction on personal grooming and weight control. Trainees for international routes get additional instruction in passport and customs regulations. Trainees must perform many drills and duties unaided, in front of the training staff. Throughout training, they also take tests designed to eliminate unsuccessful trainees. Toward the end of their training, students go on practice flights. Upon successful completion of training, flight attendants receive the FAA Certificate of Demonstrated Proficiency. Flight attendants also are required to go through periodic retraining and pass an FAA safety examination to continue flying.

Licensure and certification. All flight attendants must be certified by the FAA. To be certified, flight attendants are required to successfully complete training requirements, such as evacuation, fire fighting, medical emergency, and security procedures established by the FAA and the Transportation Security Administration. They also must perform the assigned duties of a cabin crew member and complete an approved proficiency check. Flight attendants are certified for specific types of aircraft, regardless of the carrier. Therefore, only 1-day or 2-day recurrent training, with the new carrier, is needed for those flight attendants who change airlines, as long as the type of aircraft remains the same.

Other qualifications. Airlines prefer to hire poised, tactful, and resourceful people who can speak clearly and interact comfortably with strangers and remain calm under duress. Applicants with previous experience in dealing with the public are preferred by airlines. Additionally, airlines usually have age, physical, and appearance requirements. Applicants usually must be at least 18 to 21 years old, although some carriers may have higher minimum-age requirements.

Applicants must meet height requirements for reaching overhead bins, which often contain emergency equipment, and most airlines want candidates with weight proportionate to height. Flight attendants must be in excellent health, and a medical evaluation is required. Vision is required to be correctable to 20/30 or better with glasses or contact lenses (uncorrected no worse than 20/200). Men must have their hair cut above the collar and be clean shaven. Airlines prefer applicants with no visible tattoos, body piercing, or unusual hairstyles or makeup.

In addition to education and training, airlines conduct a thorough background check, which goes back as many as 10 years, as required by the FAA,. Everything about an applicant is investigated, including date of birth, employment history, criminal record, school records, and any gaps in employment. Employment is contingent on a successful background check. An applicant will not be offered a job or will be immediately dismissed if his or her background check shows any discrepancies. All U.S. airlines require that applicants be citizens of the United States or registered aliens with legal rights to obtain employment in the United States.

Advancement. After completing initial training, flight attendants are assigned to one of their airline's bases. New flight attendants are placed on reserve status and are called either to staff extra flights or to fill in for crewmembers that are sick, on vacation, or rerouted. When they are not on duty, reserve flight attendants must be available to report for flights on short notice. They usually remain on reserve for at least 1 year but, in some cities, it may take 5 to 10 years—or longer—to advance from reserve status.

Flight attendants who no longer are on reserve bid monthly for regular assignments. Because assignments are based on seniority, usually only the most experienced attendants get their choice of assignments. Advancement takes longer today than in the past, because experienced flight attendants are remaining in this career longer than in the past.

Some flight attendants become supervisors, moving from senior or lead flight attendant, to check flight attendant, to flight attendant supervisor, then on to base manager, and finally to manager or vice president of in-flight operations. They may take on additional duties, such as recruiting, instructing, or developing in-flight products. Their experience also may qualify them for numerous airline-related jobs involving contact with the public, such as reservation ticket agent or public relations specialist. Flight attendants who do not want to travel often for various reasons may move to a position as an administrative assistant. With additional education, some flight attendants may decide to transfer to other areas of the airline for which they work, such as risk management or human resources.

Employment

Flight attendants held about 98,700 jobs in 2008. Commercial airlines employed the vast majority of flight attendants, and most attendants lived near major metropolitan airports or airports operating as hubs for the major airlines. A small number of flight attendants worked for companies that offered chartered flights.

Job Outlook

Employment of flight attendants is projected to grow about as fast as average. Competition for jobs is expected to remain keen because the opportunity for travel attracts more applicants than there are jobs.

Employment change. Employment of flight attendants is expected to grow by 8 percent, which is about as fast as the average for all occupations over the 2008–18 period. Population growth and an improving economy are expected to boost the number of airline passengers. As airlines expand their capacity to meet rising demand by increasing the number and size of planes in operation and the number of flights offered, more flight attendants will be needed.

Job prospects. Despite growing demand for flight attendants, competition is expected to be keen because this job usually attracts more applicants than there are jobs, with only the most qualified eventually being hired. College graduates who have experience dealing with the public should have the best chance of being hired. Job opportunities may be better with the faster growing regional and commuter, low-cost, and charter airlines. There also are job opportunities for professionally trained flight attendants to work for companies operating private aircraft for their executives.

The majority of job opportunities through the year 2018 will arise from the need to replace flight attendants who leave the labour force or transfer to other occupations, often for higher earnings or a more stable lifestyle. With the job now viewed increasingly as a profession, however, fewer flight attendants leave their jobs, and job turnover is not as high as in the past. According to the Association of Flight Attendants, the average job tenure of attendants is currently 16 years and is increasing.

In the long run, opportunities for persons seeking flight attendant jobs should improve as the airline industry expands. Over the next decade, however, demand for flight attendants will fluctuate with the demand for air travel, which is highly sensitive to swings in the economy. During downturns, as air traffic declines, the hiring of flight attendants declines, and some experienced attendants may be laid off until traffic recovers.

Earnings

Median annual wages of flight attendants were $35,930 in May 2008. The middle 50 percent earned between $28,420 and $49,910. The lowest 10 percent earned less than $20,580, and the highest 10 percent earned more than $65,350.

According to data from the Association of Flight Attendants, beginning attendants had median earnings of $16,191 a year in

2009. Beginning pay scales for flight attendants vary by carrier, however. New hires usually begin at the same pay scale, regardless of experience; all flight attendants receive the same future pay increases based on an established pay scale.

Some airlines offer incentive pay for working holidays, night and international flights, or taking positions that require additional responsibility or paperwork.

Flight attendants and their immediate families are entitled to free or discounted fares on their own airline and reduced fares on most other airlines. Some airlines require that the flight attendant be with an airline for 3 to 6 months before taking advantage of this benefit. Other benefits may include medical, dental, and life insurance; 401K or other retirement plan; sick leave; paid holidays; stock options; paid vacations; and tuition reimbursement. Flight attendants also receive a "per diem" allowance for meal expenses while on duty away from home. Flight attendants are required to purchase uniforms and wear them while on duty. The airlines usually pay for uniform replacement items, and may provide a small allowance to cover cleaning and upkeep of the uniforms.

The majority of flight attendants hold union membership, primarily with the Association of Flight Attendants. Other unions that represent flight attendants include the Transport Workers Union of America and the International Brotherhood of Teamsters.

Retail Salespersons

- Good employment opportunities are expected because of the need to replace the large number of workers who leave the occupation each year.
- Many salespersons work evenings and weekends, particularly during peak retail periods.
- Employers look for people who enjoy working with others and who have good communication skills, an interest in sales work, a neat appearance, and a courteous demeanor.
- Although advancement opportunities are limited, having a college degree or a great deal of experience may help retail salespersons move into management positions.

Nature of the Work

Whether selling shoes, computer equipment, or automobiles, retail salespersons assist customers in finding what they are looking for. They also try to increase sales by describing a product's features, demonstrating its uses, and promoting its value.

In addition to selling, many retail salespersons—especially those who work in department and apparel stores—conduct financial transactions with their customers. This usually involves receiving payments by cash, check, debit card, or credit card; operating cash registers; and bagging or packaging purchases. Depending on the hours they work, retail salespersons may have to open or close cash registers. This work may include counting the money in the register and separating charge slips, coupons, and exchange vouchers. Retail salespersons also may have to make deposits at a cash office. (Cashiers, who have similar duties, are discussed elsewhere in the *Handbook*.) In addition, retail salespersons may help stock shelves or racks, arrange for mailing or delivery of purchases, mark price tags, take inventory, and prepare displays.

For some sales jobs, particularly those involving expensive and complex items, retail salespersons need special knowledge or skills. For example, salespersons who sell automobiles must be able to explain the features of various models, the manufacturers' specifications, the types of options and financing available, and the details of associated warranties. In addition, all retail salespersons must recognize security risks and thefts and understand their organization's procedure for handling such situations—procedures that may include notifying security guards or calling police.

Work environment. Most retail salespersons work in clean, comfortable, well-lit stores. However, they often stand for long periods and may need supervisory approval to leave the sales floor. They also may work outdoors if they sell items such as cars, plants, or lumber yard materials.

The Monday-through-Friday, 9-to-5 workweek is the exception rather than the rule for retail salespersons. Many salespersons work evenings and weekends, particularly during holidays and other peak sales periods. The end-of-year holiday season often is the busiest time, and as a result, many employers limit the use of vacation time between Thanksgiving and the beginning of January.

This occupation offers opportunities for both full-time and part-time work. About 34 percent of retail salespersons worked part time in 2008. Part-time opportunities may vary by setting, however, as many who sell big-ticket items are required to work full time.

Training, other Qualifications, and Advancement

Retail salespersons typically learn their skills through on-the-job training. Although advancement opportunities are limited, having a college degree or a great deal of experience may help retail salespersons move into management positions.

Education and training. There usually are no formal education requirements for retail sales positions, but employers often prefer applicants with a high school diploma or its equivalent. This may be especially important for those who sell technical products or "big-ticket" items, such as electronics or automobiles. A college degree may be required for management trainee positions, especially in larger retail establishments.

Most retail salespersons receive on-the-job training, which usually lasts anywhere from a few days to a few months. In small stores, newly hired workers usually are trained by an experienced employee. In large stores, training programs are more formal and generally are conducted over several days. Topics often include customer service, security, the store's policies and procedures, and cash register operation. Depending on the type of product they are selling, employees may be given additional specialized training. For example, those working in cosmetics receive instruction on the types of products the store offers and for whom the cosmetics would be most beneficial. Likewise, those who sell computers may be instructed in the technical differences between computer products. Because providing the best possible service to customers is a high priority for many employers, employees often are given periodic training to update and refine their skills.

Other qualifications. Employers look for people who enjoy working with others and who possess good communication skills. Employers also value workers who have the tact and patience to deal with difficult customers. Among other desirable characteristics are an interest in sales work, a neat appearance, and a courteous demeanor. The ability to speak more than one language may be helpful for employment in communities where people from various cultures live and shop. Before hiring a salesperson, some employers conduct a background check, especially for a job selling high-priced items.

Advancement. Opportunities for advancement vary. In some small establishments, advancement is limited because one person—often the owner—does most of the managerial work. In others, some salespersons can be promoted to assistant manager. Large retail businesses usually prefer to hire college graduates as management trainees, making a college education increasingly important. However, motivated and capable employees without college degrees still may advance to administrative or supervisory positions in large establishments.

As salespersons gain experience and seniority, they often move into positions with greater responsibility and may be given their choice of departments in which to work. This opportunity often means moving to areas with higher potential earnings and commissions. The highest earnings potential usually lies in selling "big-ticket" items—such as cars, jewellery, furniture, and electronic equipment—although doing so often requires extensive knowledge of the product and an excellent talent for persuasion.

Previous sales experience may be an asset when one is applying for positions with larger retailers or in nonretail industries, such as financial services, wholesale trade, or manufacturing.

Employment

Retail salespersons held about 4.5 million jobs in 2008. The largest employers were clothing and clothing accessories stores, department stores, building material and supplies dealers, motor vehicle and parts dealers, and general merchandise stores such as warehouse clubs and supercenters. In addition, about 156,500 retail salespersons were self-employed.

Because retail stores are found in every city and town, employment is distributed geographically in much the same way as the population.

Job Outlook

Employment is expected to grow about as fast as average. Due to the frequency with which people leave this occupation, job opportunities are expected to be good.

Employment change. Employment is expected to grow by 8 percent over the 2008–18 decade, about as fast as the average for all occupations. In addition, given the size of this occupation, about 374,700 new retail salesperson jobs will arise over the projections decade—more jobs than will be generated in almost any other occupation.

Employment growth among retail salespersons reflects rising retail sales stemming from a growing population. Many retail establishments will continue to expand in size and number, leading to new retail sales positions. Growth will be fastest in general merchandise stores, many of which sell a wide assortment of goods at low prices. As consumers continue to prefer these stores other establishments with higher prices, growth in this industry will be rapid. Employment of retail sales persons is expected to decline in department stores and automobile dealers as these industries see a reduction in store locations.

Despite the growing popularity of electronic commerce, the impact of online shopping on the employment of retail salespersons is expected to be minimal. Internet sales have not decreased the need for retail salespersons. Retail stores commonly use an online presence to complement their in-store sales, and many consumers prefer to buy merchandise in person. Retail salespersons will remain important in assisting customers, providing specialized service, and increasing customer satisfaction.

Job prospects. Employment opportunities for retail salespersons are expected to be good because of the need to replace the large number of workers who transfer to other occupations or leave the labour force each year. In addition, many new jobs will be created for retail salespersons as businesses seek to expand operations and enhance customer service. A substantial number of these openings should occur in warehouse clubs and supercenters as a result of strong growth among these establishments. Opportunities for part-time work should be abundant, and demand is expected be strong for temporary workers during peak selling periods, such as the end-of-year holiday season between Thanksgiving and the beginning of January.

During economic downturns, sales volumes and the resulting demand for sales workers usually decline. Consequently, retail sales jobs generally are more susceptible to fluctuations in the economy than are many other occupations.

Earnings

Median hourly wages of wage-and-salary retail salespersons, including commissions, were $9.86 in May 2008. The middle 50 percent earned between $8.26 and $13.35 an hour. The lowest 10 percent earned less than $7.37, and the highest 10 percent earned more than $19.14 an hour. Median hourly wages in the industries employing the largest numbers of retail salespersons in May 2008 were as follows:

Automobile dealers	$18.91
Building material and supplies dealers	11.95
Other general merchandise stores	9.22
Department stores	9.14
Clothing stores	8.94

Many beginning or inexperienced workers earn the Federal minimum wage of $7.25 an hour, but many States set minimum wages higher than the Federal minimum. In areas where employers have difficulty attracting and retaining workers, wages tend to be higher than the legislated minimum.

Compensation systems can vary by type of establishment and merchandise sold. Salespersons receive hourly wages, commissions, or a combination of the two. Under a commission system, salespersons receive a percentage of the sales they make. This system offers sales workers the opportunity to increase their earnings considerably, but they may find that their earnings depend strongly on their ability to sell their product and on the ups and downs of the economy.

Benefits may be limited in smaller stores, but benefits in large establishments usually are considerable. In addition, nearly all salespersons are able to buy their store's merchandise at a discount, with the savings depending on the type of merchandise. Also, to bolster revenue, employers may use incentive programs such as awards, bonuses, and profit-sharing plans to the sales staff.

Housekeeping

Housekeeping or housecleaning is the systematic process of making a home neat and clean in approximately that order. This maybe applied more broadly that just an individual home, or as a metaphor for a similar "clean up" process applied elsewhere such as a procedural reform. It can also be called household management, which is the act of overseeing the organizational, financial, day-to-day operations of a house or estate, and the managing of other domestic concerns.

In the process of housekeeping general cleaning activities are completed, such as disposing of rubbish, storing of belongings in regular places, cleaning dirty surfaces, dusting and vacuuming. It is also the care and control of property, ensuring its maintenance and proper use and appearance. In a hotel, "housekeeping" is also a term for the cleaning personnel.

Some housekeeping is housecleaning and some housekeeping is home chores. Home chores are housework that needs to be done at regular intervals, Housekeeping includes the budget and control of expenditures, preparing meals and buying food, paying the heat bill, and cleaning the house. Outdoor housecleaning chores include removing leaves from rain gutters, washing windows, sweeping doormats, cleaning the pool, putting away lawn furniture, and taking out the trash.

Tools include the vacuum cleaner, broom and mop. Supplies such as cleaning solutions and sponges are sold in grocery stores and elsewhere. Professional cleaners can be hired for less frequent or specialist tasks such as cleaning blinds, rugs, and sofas. Professional services are also offered for the basic tasks. Safety is a consideration because some cleaning products are toxic and some cleaning tasks are physically demanding. *Green cleaning* refers to cleaning without causing pollution. The history of housecleaning has links to the advancement of technology.

Reasons

People perform house cleaning for the home to look better and be safer and easier to live in. It is in response to clutter, disorder, litter, dirtiness or to prevent such. Without housecleaning limescale builds up on taps, mold grows in wet areas, bacterial action make the garbage disposal and toilet smell and cobwebs accumulate. With organisation belongings are easily found and table tops are clear.

Indoor Litter

Disposal of rubbish is an important aspect of house cleaning, the reasons for this are psychological, social and practical. Plastic bags are designed and manufactured specifically for the collection of litter. Many are sized to fit common waste baskets and trash cans. Paper bags are made to carry aluminum cans, glass jars and other things. Recycling is possible with some kinds of litter.

Clutter Problem

Clutter is belongings that have not been put away into storage locations designed for them. If there are not enough shelves and drawers and hangers and there can't be more, this is a cause of clutter. There is a limit to the number of possessions that can be neatly stored in a home. A tangled pile of old coats, mittens, scarves, hats and boots occurs in some hall closets. Pawnbrokers, thrift shops and garbage collectors are involved in the prevention of clutter.

Dustiness

Over time dust accumulates on household surfaces. As well as making the surfaces dirty, when dust is disturbed it can become suspended in the air, causing sneezing and breathing trouble. It can also transfer from furniture to clothing, making it unclean. Various tools have been invented for dust removal; Feather and lamb's wool dusters, cotton and polyester dust cloths, disposable paper "dust cloths", dust mops for smooth floors and vacuum cleaners. Vacuum cleaners often have a variety of tools to enable them to remove not just from carpets and rugs, but from hard surfaces and upholstery. This way can help your things well organize. Things will look so clean likewise neat.

Dirtiness

Although one meaning of housecleaning is "improvement," the primary meaning of housecleaning is "the cleaning of a house." A goal of housecleaning would be the removal of mold from shower grout or smudges and splatters from a kitchen wall. Examples of dirtiness or "soil" would be dry coffee spills and jelly drips or muddy footprints on carpet. Soap and water is a "cleaner." Equipment used with a cleaner might be a bucket and sponge. A modern tool is the spray bottle, but the scientific principle is the same. Cleaning supplies have directions and are sold at janitorial and other stores. Cleaning specialists such as carpet cleaners are listed in phone books. Housecleaning is done to achieve and to enjoy a cleaner house.

Training

In the early 1800s throughout the industrialized world there was a campaign to teach girls the domestic arts (cooking, cleaning, hygiene, sewing, art, decor, etc) in school. In the early 1870s there were college courses in home economics and by 1880 there were high school courses. There continues to be high school and vocational school courses and college degrees in home economics, which prepares students for various employment, as well as home and family management. Home economists are taught and teach about relationships, children, economy, shopping, management of home and family, sewing and interior decoration. Although boys have not been required to learn cooking and cleaning in school, a few have taken a course or two.

Household Chemicals

Various household cleaning products have been developed to facilitate the removal of dust and dirt, for surface maintenance, and for disinfection. Products are available in powder, liquid or spray form. The basic ingredients determine the type of cleaning tasks for which they are suitable. Some are packaged as general purpose cleaning materials whilst others are targeted at specific cleaning tasks such as drain clearing, oven cleaning, lime scale removal and polishing furniture. Household cleaning products provide aesthetic and hygiene benefits but are also associated with health risks for the users, and building occupants. The US Department of Health and Human Services offers the public access to the Household Products Database. This database provides consumer information for over 4,000 products based on information provided by the manufacturer through the Material Safety Data Sheet. Consumers can search for products by brand name, manufacturer, ingredients, product recalls, and health effects.

Surfactants lower the surface tension of water, making it able to flow into smaller tiny cracks and crevices in soils making removal easier. Alkaline chemicals break down known soils such as grease and mud. Acids break down soils such as lime scale, soap scum, and stains of mustard, coffee, tea, and alcoholic beverages. Some solvent-based products are flammable and some can dissolve paint and varnish. Disinfectants stop smell and stains caused by bacteria.

When multiple chemicals are applied to the same surface without full removal of the earlier substance, the chemicals may interact. This interaction may result in a reduction of the efficiency of the chemicals applied (such as a change in pH value caused by mixing alkalis and acids) and in cases may even emit toxic fumes. An example of this is the mixing of ammonia-based cleaners (or acid-based cleaners) and bleach. This causes the production of chloramines that volatilize (become gaseous) causing acute inflammation of the lungs (toxic pneumonitis), long-term respiratory damage, and potential death.

Residue from cleaning products and cleaning activity (dusting, vacuuming, sweeping) have been shown to impact indoor air quality (IAQ) by redistributing particulate matter (dust, dirt, human skin cells, organic matter, animal dander, particles from combustion, fibers from insulation, pollen, and polycyclic aromatic hydrocarbons that gaseous or liquid particles become adsorbed to. The particulate matter and chemical residual will of be highest concentrations right after cleaning but will decrease over time depending upon levels of contaminants, air exchange rate, and other sources of chemical residual. Of most concern are the family of chemicals called VOCs such as formaldehyde, toluene, and limonene.

Volatile organic compounds (VOCs) are released from many household cleaning products such as disinfectants, polishes, floor waxes, air-freshening sprays, all purpose cleaning sprays, and glass cleaner. These products have been shown to emit irritating vapors. VOCs are of most concern due to their tendency to evaporate and be inhaled into the lungs or adsorbed to existing dust, which can also be inhaled. It has been found that aerosolized (spray) cleaning products are important risk factors and may aggravate symptoms of adult asthma, respiratory irritation, childhood asthma, wheeze, bronchitis, and allergy.

Other modes of exposure to potentially harmful household cleaning chemicals include absorption through the skin (dermis), accidental ingestion, and accidental splashing into the eyes. Products for the application and safe use of the chemicals are also available, such as nylon scrub sponge and rubber gloves. It is up to the consumer to keep themselves safe while using these chemicals. Reading and comprehending the labels is important.

There is a growing consumer and governmental interest in natural cleaning products and green cleaning methods. The use of nontoxic household chemicals is growing as consumers become more informed of the health effects of many household chemicals, and municipalities are having to deal with the expensive disposal of household hazardous waste (HHW).

Tools

"Modern housecleaning tools" is almost an oxymoron. There are few areas of employment where someone from 50 years ago could step into the same job today, but housecleaning is one area where there has been very little change. Brooms remove debris from floors. Brushes clean cracks and crevices. Buckets hold cleaning and rinsing solutions. Carpet sweepers remove surface dust and debris. Chamois do lint-free drying of windows. Clotheslines hold doormats and rugs for cleaning. Clothespins fasten things on clotheslines. Dishwashers are machines that wash dishes placed inside them. Dryers dry textiles placed inside them. Dusters are soft cloths for wiping dust, or are various dust sweepers. Dustpans carry dust and debris swept into them. Floor machines remove and apply floor finish. Rubber gloves protect hands from dish water and other cleaners. Dust mops remove dust from smooth floors. Wet mops are for washing floors. Paper towels wipe up grease and other materials difficult to rinse from a cloth. Polishing cloths are for applying polish and removing excess polish. Sponges apply cleaning solution and remove soil. Spray bottles apply cleaning solution to be removed by another tool. Squeegees remove solutions from glass. Steam cleaners are machines that help wash carpet. Vacuum cleaners remove dust from inside carpet. *Upright vacuums* are best at carpet vacuuming. *Canister vacuums* are best at upholstery and bare floors. *Wet-dry vacuums* can be used to remove spills and spot removers. Washing machines clean textiles such as dust cloths.

Yard

A home's yard and exterior are sometimes subject to cleaning. The first impression of a home's cleanliness is given by its yard and entranceway. Exterior cleaning also occurs for safety, upkeep and usefulness. It includes removal of paper litter and grass growing in sidewalk cracks. Rain gutters, doormats, pools and the screens and glass of windows are also cleanable. Yard junk-removal might occur and porch clutter removal. The paint of door frames might be washed or an old pinata thrown away.

Professional Cleaning Services

There are many professional house cleaning services located around the world. In recent years, they have grown in popularity due to the increase in both spouses needing to work.

Investment in Property

Funding Real Estate Projects for the Hospitality Industry: Emerging Perspectives

Up until 2007, most hoteliers, investors and developers were buoyant when it came to the growth prospects in the hospitality industry. They had enough reason to be optimistic as every factor which would influence the industry, directly or indirectly, was on a growth trajectory.

The GDP was growing like never before and the whole world had its eyes on the Indian growth story. Plans of expansion filled the newspapers and press releases and investors were keener than ever to get a fair share of the pie.

The recession, however, had plans of its own and devoured most of the pie. The global economic slowdown and its effect on the Indian economy has doused the fire of excitement of even the most optimistic developers and investors. It has resulted in an extreme crunch for investment in the hospitality sector, coupled with the decrease in demand for rooms. This double whammy put to rest most of the ambitious plans of expansion across the country.

All players have been reviewing their plans of development, owing to the increasingly challenging macro economic situation at the moment. The total number of rooms estimated to be added is today nearly half of what was announced earlier. One-fourth of the announced plans have fallen completely flat and the rest are hanging on the edge of viability. DLF, Parsvnath and other developers of similar cadre have scaled down or slowed down their plans of expansion.

Parsvnath, which had plans of adding at least 10,000 rooms, has now stopped acquiring land for any further plans other than the twenty hotels for which they have already done the same. There have been reports that DLF has been in talks with various hotel companies to sell eight to nine of their land parcels demarcated for hotel projects to raise funds. Unitech has sold its Gurgaon hotel project to reduce its huge debt burden.

Developers are keener to finish the projects on hand rather than plan further. Divesting the investment heavy hotel plans seems to be the best way out for the cash strapped, heavily indebted players to survive the present-day economic scenario.

Financial Projections Going Awry

The seeds were sown, the crops were nurtured through the tough inflationary times but when the time to harvest came, the floods of recession washed away the anticipated bounty. Cost and revenue assumptions made during the good times have thus gone for a toss. When it comes to loan disbursements, real estate is presently the black sheep of the family.

Private banks from which loans were freely available earlier have dried up. Public sector banks which continue to lend, albeit cautiously, now require a higher collateral to lend the same amount.

Non-banking finance companies are either not lending at all or looking at returns in the post 20 per cent range. Private equity interest in the hospitality sector has all but dried up. Due to the severe global liquidity crunch and flight of capital to 'places of origin', there is a diminishing interest for private equity players in foreign markets. This has added to the financial woes of the capital thirsty developers.

The risk associated with a hospitality project being relatively larger, the premium at which funding is available has gone up. Due to this, only the most stable projects in the market would be able to take up the risk of delivering higher returns to the lenders.

Many developers had invested heavily in land in the past when the land values were significantly higher. At present, the value of the same land parcels has come down significantly. The dependency on the appreciation of these assets has turned out to be a major dampener to the development plans of the various developers. The lower value of land means that the value of collateral has come down for project loans.

The cycle of cost of construction has taken the industry on a roller coaster ride over the past couple of years. The global commodity cycle has drastically changed its course. Steel and cement which form a significant chunk of the civil construction costs have lost up to 40 per cent from their historic highs twelve months ago.

The hotels which have opened recently have faced the brunt of the cost fluctuations in a similar fashion. Greater costs were incurred, owing to the period in which their construction phases passed through. The cost of materials was higher, the market was booming and along with the high material costs, the various architects and consultants demanded a premium as a result of a never-before-seen demand. Despite the increased amount of investment that the developers had to put in, they now face a world with reduced revenue prospects.

The main factor that has directly and indirectly influenced the stability of revenue-side financial projections in the hotel industry is the lack of 'stickiness' relative to other real estate sectors.

Stickiness of the hotel industry is low. In order to explain, take lease agreements into consideration. These are long term in nature and hence revenues are more secure in the case of an office or retail space as they have a considerable lock-in period. However in case of the hospitality industry, the revenues are more directly susceptible to market conditions. This being the reason as to why other sectors have been relatively less affected by the present day scenario.

The main factors influencing this stickiness are occupancy rate and Average Room Rate (ARR).

Occupancy rate is a function of supply and demand. The present scenario is affected by both the demand and supply factors, with demand having the more potent influence. The two main demand drivers, the leisure and business travellers, have contributed to the reduction in occupancy rates. Overseas travel has been affected to a large extent due to the economic slowdown.

Corporates have found innovative ways to cut down on their expenses and there is a growing need for them to rationalise business travel. They have reduced their travel budgets, are staying at serviced apartments and guesthouses or even looking at options where they can avoid staying overnight. MNCs with significant exposure to the developed markets are taking the lead to drive travel associated business expenditures down as a part of their global strategy. Spending sentiments of consumers has been hit to a large extent owing mostly to fears of job loss and a resulting lack of confidence and low morale. The leisure consumers are hence looking to spend lesser on travel.

In addition to the demand slowing down, the supply is on the increase which would mean that the occupancy rates are set to reduce further at least for the next one or two years. All these factors contribute to the occupancy rate reducing significantly and this is a major reason contributing to the instability of the financial projections made by the various players. On the supply side, although there is an inherent demand for more supply in the long run, occupancy rates would see an improvement only with the revival of the economy.

Due to the hit on occupancy rate, hoteliers have been forced to cut down on the ARRs to attract both their business and leisure customers. The occupancy rate has also negatively affected the other closely linked revenue sources such as food and beverage, conferences and banquets.

Role of Funding Options

Traditionally, most developers have tended to plough back the surplus that they earn, into their business via investing in land banks. This makes them highly dependant on external sources for funding. The various equity funding options available in the market till now have been public or private equity which can be foreign (FDI) or domestic funding. In the present market scenario, there is a lot more uncertainty in cash flows associated with hotel projects than usual. This has led investors to be quite cautious when it comes to investing in or lending to hospitality projects.

With many of the real estate companies trading below book values, the public equity scenario is dismal. IPO market is almost non-existent. The last high profile real estate IPO which failed was the EMAAR MGF IPO in February 2008. Real Estate Index has fallen up to 80 per cent from its peak. Going ahead with secondary offerings or rights issues would likely meet with a negative investor response.

Private equity, while still being an option, has seen a slowdown. Investors are worried about the market bottoming out and there is a feeling that the correction in the hospitality sector is still not complete. PE players are avoiding common equity in SPVs but looking at structured investments with greater security and preferred returns. However, there are a number of funds which are actively looking to buy out or invest in distressed assets at enticing valuations.

Having said that, owing to the severe capital crunch, the market for new PE capital raising especially in real estate is difficult right now and is likely to remain so for the next two to three years. Where funds have already been raised, there have been cases of Limited Partners (LPs) not honouring their capital commitments.

Project loans for under construction projects are harder to come by with only the public sector banks lending. These loans are being disbursed primarily to promising projects with substantial asset cover guarantees. We are also witnessing cases of liquidity parched developers borrowing from HNIs at extremely high rates.

Bailing out Stranded Projects

A million dollar question on everyone's mind would be on how to bail oneself out of stranded projects.

Divesting a part of the stake in the project to gain capital may be one of the options. This may not be very easy in today's market. The project maybe valued at a much lower price than what is expected and may leave the seller with a raw deal from the transaction made. One could also think of repositioning the project. Instead of increasing the investment requirement for a project by planning a high end luxury hotel, one could look at serviced apartments and budget hotels at the moment to get through the times of credit crunch.

Another option would be to reduce the scale of the project. This can be done in one go or in phases. Phasing the project out in stages where part of the hotel could be operational in a relatively lesser time and with lesser investment than earlier planned would help ease the credit and liquidity crunch. There are quite a few operators who take a stake in the project as well. Accor is a good example of such an operator who have significant expansion plans in India. Tying up with the right investing operators would however not be as easy as it may look as these operators would choose only the best of the options available and they would have their own plans in place already.

Going back to the lender may be an option worth visiting, to see if they could restructure the existing loan. One could also go for refinancing or extending the loan. If the borrower has a good record, they could also look at finding a new lender as well, probably an HNI who would be willing to invest. However, if the only option left is to exit the project, the timing would need to be well thought out. If one waits too long for a good price, the price might just go lower. On the other hand one also needs to assess the urgency to exit the project as we would not want to end up in a situation where we would be forced to accept a price which would normally be unattractive.

Liberalisation of FDI Norms and its Impact on Expansion Plans

FDI has the promise to be a major factor in the economic development of the many developing nations of the world. With tourism being a major revenue earner for countries across the world, FDI norms liberalisation in this sector is a definite boost for the Indian economy.

The government has been very liberal when it comes to FDI regulations in the hotel and tourism industry. According to the Government of India-Ministry of Commerce and Industry, 100 per cent FDI is permissible in the hotel and tourism sector on the automatic route subject to the automatic approval clauses. The additional restrictions, applicable to some sectors of real estate, such as area of development being at least 50,000 square metres, 50 per cent of the project to be completed before five years, no repatriation of funds before three years from date of minimum capitalisation released in 2005, are not applicable to the hotel and tourism industry.

The government has thus made a conscious effort knowing the fact that tourism can be a major source of revenue for the country which is still relatively untapped. Hence, the only effect that existing FDI norms can have on the industry is on the positive side. It is only a matter of time before investments in the hotel and tourism sector start flowing in freely once again. These investments would be more dependant on the inherent demand in the industry and the overall economic scenario. Once the credit crunch situation gets better, the inherent demand in the industry that one senses should help attract funds easily as compared to some of the other sectors.

Some say the worst is over and India will be getting back on its feet soon. However, the key is not just to wait and watch but to try and be one step ahead. Be ahead and decide on when to stop waiting. Only the best would survive and we would be lying if we said we weren't all eager to see who they really are.

The Hotel Organisation Framework

Both people and organizations need to establish a strategic framework for significant success. This framework consists of:

- a vision for your future,

- a mission that defines what you are doing,
- values that shape your actions,
- strategies that zero in on your key success approaches, and
- goals and action plans to guide your daily, weekly and monthly actions.

Your organization's success and your personal success depend on how well you define and live by each of these important concepts. In fact:

- Companies whose employees understand the mission and goals enjoy a 29 percent greater return than other firms (Watson Wyatt Work Study).
- U.S. workers want their work to make a difference, but 75% do not think their company's mission statement has become the way they do business.

Read more to find out how to develop a successful strategic framework for your organization and yourself.

Vision Statement

A vision is a statement about what your organization wants to become. It should resonate with all members of the organization and help them feel proud, excited, and part of something much bigger than themselves. A vision should stretch the organization's capabilities and image of itself. It gives shape and direction to the organization's future. Visions range in length from a couple of words to several pages. I recommend shorter vision statements because people will tend to remember their shorter organizational vision.

Vision Statement Samples

"Year after year, Westin and its people will be regarded as the best and most sought after hotel and resort management group in North America."

"To be recognized and respected as one of the premier associations of HR Professionals."

Personal Vision Statement

Your personal vision for your life can be as simple as a couple of words or as lengthy as 200 or more items you want to attain or accomplish.

Mission or Purpose is a precise description of what an organization does. It should describe the business the organization is in. It is a definition of "why" the organization exists currently. Each member of an organization should be able to verbally express this mission.

Additionally, each person needs a mission for his or her life. The alignment of your life mission with your organization's mission is one of the key factors in whether you are happy with your work and workplace. If they are incongruent, you are likely dissatisfied with your work choice.

Mission Statement Samples

"Our goal is simply stated. We want to be the best service organization in the world." (IBM)

"FedEx is committed to our People-Service-Profit Philosophy. We will produce outstanding financial returns by providing totally reliable, competitively superior, global, air-ground transportation of high-priority goods and documents that require rapid, time-certain delivery."

"To give ordinary folk the chance to buy the same thing as rich people."

"Our mission is to earn the loyalty of Saturn owners and grow our family by developing and marketing U.S.-manufactured vehicles that are world leaders in quality, cost, and customer enthusiasm through the integration of people, technology, and business systems." "In order to realize our Vision, our Mission must be to exceed the expectations of our customers, whom we define as guests, partners, and fellow employees.(mission) We will accomplish this by committing to our shared values and by achieving the highest levels of customer satisfaction, with extraordinary emphasis on the creation of value. (strategy) In this way we will ensure that our profit, quality and growth goals are met." (Westin Hotels and Resorts)

Values are traits or qualities that are considered worthwhile; they represent an individual's highest priorities and deeply held driving forces. (Values are also known as core values and as governing values; they all refer to the same sentiment.)

Value statements are grounded in values and define how people want to behave with each other in the organization. They are statements about how the organization will value customers, suppliers, and the internal community. Value statements describe actions which are the living enactment of the fundamental values held by most individuals within the organization.

The values of each of the individuals in your workplace, along with their experience, upbringing, and so on, meld together to form your corporate culture. The values of your senior leaders are especially important in the development of your culture. These leaders have a lot of power in your organization to set the course and environment and they have selected the staff for your workplace.

If you think about your own life, your values form the cornerstones for all you do and accomplish. They define where you spend your time, if you are truly living your values. Each of you makes choices in life according to your most important four – ten values. Why not take the time to identify what is most important to you and to your organization.

Why Identify and Establish Values?

Effective organizations identify and develop a clear, concise and shared meaning of values/beliefs, priorities, and direction so that everyone understands and can contribute. Once defined, values impact every aspect of your organization. You must support and nurture this impact or identifying values will have been a wasted exercise.

People will feel fooled and misled unless they see the impact of the exercise within your organization. If you want the values you identify to have an impact, the following must occur.

- People demonstrate and model their values in action in their personal work behaviours, decision making, contribution, and interpersonal interaction.
- Organizational values help each person establish priorities in their daily work life.
- Values guide every decision that is made once the organization has cooperatively created the values and the value statements.
- Rewards and recognition within the organization are structured to recognize those people whose work embodies the values the organization embraced.

- Organizational goals are grounded in the identified values. Adoption of the values and the behaviours that result is recognized in regular performance feedback.
- People hire and promote individuals whose outlook and actions are congruent with the values.
- Only the active participation of all members of the organization will ensure a truly organization-wide, value-based, shared culture.

The following are examples of values: ambition, competency, individuality, equality, integrity, service, responsibility, accuracy, respect, dedication, diversity, improvement, enjoyment/fun, loyalty, credibility, honesty, innovativeness, teamwork, excellence, accountability, empowerment, quality, efficiency, dignity, collaboration, stewardship, empathy, accomplishment, courage, wisdom, independence, security, challenge, influence, learning, compassion, friendliness, discipline/order, generosity, persistence, optimism, dependability, flexibility.

Although important aspects of your life and attention, these are not values: family, church, professionalism. If you define what you value about each of these, you are identifying the core value. As an example, the core value in family might be close relationships; in church, spirituality.

Want to see samples of values and value statements? These give you an idea of the depth and breadth in which organizations write their values. Search online for values and value statements and you'll find some that stretch to several pages, too.

At Merck, "corporate conduct is inseparable from the conduct of individual employees in the performance of their work. Every Merck employee is responsible for adhering to business practices that are in accordance with the letter and spirit of the applicable laws and with ethical principles that reflect the highest standards of corporate and individual behavior...

"At Merck, we are committed to the highest standards of ethics and integrity. We are responsible to our customers, to Merck employees and their families, to the environments we inhabit, and to the societies we serve worldwide. In discharging our responsibilities, we do not take professional or ethical shortcuts. Our interactions with all segments of society must reflect the high standards we profess.".

Our Employees

- Our employees are the most valued assets of our company, essential participants with a shared responsibility in fulfilling our mission.
- We recognize that the quality, motivation and performance of our employees are the key factors in achieving our success.

"Accordingly, our Human Resources policies and practices are built on:

- Dedication to assisting every employee in reaching his or her full potential in both performance and reward.
- Commitment to diversity, equal opportunity and fair treatment.
- Promotion based on merit, and from within whenever possible.
- We want our organizational structure and culture to promote employee involvement, open communication, teamwork and cooperation."

Strategies are the broadly defined four or five key approaches the organization will use to accomplish its mission and drive toward the vision.

Goals and action plans usually flow from each strategy. One example of a strategy is employee empowerment and teams. Another is to pursue a new worldwide market in Asia. Another is to streamline your current distribution system using lean management principles.

A university Human Resources Development department established several broad strategies for growth.

These included becoming the training and education resource of choice for all employees by offering one-stop access to any and all existing education and training resources. Additionally, they determined key strategies for expanding their funding base and moving courses online for customer convenience.

A Human Resources department devised strategies to develop a superior workforce. These included eliminating poor performers; hiring from several choices of excellent candidates, not just "settling" on a candidate; developing succession planning; and increasing training and cross-training opportunities.

Sample Strategies

"The Human Resource Association of Greater Detroit's (HRAGD) efforts to advance its mission will include: The promotion of voluntary member interchange, observance of ethical and professional standards, the conduct of meetings and workshops on relevant human resources topics and issues, communication of our purpose and activities to the broader business community, cooperation with the Society for Human Resources Management (SHRM), as well as, other SHRM professional and student chapters and related Human Resources organizations and the community involvement of our membership. The Association regularly publishes newsletters throughout the year which cover items such as monthly meeting highlights, future programs, Executive Board announcements, SHRM and legislative updates and general human resources news. In addition, a Membership Directory and member skills listing are published."

The San Antonio Express News developed these strategies.

- "Expand our customer base and enhance the franchise by pursuing multimedia opportunities.
- Deliver an award-winning level of journalistic excellence, building public interest, trust and pride.
- Provide vigorous community leadership and support.
- Instill an environment of internal and external excellence in customer service.
- Empower and recognize each employee's unique contribution.
- Achieve the highest standards of quality.
- Improve financial strength and profitability."

Goals and Action Plans

After you have developed the key strategies, turn your attention to developing several goals that will enable you to accomplish each of your strategies. Goals should be SMART: specific, measurable, achievable, realistic and time-based.

In the example above, the HRAGD group might consider setting one goal to hold a monthly chapter meeting. Another goal that supports their strategies is to schedule a relevant seminar quarterly. Another goal might include holding informal dinners and cocktail hours to support voluntary member exchange.

Once you have enabled strategy accomplishment through setting SMART goals, you will want to develop action plans to accomplish each goal. Continuing with HRAGD as the example, to offer a quarterly seminar, you will need to follow an action plan:

- Establish a cross section of professionals as a committee and meet to plan the sessions.
- Determine budget.
- Perform HRAGD member needs assessment.
- Select topics based on member needs assessment.
- Locate exceptional speakers.
- Pick speaker and negotiate workshop length, pay, topic and objectives.
- Determine location and schedule the seminar.
- Plan advertising strategies, and so forth.

Make action plans as detailed as you need them to be and integrate the individual steps into your planning system. An effective planning system, whether it uses a personal computer, a paper and pen system, a handheld computer or a Palm, will keep your goals and action plans on track and on target.

5

The Hotel Organization of the Future

No hotel company operating today can be unaware of the swift pace of global change and its impact on every facet of the hospitality industry. With just five years left in this century, we can expect change to be the only constant. New business practices are evolving virtually as fast as our technologies, while resistance to change has become one of the primary causes of business failure.

The specter of constant change raises fundamental questions as to the creation of shareholder wealth in a capital-constrained, highly competitive environment. How will hotel organizations build shareholder wealth, and what key drivers will result in success? What future products and services will be essential in a technology-driven, global environment marked by rising customer expectations? Moreover, what alternative approaches and skills must organizations develop to ensure market success?

The future success of hotel organizations will be driven in large part by the ability to foresee — and capitalize — on change. Beyond this truism, however, there is an urgent need to identify what will be required in the competitive environment of the future with its intense focus on serving customer needs. The hospitality industry — as is the case with business generally — is subject to deep currents of change set in motion as economic and social systems shaped in the industrial era evolve to a knowledge-based era driven by technology advances.

In this period of global transition, it behooves hotel organizations to examine the key factors that will not only define success, but the ability to survive in coming years. Many of these issues were spotlighted in a global study undertaken by the Economist Intelligence Unit and co-sponsored by Arthur Andersen. The Successful Corporation of the Year 2000 surveyed more than 600 senior executives around the world. Its mission was to identify the characteristics needed to lead successful businesses in the next century. These executives offer a number of compelling messages regarding the key success factors of the future.

Customers will have the strongest influence on the corporation in the year 2000. Indeed, these executives believe that the customer will be "king" in the new century. Exceptional leadership was by far the attribute most frequently cited by CEOs and senior executives; the consensus appears to be that successful companies in the year 2000 will be led by corporate visionaries. A strategic planning focus is not only essential, but must embody a concept of planning for the future that anticipates change, rather than being based exclusively on historical models. In structuring organizations for the future, companies must build management capabilities to deal with one of the most critical challenges — diversity in the marketplace. Employing information technology to drive business success in this information-driven era is not only the path of least resistance, but vital to virtually every aspect of operations.

The study's top-line results create an excellent backdrop to address key issues confronting the hotel industry, and what factors will lead to membership — rather than rejection — in the elite club of the world's corporate success stories in the year 2000.

From an Asset to Customer Focus

Recognizing that the hotel industry has a somewhat split personality reflecting the inherent conflicts between its real estate and operational aspects, it is important to understand the industry's real estate origins and how they are shaping the challenges ahead.

The origins of the industry's real estate persona are embodied in the classic theory of location-"if we build it, they will come." As a result of this "building" complex, the industry has tended to have a real estate and asset orientation, rather than a customer focus. From the hotel company perspective — especially that of the brand-oriented "chain" — the varied interests of a diffused property ownership group can be quite different than the singular interest of the chain that operates and markets the properties.

Even when the ownership of geographically dispersed hotel properties is controlled by a single hotel organization, the financial structuring tends to be property-specific. Corporate financial strategies are frequently subjugated to the needs of the last property deal brought into the company's fold. Each property in a so-called "chain," is frequently the subject of a unique and distinctive ownership and financial structure. This phenomenon — quite common in the real estate sector, but unusual for business enterprises generally — makes for elusive economies of scale in the structuring and financing of property-driven expansion.

Collectively, these factors have produced low comparative returns in real estate, although criticism leveled at commercial real estate returns is somewhat less germane to the hotel industry, where management and franchise fees can produce high returns for those companies where property ownership is held by third parties. Nevertheless, average returns in the real estate industry in the United States, for example, are just over 10 percent, compared to small company stock returns at almost 20 percent and large company stocks at an average of about 15 percent.

While hotel chains have adopted traditional corporate frameworks, there are a number of predominantly real estate-driven, family-owned businesses in the hotel sector that continue to operate as relatively unstructured organizations. In meeting the future, these businesses will need plans, people and processes in order to establish viable corporate forms that can compete in tomorrow's marketplace and capitalize upon its opportunities.

In today's changed environment, the hotel organization must deal with a number of new realities. Investors in our industry are no longer satisfied with long-term capital appreciation and psychic income that heretofore were often the justification for otherwise seemingly uneconomic investments in hotel property or, indeed, hotel chains. The first reality is that there is a very specific and identifiable relationship between bottom line performance and value. Improvements in business operations raises values. It is not surprising, therefore, that the new owners attracted to this industry in recent years have new sets of demands. This transformation from an old-guard group of investors and owners to income and return-driven newcomers has meant that the once "quiet enjoyment" of operators in their management of hotels for third parties is being disturbed, interrupted and overturned.

These challenges all take place in an environment where capital has become extremely selective in markets that have little stability. A global shortage of capital will not remain a short-term problem, and future hotel organizations must have a stronger alignment to capital providers — a critical "customer" group. Hotel companies will need to compete by offering better returns and performance than in the past. Hotel chains have found their development timetables quashed in recent years, making it difficult to achieve goals of critical mass often required to improve performance. These factors are driving consolidation in the brand "sweepstakes." Capital markets, therefore, continue to favour well-established companies, a reality that must drive entrepreneurial organizations to meet the future now by planning for an evolving corporate context in which to operate.

Key Success Factors-The Future

Within this broad context, hotel developers, owners and management companies will all need to develop new strategies, skills and processes that look forward to the competitive demands of the future. These ultimately must address issues related to vision and planning, as well as organizational skill sets and processes to attract and retain customers. To stake a claim in the future, current business practices should be examined in light of what can be expected to be the key success factors in the year 2000.

Embrace a global change orientation. As the information age produces greater worldwide integration of business activities, a global knowledge base will become invaluable. Success in local and regional hotel markets will be shaped decisively by a global business environment that defines capital movement, customer expectations and applications of new technologies.

Focus on the Customer. If the customer is "king" in the 21st century, hotel organizations will be best served by focusing less on their hotel assets as measures of success, and more on their customers.

This involves a fundamental shift in viewing the real estate asset as the wealth creator — to the customer as the key to building shareholder wealth. A customer focus must imbue business decisions at all levels of developing and operating a hotel organization. Pursuing such a course will inevitably impact shareholder wealth. To accomplish this, however, customers need to participate in the product development process.

Fully realizing a customer focus in the industry poses a significant challenge. The hotel industry must confront problems due to conflicts between operational needs and real estate goals. Quite simply, an operator must remain customer-focused, but the short-term strategies to meet these needs may be inconsistent with the long-term objectives of property owners. Balancing those goals will be essential. A customer. focus implies a significant shift in what drives hotel development — placing primary emphasis on the customer with the locations to follow. Nevertheless, a hotel organization with its large investment in fixed assets — the real estate — can never be as nimble as a consumer products company in adjusting products and services to match rapid shifts in the marketplace.

The Japanese taught us that the concept of "zero defects" in products and services can yield tremendous benefits. But today an even more rigorous standard dominates — quality that surprises. In practical terms, the hotel industry finds it extremely difficult to meet the standard of zero defects in service. Hotel services are based primarily on people, not computers or other equipment. Quality that surprises takes the concept of zero defects a step further. Yesterday's surprising product or service is today's status quo. Twenty years ago, a business executive did not expect a consistent and predictable level of service wherever he or she travelled in the world. Today that is a standard — not the exception — as is the expectation for sophisticated technology in hotel rooms to support business needs. With customer discrimination so acute, it is not surprising that brand loyalty is a diminishing "commodity" in the hotel industry.

Find the ingredients for visionary leadership. Today's hotel organizations need to recognize the need for visionary leadership. The ability to forecast the future — to anticipate change rather than react to it — will be one of the single greatest determinants of market dominance in the years ahead. The old "command and control" model of leadership is giving way to a focus on leadership in ideas, information, inspiration, vision and teamwork. Warren Bennis, an authority on leadership in the U.S., puts it this way —

"For the most part, failing organizations tend to be over-managed and under-led. The leader sets the tone for the moral character, the vision, the corporate culture and the fiber of the institution."

While visionary leadership is essential, it must be linked to business operations and foster a risk bias, rather than a procedural bias. This will allow the organization to stretch and, in turn, change. And it must be shared by empowered professionals and staff throughout the organization, including those who meet the customer. Overcoming the resistance to change can be a daunting task, particularly in large hotel organizations in which diversions from the status quo may threaten established management lines. It suggests that a culture based on conformance may need to be replaced by an emphasis on flexibility, learning and cooperation. Management competencies will need to be aligned in order to achieve the desired result. For many organizations, this may mean a shift from traditional hierarchies typical of companies in an industrial era to a flatter organization with a more transparent interface between leadership, organizational functions and employees.

Create a defensible position through corporate strategy. For many of the industry's leaders, vision is driven by the strategic planning process, a function which has become critical for success.

Strategic planning, however, has at times been a step-child in the hotel industry, and it is often the first to be cut when organizations are downsized. It is clearly in transition. There also has been a tendency to decentralize and simplify this function – both actions of potential benefit. Strategic planning must be led by the top people in the organization – the CEO and COO. On the other hand, it should be close enough to the customer to ensure that planners can "listen" to and be influenced by customer needs.

Empower Management. Beyond the ability to envision the future, core management capabilities will make the difference – they are essential. A clear vision without the management skills to support it cannot be a recipe for success. First and foremost, hotel management must have strategic development skills and the ability to integrate complex factors affecting success. Market volatility has become the norm, in part caused by the rapidly changing tastes of customers. Customers are increasingly approaching the hotel industry with widely different social, economic and political backgrounds, to say nothing of employees. Being able to deal with these diversities in a positive and constructive fashion that capitalizes on the differences, rather than working to find ways to mitigate them, is the clear path for successful management in the future.

The organization will also need to be imbued with a sense of entrepreneurship that reacts proactively to the market's diversity. Traditional organizations that follow well-documented rules must give way to leaders who can balance a sense of discipline with that of flexibility. Talent and resources must be marshaled and leveraged. In an industry with high fixed costs and labour intensity, the concept of leverage in the hotel business is an all-important one. Improving labour productivity through technology must be a goal for today's forward-looking hotel organization. Management must also be able to narrow the gap between the employer and the employee, forcing a flatter organization in the process. This will put management closer to the customer and speed the two-way communication process up and down the organization.

Be in the information fast lane. The traditional role of information technology (IT) as a back office support for accounting and bookkeeping has clearly moved front and centre stage. IT today influences all aspects of business from corporate strategies to organizational structure — and from the very business processes it is designed to support to performance measurement. In a world where the customer is "king," IT must also deliver in two critical areas: sales and marketing and customer service.

Technology was once viewed as a way to reduce costs by replacing people. That attitude has been firmly supplanted by one that seeks IT support for the creative work that all organizations must pursue. IT must allow organizations to react more speedily to market needs and, of course, produce the fulfilment of customer demands both quickly and accurately. To do this IT must operate on a decentralized basis. IT delivers, but it has to be the right information to the right people, and it needs to be done on a timely basis.

Human Resource Development

The traditional constraints of the hotel, catering and tourism industry – long, antisocial working hours, low pay, unstable, seasonal employment, low job status, etc. – make employment within the industry appear unattractive to many. A study carried out in 1996 in Germany found that employment in the hotel and catering trade was not the first choice for nine out of ten employees, while only one employee in seven was satisfied with the trade as a choice of career. Nevertheless, the industry does attract some people either on a short-term basis or for a long-term career.

The immediate and most obvious consequences of such a situation are the difficulty of recruiting suitable staff and high staff turnover; both these effects are costly to the industry. There is therefore a perceived need for human resource development, to raise the profile of the industry, increase productivity and provide decent, sustainable employment within the sector.

Estimating Labour Productivity

A wide range of technological developments in service in hotels may be affecting productivity. Integrated management systems are enabling hotel companies to computerize day-to-day reception operations. Clients are thus able to make their own reservations via the Internet, while electronic in-room installations make it possible to settle accounts from the hotel room. This technology will also make it possible to monitor the productivity of personnel, while new techniques in food preparation and storage are reducing the skills needed in the kitchen and the time required for food preparation. Hotels are therefore seeking new ways to measure service delivery that take into account customer satisfaction and return visits, rather than sticking to a narrow "input/output" system. In Europe, tourist-related activities account on average for 5.5 per cent of GDP in all European Union Member States and for a total of 9 million employees, representing 6 per cent of the total workforce. The precise percentages vary from country to country. According to WTTC simulated figures, the tourism industry's labour force represents about 3 per cent of the world's total labour force and produces about 4 per cent of total world GDP. The industry can therefore not be regarded as labour intensive throughout.

New Forms of Work Organization

Flexible Work

The First World Travel and Tourism Summit, held in 1977 in Vilamoura, Portugal, recognized that travel and tourism create an unparalleled number of entry-level jobs for young people and women and provides part-time or seasonal employment for people seeking flexible working arrangements. The Summit called for the reduction of rigid practices in labour markets to encourage greater staff mobility, productivity and innovation in a progressive employment environment, with emphasis on a flexible market economy, avoiding protectionist regulation. The Conclusions and Recommendations of the European Union's High Level Group on Tourism and Employment drew attention to the fact that notable adjustments were taking place in European tourism, that these were critical to its competitiveness, and that they would lead to important changes in the tourism labour market. Those are: a refocusingof core competencies; a deskilling of operational tasks in some sub-branches; upgrading of skills and specializations, in particular in large enterprises and tourist organizations and in complementary services; and the creation of new professional profiles to meet tourists' needs and preferences. The document draws attention to a tendency within the industry to transfer work operations from traditional core sectors to ancillary service suppliers.

A positive example of flexibility is provided by the Sheraton-Denver West Hotel in the United States, where two experienced sales managers share one full-time job, thus enabling the company to benefit from the energy and experience of two persons for the price of one. In this instance, both managers wanted to work part time to accommodate their personal and family needs. The arrangement was particularly effective, since both managers were in continual contact. Job-sharing opportunities of this kind will be even more viable in the future, as information becomes more comprehensively shared and more easily transmitted.

Seasonal Employment

One opportunity which has been insufficiently investigated is the possibility of using the inter-season period as a time for training to impart new skills, guaranteeing re-employment of qualified staff in successive seasons so as to retain their services. A hotel located in Savonlinna (South-Savo, Finland), a city famous for its summer opera festivals, has adopted this approach. To deal with the multicultural and demanding clientele drawn by the summer festival, the hotel pays its core staff to attend off-season training courses in language skills, knowledge of food and wine and leadership skills. Employee development is seen not as a cost but as an investment which pays good returns during the summer season.

Multiskilling

The employers argue that one way to create sustainable, realistic employment in the industry is to implement a policy of "multiskilling". This is also viewed as a means of reducing the problems of recruitment. Multiskilling has always been practised in small enterprises, but it is only recently that particular attention has been paid to it. As demand for general competencies in small enterprises as well as in major hotel and restaurant chains has grown, and as appropriate means of training for these competencies have been developed, awareness has grown of the importance of multiskilling in that segment. One person fulfilling several roles at different times of the day combines the tasks of several (part-time) jobs into one job. Multiskilling is also seen as a way to create or preserve a number of full-time jobs, as opposed to part-time jobs, since the tasks may be performed at any time of the day. Instead of employing specialists on a less than full-time basis, employees are trained to perform the tasks of several specialists, often supported by facilitating technology. In Finland, a relatively small hotel has adopted a "multitask" policy. All its employees must be willing to perform any of the tasks that are necessary to operate the hotel. When hiring staff, the hotel manager gives precedence to "right personality" over all other criteria. Some workers left when this decision was taken which suggests that the approach is not universally appealing to employees. According to the CBI, "... skills flexibility is indispensable for functional flexibility. It requires a strong basic education system and a commitment on the part of employers and employees to the acquisition of new and transferable skills. It helps maintain high employability and reduces frictional unemployment associated with skills mismatch". The IUF, on the other hand, considers that such multiskilling may have the effect of devaluing specific skills, since the flexible worker, as viewed by the employer, has no specialized skills or job qualifications, and performing a variety of tasks requires a lower level of knowledge for each of them. The highly skilled, and consequently better remunerated, specialist worker may become a thing of the past. However, the unions also concede that an employee able to perform a variety of tasks is more valuable to an employer and should be remunerated accordingly.

New Mnagement Methods

Corporate organizations are downsizing and restructuring, which means that they are cutting back on layers of management. This means that less direction is being imparted to employees, who are more frequently required to accept a greater degree of responsibility and accountability. Increased use of technology in the workplace also means an added responsibility for individual workers. It is estimated that the "knowledge revolution", by providing clear information via the Internet on all the industry's tangible elements (illustrations of accommodation and hotel facilities) will make the intangible elements (those imparted by personal contact and service) all the more important. Lower levels of staff will be empowered to act autonomously. Command and control structures are thus largely giving way to a participatory teamwork approach. Human resources trained to fit in with new working methods will have to be regarded as an asset in which investment must be made, rather than merely as a cost, or employees will seek employment elsewhere. Management is developing ways in which to attract and retain employees.

The advent of new technology will not stop the industry from being a supplier of entry-level jobs; clearly, a large number of routine jobs will continue to exist. However, the question of staff retention will remain a management problem. Information technology will make potential entrants to the industry more aware of the possibilities available, compounding the problem for the industry. In order to retain staff, certain companies have already set up an incentive system. McDonalds introduced a broad-based stock ownership programme in 1995 to improve staff morale and productivity, while in Europe, one major hotel chain has established the CHAMPS reward programme, in which employees earn points for cleanliness, hospitality, accuracy, product quality and speed. These points can be used to buy catalogue merchandise.

Career Development

Truly structured careers, in which workers have genuine prospects of career development, are not numerous in the hotel, tourism and catering sector, and efforts to retain employees through incentives or promotion are the exception rather than the rule. Not only do people tend to "pass through" the sector, but research has shown that it is often the most talented who leave, since they are the most confident of finding other employment, while the less confident stay for fear of becoming unemployed. However, for many young people the industry is an entry point to the world of work. It brings workers into direct contact with the public and can provide opportunities for travel. Moreover, for young people, the provision of food and lodging – a common practice in the industry – facilitates entry into active adult life. These factors combine to make tourism a major motor for the social and professional integration of the young.

New and Changing Occupational Profiles

With the advent of new technologies and an increasingly discerning public able to keep informed through the Internet, the hotel sector is being forced to widen its sphere of action beyond the traditional provision of food and accommodation. In the pursuit of improving the intangibles, major hotel chains are seeking to provide more services, both in response to customers' needs and in an effort to provide an "experience" rather than simple lodging. For example, the French Accor Group has expanded into travel agency services, car hire, casinos and on-board train services, while other groups have established connections with sectors that are indirectly linked to tourism, such as insurance, travel articles and health and beauty services. The range of services now expected by customers naturally requires an upgrading of skills among front-desk staff, who will for the most part be required to administer these services. This will call for motivated personnel with excellent social skills and an understanding of what people want.

Advances in computer technology allow far more rapid and detailed generation of information on quality and economic performance. Hotel managers will thus be called on to react more quickly, to analyse situations and take appropriate decisions. The wider range of services on offer will also call for greater marketing skills than were previously necessary. In large hotels and hotel chains this is resulting in the creation of posts which are new to the industry, but which already exist in other fields, such as budget analysis and management accounting expert, quality manager, yield manager, technical and computer services manager. With greater emphasis being placed on environmental protection, there is also an increasing need for experts on the environmental impact and planning of tourism development. Similarly, greater concern over food safety is creating a growing need for food safety and health experts. As the hotel sphere increasingly includes services catering for customers' entertainment needs, sports and games specialists as well as specialized tour guides are opening up as careers in the tourism sector.

Women's Careers

Women traditionally play an important role in the hotel, restaurant and tourism sector. However, their access to the higher levels of the corporate structure remains problematic. Moreover, they represented only 4 per cent of the industry's highest ranking officers, and 4 per cent of its top earners. To an extent this is the result of friction between family and work responsibilities, especially given the prevailing long working hours in the food-service business. The lower wages paid to women make it more feasible for them to take time off from work to look after family needs than for their husbands to do so. To help resolve this problem, enterprises are starting to introduce family-friendly programmes involving flexi-time, tele-commuting and childcare schemes.

At the level of line employees, a United Kingdom hotel has found an innovative solution to problems it had been encountering in recruiting and retaining room service staff. The hotel decided to target its recruitment efforts on mothers of school-age children and agreed to provide a play leader to look after the children during school holidays. The cost of the play leaderwas made up by saved advertising and recruitment costs previously incurred as a result of high staff turnover. Nonetheless, it remains generally true that there is a gender-based income disparity across all segments of the hotel, catering and tourism industry.

Measures to Promote Career Building in the Enterprise

New divisions of labour and changes in the nature of jobs within the tourism sector mean that the industry is employing an increasingly varied range of employees. However, although tourism is a diverse sector which can provide many working opportunities for a wide range of skills, there is a shift within Europe away from specific skills towards broader, more generic competencies. Good practice in training is largely limited to large hotel chains, and small, individual enterprises tend to rely on training given "on the job". According to research in Spain, managers of three-star hotels recognized that older workers rarely had any of the formal training required to deal with a more sophisticated clientele, and younger workers lacked industry-specific practical skills. However, they were generally reluctant or unable to invest in training, on the grounds that the cost could not be sustained by their operations. The key training needs established by employers and trade unions are food safety, IT, environmental awareness and foreign language skills. The industry provides few post-experience training or retraining opportunities, and, indeed, commitment by the private sector to human resource development appears slight, especially where such development lies beyond their immediate operational needs: "European companies, especially smaller businesses, provide little by way of financial and practical support for human resource development within the wider educational and training framework."

Within the multinational hotel industry, however, there is a trend towards investment in education, training and development, to meet the need for a higher level of customer-oriented service. The Radisson Hotel Group acknowledges that the success of the company depends on the knowledge, skills, abilities, motivation and dedication of its employees, and consequently has a well-developed internal training system, with links to outside training establishments as well, to which 0.4 percent of each hotel's total revenue is dedicated. Through the Radisson SAS climate analysis system, outstanding efforts and exceptional results, both individual and on a team basis, are rewarded through local incentive schemes. The training emphasis is shifting towards continuous learning and increasing the potential of individual employees. A total of 515 employees were trained in different areas in the Radisson SAS Management School in 1999, with specific training in business finance, revenue management, euro handling and business planning. Efforts have been made by the enterprise to establish relations with European and American hotel schools, so that a steady flow of students takes up internships at a Radisson hotel. The Per-Axel Brommesson Scholarship enables four talented employees a year to develop management skills through professional development programmes at institutions such as Cornell University, and other business schools.

In order to bring the training provided by formal education institutions into harmony with the requirements of the everyday operation of the trade, the industry has entered into partnership with teaching establishments, to ensure that the content of their courses is relevant to work in the sector, and to offer students, through that linkage, practical experience in all fields. In the United States in 1996, the Hospitality Business Alliance (HBA) was formed between the National Restaurant Association and the American Hotel and Motel Association to create a school-to-career programme. Worksite experience is an integral element of the training. During the school year, students work between 15 and 20 hours a week in the enterprise, gaining experience in front-desk operations, housekeeping, room service, safety and health, reservations, sales and marketing and convention services. The system has grown from involving three high schools in 1997 to 600 high schools in 1999, covering 25 States and 11,000 students.

One hotel group in the United Kingdom noted a training gap which was preventing the company's (multi-)unit managers, whose role is a largely implementational one, from progressing to a more strategic role within the enterprise. The company's human resource department has organized strategic management development schemes at a number of leading business schools in the United Kingdom and the United States. The courses are designed to expose area managers to the strategic concepts of operational management, including corporate governance, finance, marketing and human resource strategy. This move to supply appropriate training is appreciated by unit managers aspiring to strategic, policy-creative posts.

A number of hotel chains have introduced schemes to enhance careers within their structures, with a view to reducing staff turnover. Choice Hotels International in the United States analysed the requirements for its senior executives on the basis of suitable existing competency models, then assessed the competencies of current top executives and compared these with the competencies needed for the future. This enables the company to carry out annual readiness assessments and to establish a genuine career structure within the group, thus avoiding the disruption and expense of replacing executive staff. A further example is provided by Motel 6, which has established an HRD approach whereby every employee is eligible to become a manager, via a three-tier training scheme. By early 1998 this system had allowed around 300 Motel 6 employees to reach the grade of general managers, thereby helping to fill a need for qualified managers by providing employee training and the basis of a career structure.

Developing Language Skills

An increasingly culturally diverse clientele has necessitated specialist training in the field of knowledge building for staff. ITT Sheraton operates a number of resort hotels in the Hawaiian islands, where the presence of Japanese clients has encouraged the creation of Japanese language and culture courses. This initiative has resulted in a significant increase in the number of Japanese guests frequenting the hotels, while the courses themselves have become problem-solving sessions with staff. In 1992, the Four Seasons Hotel and Resort developed the Self-Access Learning Centre in Indonesia, where the company was opening a new resort, to teach English to locally recruited staff. The courses were designed to take account of the fact that around 80 per cent of the staff had no more than primary-school education. The centre now teaches French and Japanese as well as Bahasa Indonesia. Employees are rewarded as they complete each of the five levels of the course with bonuses ranging from Rps.100,000 to Rps.250,000 (about $8-20), and a certificate of achievement. Turnover at the resort is low, at 4-6 per cent.

Career Enhancement through Increased Employee Responsibility

The Ritz-Carlton Company has identified the empowerment of individual staff members as a way to retain staff through increased job satisfaction. Employees were invited to take on certain management duties: the front-office employees, for example, were invited to take over the role of the front-office manager. As an incentive, the hotel proposed dividing half of the savings obtained through the elimination of the post among the employees who had taken on the duties (about $1.00 each an hour). The replaced staff members were not sacked, but redistributed elsewhere in the company. At another hotel, a system of self-directed housekeeping teams was established and responsibility given to the teams for choosing their own work areas, evaluating room quality and conducting room inspections; this has increased the staff retention rate and morale among room attendants. In 1993, Accor launched a three-year programme to "re-engineer" the structure of Sofitel North America. The programme was designed to empower employees to make decisions to benefit guests, and called for volunteers eager to make improvements in services provided by the hotels. Since suggestions for improvements and alterations were now originating from the employees, peer resistance within each department was minimal: a culture of trust and communication was established. The result has been an increase not only in customer satisfaction, but in employee satisfaction as well. Staff turnover fell from 58 per cent in 1993 to 39 per cent in 1998, below the industry average.

Among the reasons frequently cited for reluctance to taking up employment in the hotel, tourism and catering trade, lack of promotion possibilities features prominently. The broad pyramid of the hierarchy within the industry renders interpretation of the word "career" difficult. While careers are possible in the sector, and it is theoretically possible to progress from waiter to managing director of a major hotel chain, the increasingly flat management structures can only make this increasingly difficult. On the other hand, systems designed to reward staff financially for their performance, with the aim of reducing staff turnover and encouraging a feeling of "belonging" to the enterprise, are not yet accepted by all staff, and vertical career aspirations are still widespread. Modern-minded employers trust that job satisfaction is tending to shift away from hierarchical feelings. Bonuses to enhance job satisfaction can be awarded (and sometimes withdrawn) at any time, according to individual or collective performance.

Tourism Education and Training

Recognizing the Need for Tourism Education and Training

Employers maintain that many enterprises, especially SMEs, cannot pay wages commensurate with formal training and recognized qualifications. Others argue that the greater productivity made possible by training will make higher wages possible. In general, many of the operational activities in the industry require learning on the job, rather than formal training, and managers frequently state their preference for recruitment on the basis of personality rather than formal qualifications. More than 60 per cent of operational staff in Germany and more than half the labour force in Austria have had no formal training. The industry displays a reluctance to give formal recognition to acquired skills, and this may reflect a wish to avoid claims for higher wages and prevent undesired mobility.

On the other hand, a recent study also suggests that practical training and experience is more highly valued in the countries covered than formal, accredited training qualifications. Moreover, high staff turnover in the industry makes returns on training investment hard to evaluate. Employees, who may not wish to develop a career in the industry or may be discouraged by poor scholastic performance, also avoid measurement by public standards.

At middle management level and higher, however, tourism education is a formal requirement. In Canada, it is estimated that more than one-third of jobs in hotels require post-secondary education, including language proficiency, but a Brazilian study shows that only 12 per cent of hotel and restaurant staff have completed secondary school.

Tourism-related degree programmes have been slow to acquire recognition as a truly academic discipline although, given the increasing social and economic importance of tourism, a sound knowledge of its economic, social, cultural, environmental and political dimensions is essential. This is particularly the case in countries, including developing countries, where tourism is growing rapidly. In Europe, tourism training is seen as a means of boosting employment and recouping Europe's dwindling market share in the industry.

New Skill Requirements

In the Rhone-Alpes region of France, 7,000 new hotel and restaurant workers are required. Half the posts do not match formal training schemes. The bipartite committee on vocational training is therefore proposing that graduates acquire additional certificates to become waiters or wine-cellar specialists, as well as cooks, and is considering replacing the certification system with a system listing a variety of competencies. Given the higher customer expectations of quality in a one-to-one relationship with the service personnel, an important part of the required skills concerns personal behaviour and communication, as opposed to specialized operational skills.

The new skill requirements have an undeniable vertical element. The joint vocational training committee in Rhone-Alpes therefore recommends recruiting waiters with higher school qualifications (baccalaureate). However, workers with that level of education rarely seek employment as waiters.

More complex workplaces have brought about a shift in training concerns from operational or vocational skills to personal and social skills. Operational skills are still required, but are increasingly focused on technological innovation. A capacity to learn and develop activities, and to assimilate all elements of a complex process, and effective communication skills, including negotiation in cases of conflict, are among the skills needed to enable today's worker to attain the necessary autonomy at work. This presents a challenge for training institutions geared towards operational skills, rather than "soft" skills.

New technical skills which need to be acquired by line-level employees include: deeper and more up-to-date knowledge of materials and production processes; knowledge of computer programs and other new technologies employed in kitchens and the concomitant new working methods; awareness of safety and health issues, an understanding of the house "business culture"; and an ability to impart an increasingly broad range of information to customers. Language knowledge and a developed inter-cultural sensitivity are key skills for tourism personnel who have direct contact with customers.

Management-level requirements mirror the qualities listed above, but also embrace a new approach to human resource management and development. Enterprises are espousing a philosophy by which workers receiving "good service" from their superiors are more likely to provide "good service" to customers. Another important area of innovation and emphasis for management training is quicker response to – or anticipation of – market developments. This requirement is nothing new for top chain hotel managers, but it is new for many managers of smaller units and for department chiefs or supervisory-level managers. Adjusting in an autonomous way and developing innovative strategies require a capacity to generate the necessary flux of market information, and consequently also the ability to manipulate computer programmes. This marks a significant departure from the traditional picture of the independent hotel manager as "a jack of all trades" who does not work within budgets or performance targets.

The Importance of Continuous Training

Formally structured initial or primary training, including apprenticeships with practical and technical schooling, seems less adapted to the new "soft" skill requirements of today's industry than continuous training, and current thinking holds that it might be restricted to a minimal, multisector learning platform to raise the employability of young people and their mobility between different sectors. Continuous training, which has the advantage that it may be used to react quickly to changing circumstances, is being directed towards imparting the new skills.

Learning for Competencies

Exchanging the concepts of skills, capacities and qualification for that of competencies is consonant with the idea of the enterprise as a learning organization in which personnel have enhanced strategic and problem-solving capacities at all levels. Competencies are described in terms of the results to be achieved, whereas earlier methodologies prescribed tasks, abilities and desired attitudes, leaving the responsibility for the result to the hierarchy. To promote the new concept, the European Working Group on improving training in the tourism industry" convened by the European Commission recommends that research should be undertaken into ways to develop individuals' capacity to make full use of general, technical and personal skills as well as the "soft skills" needed to make use of the other skills, and into how the enterprise can engage and combine the competencies of individuals in an organic manner. The concept of competencies and their standardization and certification can more easily be introduced where training schemes are flexible. Modular training has always been the basis of training systems in countries where no neat distinction was made between initial training and continuous training. Courses of varying duration, institutional backing, and funding modalities were extended to students of all ages. The new concept of competencies can therefore be introduced speedily to satisfy an increasing need for certification arising from more flexible employment relationships. Training systems in Costa Rica, the Dominican Republic and Mexico now provide standards for competencies in the hotel, restaurant and tourism sector. Whilst employers offer "earning with learning" to encourage multiskilling, i.e. each acquired competency leads to an increment in salary, trade unions observe that the acquisition of various competencies by workers who occupy jobs outside conventional job classifications tends not to be remunerated appropriately. Bargaining for appropriate remuneration is more difficult where qualifications are diffuse and do not fit into any pre-established scheme. Moreover, bargaining collectively can hardly take account of all possible individual skill combinations. Indeed continuous training has been far less subject to social dialogue than has initial training. Where training for competencies has been introduced, standardization and certification of acquired skills are therefore essential.

Certification

Globalization of the travel and tourism industry and the increased use of e-commerce require a common international understanding and certification of core skills in order to facilitate distance business transactions and assure buyers and sellers that the services they deal with meet certain standards anchored in the qualifications of the labour force. The competitiveness of small tourism enterprises will increasingly depend on the credibility and reliability of the services they can offer. Hotel and restaurant management training provided by colleges and universities is quite transparent even across national borders, but for operational level workers it is often developed by industry associations of the different sectors involved, and it is difficult to avoid overlapping even at the national level.

In recent years, the certification of skills has also been debated as a means of improving the functioning, transparency and permeability of local and national labour markets. Greater workers' mobility between different employers, seasonal locations and ultimately across borders would enhance human resources allocation and create benefits for all players in the sector. On the other hand, there could be immediate disadvantages for some. Increased mobility of workers would counteract efforts made by employers to promote in-house human resources development, as the training and incentives provided would not necessarily pay off within the enterprise. Where elaborate initial training systems exist, they are regarded by trade unions as an acquired right. Certification of skills is therefore not endorsed as a substitute for formal initial training (where it exists), but only as a new way of presenting its results.

Greater international recognition of certification is needed where economic integration creates greater mobility within the labour market. In Latin America, an ILO project in the 1990s assisted nine countries on an inventory of qualifications with a view to agreeing on a common classification at a later stage. The European sectoral social partners are considering a proposal to make the description of acquired skills compatible between the European Union countries. The ECF-IUF and HOTREC are examining the possibility of implementing a "European qualifications passport" for the hotel and restaurant sector. Objections have been voiced on the grounds that certified skills for migrant workers might lead to higher wage claims; however, a qualifications passport could also help employers to find and recruit the right personnel much more easily.

Providers of Continuous Education and Training

There is a very wide range of private, public and semi-public institutions offering continuous education and training in the HCT sector. In some countries, such as Austria, entrepreneurs are required to obtain an entry certificate to the industry from the public authorities. In Switzerland, this practice has been abolished by most local governments. In these countries, and in others with a strong tradition of public training, the social partners run institutions to deliver continuous training, especially at a higher or middle level. Although continuous training features frequently in public debate in Austria, only 5 per cent of the workforce had recourse to it in 1996. This may be explained by the reluctance of employers to give workers time for training or to pay for the courses, or it may be caused by the workers' own disinclination to undergo training.

Private and Semi-private Institutions

Private hotel and restaurant training facilities are many and varied and employers as well as students tend to criticize the weakness or absence of public or joint (employer/government) control of private training establishments unless they have the authority to issue government-guaranteed certificates. In Switzerland, tight public control is exercised over the six establishments that issue government certificates. Their owners include government, employers' organizations, a workers' organization, a mixed foundation, and a fully private institution. The remaining 31 private hotel and restaurant schools in Switzerland are not publicly monitored: the Swiss Association of Hotel and Restaurant Schools performs this function. These establishments tend to recruit students from abroad and charge annual fees of up to Sw.frs.20,000. The training provided by the Swiss schools has already assimilated the requirements of the new skills and concentrates on continued general education, languages, and personality skills for managers. On the technical side, the emphasis is on marketing and product development, while more basic skills are dealt with in training blocks.

In the 1960s and 1970s, universities and colleges in the United States were the first to offer hotel and tourism degrees at the tertiary level. Since then, hotel and tourism curricula have been established at college and university level in Germany, Austria and Switzerland. In Spain, tourism schools used to have agreements with British universities to issue college certificates, but they have now linked up with local universities and their work has been integrated into the official Spanish education system. The training at universities, colleges and generally private specialized schools focuses on management of tourism enterprises or developing tourism destinations and also provides a grounding in both conceptual and practical skills geared to a sector dominated by small and medium-sized enterprises. The schools are responding to criticism, heard mainly in developing countries, regarding a lack of practical skills in their graduates. In recently industrialized countries, such as Brazil and China, local centres are upgrading their curricula through cooperation with renowned American and European hotel and restaurant schools.

Tourism education and training provided by trade associations is widely available in many industrialized countries. This in general consists of non-degree programmes of a more practical nature. In the United States, as an outstanding example, the Educational Institute of the American Hotel and Motel Association has provided educational services to almost 300,000 persons within the country and elsewhere. The institute offers its own diplomas and certificates in six areas of specialization using textbooks and distance learning materials produced by leading educators from various universities. Distance training systems with interactive Internet technology and worldwide outreach are starting to operate in all sectors, to the benefit of employees unable to leave work.

New work structures require more direct customer contact. Training institutions will accord greater attention to this area which is critical to improvement in productivity. However, there is little information available about changes in the area of traditional apprenticeships, through which (in Austria, for example) apprentices continue to be trained for the classical occupations of cook or waiter. It is probable, in view of the emphasis on personality and social skills, that training will become less formalized. These changes pose a considerable challenge as regards certification of skills for career purposes.

Training Provided by the Employer

Elaborate human resource development strategies are usually linked to long-term business development plans, and these are more frequently associated with large enterprises. They are based on a budget set aside for training and providing for trainers to be contracted from outside the hotel. Training budgets can account for up to 3 per cent of a hotel's financial turnover although 1 per cent of payroll is considered substantial. A system of assessing training requirements through frequent staff appraisal is found at establishments where staff development is taken seriously. Where training is less formalized, on the other hand, it is done by managers or supervisors who are not training specialists; there may be no budget set aside for it in spite of a declared willingness to offer training to staff. In such cases, training is often reactive rather than proactive, i.e. restricted to induction training for newly recruited staff and statutory (compulsory) safety and health training. It is also common for scheduled training sessions to be cancelled when employees are not replaced at their workplaces and therefore fail to turn up.

Major hotel chains rely largely on their own internal training systems. The Accor Group employs about 140,000 people in 132 countries. Five per cent of staff-related expenditure goes on training in three main areas: initial training for basic qualifications or as an introduction for new employees (delivered in-house); continuous training for director-level employees (department chiefs and others), covering areas such as sales, leadership, customer contacts and so on; and inter-cultural education. Accor's training is delivered by the group's own Paris-based academy which has training centres in various locations and countries. The Accor academy receives 14,000 trainees each year. In addition, the group has concluded agreements with a number of schools to accept Accor personnel for certain courses and to run fellowship programmes for Accor.

In spite of notable efforts by employers, the HCT industry comes bottom of a table of 16 industries in Germany in terms of the percentage of its enterprises that provide training for their employees (24.4 per cent, the median being about 70 per cent). On the other hand, continuous training for employees of hotel chains is quite common at management level. The Hyatt Group, to give one example of many, runs a "corporate management training programme". In-house training at management level generates a strong commitment to the company culture among beneficiaries and yields very high dividends in terms of competitive advantage. In the United Kingdom, a recent survey showed that 60 per cent of all hotels, 53 per cent of restaurants and 70 per cent of pubs and caterers arranged some form of continuous training. Enterprises employing 11 or more workers provided significantly more continuous training than smaller establishments, as did hotel chains, as opposed to individual, private hotels. This was also the case in Brazil, where research shows that it is generally large or medium-sized hotels that provide training, and that courses are short (21 hours on average). Since the larger hotels also tend to offer better employment conditions in other respects too, they can lure workers away from smaller hotels, to the detriment of any staff development policy in the independent hotels.

An example of the way in which some independent hotels address the problem of skills deficiencies is provided by one group of United Kingdom hotels. The group in question has formed a training consortium which works with a regional college to run an employee training and development programme, thus allowing economies of scale. All the hotels in the group can send one or two staff members to attend the courses as required.

Defining the Training Gap

The hotel and restaurant industry suffers from a discrepancy between training supply and demand. The specialized training institutions tend to lag behind developments in the industry, and these developments are particularly radical at present. The current skills gap is felt to be at the operational level, whereas training institutions, especially private institutions, are largely geared towards management training. This situation is seen in Brazil, where a study shows that training institutions are relevant only for the higher qualification levels and the majority of staff recruited by enterprises have not undergone any formal.

New Techniques of Training Delivery

Education and training are benefiting from developments in information and communication technologies and are increasingly being delivered through multimedia devices such as interactive on-line connections and CD-ROM. Investments in competitive training packages can be immense: the cost of a recent training CD-ROM for the hotel and restaurant sector was US$1 million. Large chains of hotels are also making use of this technology to fulfil their training needs: Holiday Inn spent US$2.5 million in 1995 to create online training multimedia for its employees. In 1998, Cendant's Days Inn launched an interactive web-based training programme to maximize the efficiency of the training budget and employee time.

Traditional schools are finding themselves in competition with "cyberschools", and where multimedia training devices are used within traditional schools, teachers are moving away from their traditional role as sources of knowledge towards a new role as "coaches" who help students to tap into much better (electronic) sources of knowledge. Hotel and restaurant firms are already developing and using multimedia components to guide employees through everything from making a pizza to providing a help desk for night auditors. Students will be able to chose when and where to undergo their training, and to adapt it to their individual learning speed. Education and training will shift from being teacher-centred to being learner-centred.

In the Netherlands, the Hotel School of The Hague has developed an innovative teaching method. There are no traditional classes. Students are set problems individually or in groups and then seek the information they need to solve them, coached by former teachers. In order to do this they have to develop technical and behavioural skills of various kinds and in different areas which hitherto were taught separately. Students are expected to return to the school throughout their professional life for recycling and "lifelong learning", supported by more or less permanent on-line learning. Increased motivation has been noted both among staff and students. However, performance measurement was harder, and prospective employers will have to adjust their selection criteria in order to assess the new type of training.

Conditions for electronically supported learning are almost ripe for a further "quantum leap". The interconnection of individuals and the formation of virtual learning groups, as well as the ability to call up from a local workstation all the knowledge accumulated by a company or made available through leasing contracts, will change lifelong learning into a continuous updating of personnel. Expert support will be made available on line and in real time, and there will be virtually no limits, other than those of cost, to the instant accessibility of the multimedia training material needed for individual learning plans.

Social Dialogue on Training

Tripartite or bipartite cooperation on training policies is common in many countries, at central or local levels. In many countries, developed or developing, staff training is guided by tripartite bodies, some of them sectoral. In Canada, the Hotel Employees and Restaurant Employees International Union (HERE), the Canadian Auto Workers (CAW) and the United Food and Commercial Workers sit beside management on the board of the Canadian Tourism Human Resource Council (CTHRC) which provides labour-oriented input to new certification and training programmes.

The dual system of initial training common in a number of European countries has long been based on a firm consensus between employers' and workers' organizations and on detailed legislation. Proposals for changes in pertinent legislation go through solid consultation procedures before they can be adopted by the competent authorities. Quicker action and intensive consultation is required in the sphere of continuous training, particularly where the improvement of workers' skills is part of a broader strategy for the development of the hotel, catering and tourism sector on a national or regional basis.

Spain provides an example of an effort to rapidly improve the quality of the tourism product in the face of increased international competition. Joint sectoral committees composed of delegates from representative workers' and employers' organizations, technically supported by the Foundation for Continuous Training (FORCEM), appraise training plans with a view to submitting recommendations for public funding to a central (inter-sectoral) joint committee. The sectoral committees propose certification criteria for continuous training courses in accordance with a national qualification system. Women's training heads the list amongst the target group criteria of the Spanish joint committee on hotels and restaurants.

In a number of Latin American countries, tripartite committees on vocational training have been in existence for decades and have influenced some vocational training policies. However, as most efficient vocational training systems were run by sectoral employers' organizations using payroll-based funding modalities (Brazil, Colombia), unions felt that their participation in steering committees did not always have the desired effect. Designing standards for competencies is a new area in which tripartite cooperation is developing at a rather technical level.

In the European Union, an important step was taken by the ECF-IUF and the European Federation of Contract Catering Organizations (FERCO). In 1999 they concluded an "Agreement on vocational training in the European contract catering sector," which provides for joint initiatives in the area of continuous vocational training. In particular, it refers to non-discrimination between men and women, full-time and part-time employees and professional categories, in respect of access to continuous training measures. Before the agreement, the ECF-IUF prepared a survey on continuous training in the European contract catering industry based on a questionnaire. It produced a very heterogeneous picture across the countries in terms of regulations (none at all, legislation or collective agreements), volume (in terms of percentage of payroll spent on continuous training), distribution (between blue-collar and white-collar workers), participation of workers' representatives in planning, certification, and other areas. The survey concluded that continuous training was provided by enterprises, and that the skills required were not recognized officially. It noted that such training still helped workers to advance in their careers or to find alternative employment. However, such training did not fully meet workers' expectations, and there was inadequate trade union involvement.

Social Dialogue

The social dialogue relationship between the social partners in the hotel, catering and tourism sector in general seems to need more development. Both workers and employers agree that much remains to be done. There are differences, however. Trade unions' concerns are centred on being recognized as partners for social dialogue everywhere, as pointed out below. Employers generally favour greater social responsibility of the enterprise, but not all employers actively promote partnership with trade unions as a means of achieving their social goals. Whatever the current and future shape of partnerships, the understanding of the International Hotel and Restaurant Association (IH&RA) is that the social role of enterprises will be determined by a general trend towards democratization.

Employers also see better partnership between management and labour arising from a common response to the challenges of global competition. They anticipate that workers' organizations will adjust to the discipline that capital markets impose on business, while trade unions are worried by practices such as subcontracting and franchising which they feel create divisions among those working at the same location. They also favour the ratification by ILO member States of the Working Conditions (Hotels and Restaurants) Convention, 1991 (No. 172), and the promotion of equality between women and men at the workplace.

A trend towards improving social partnership can be observed in the Caribbean, where the tourism industry is by far the most important economic sector and where employers' "increasing recognition of the need to engage the cooperation of labour is matched by an increasing recognition on the part of labour that the transformation of business into more productive and competitive operations could mean higher levels of employment and income security".

Organizations

The coverage by workers' and employers' organizations of the hotel, catering and tourism sector can vary from country to country and from region to region. In general, workers' organizations are more diverse than employers' associations. For historical reasons, trade unions either: (a) cover a number of sectors, of which the hotel, catering and tourism sector is only one; such is the case of those trade unions that represent the entire food production chain from farms to restaurants or groceries; or (b) cover a proportion of workers in the hotel, catering and tourism sector as a result of overlapping with their main sectors, such as office workers (travel agencies), transport workers, workers in services in general (France) or in personal services in particular (Austria).

On the other hand, employers' organizations in the HCT sector are more uniform, as hotels and restaurants form a clear majority amongst their membership. As far as the restaurant subsector is concerned, however, representation of employers in a number of countries is subdivided into three different types of specialized organizations covering conventional restaurants, collective or institutional catering, and, more recently, fast-food restaurants, as in Germany.

At the European level, there are two federations of employers' organizations: the Confederation of National Associations of Hotels, Restaurants, Cafes and Similar Establishments in the European Union and European Economic Area (HOTREC), for conventional hotels and restaurants; and the European Federation of Contract Catering organizations (FERCO), for collective or institutional restaurants.

The International Hotel and Restaurant Association (IH&RA) is the largest organization of hotel and restaurant employers at the international level, representing over 750,000 establishments in more than 150 countries. Among its affiliates are some 50 national and international hotel and restaurant chains, many independent hotel operators and restaurateurs, over 110 national hotel and restaurant associations, a number of industry suppliers, and 130 educational institutions in the hotel and restaurant industry.

The largest workers' organization at the international level, the International Union of Food, Agricultural, Hotel, Restaurant, Catering, Tobacco and Allied Workers' Associations (IUF), has 326 affiliated organizations representing 10million workers in 118 countries. Other international trade secretariats, the International Transport Workers' Federation (ITF), and Union Network International (UNI), which represents workers in travel agencies, coordinate their action with the IUF. At the European level, this coordination has resulted in a special European Trade Union Liaison Committee on Tourism (ETLC).

Obstacles to Workers' Organizing

Workers in the hospitality sector are in general organized in trade unions to a lesser degree than workers in other sectors. This is due to a number of circumstances including the following:

- *The small size of enterprises:* Owing to the prevalence of small enterprises, trade union affiliation in the HCT sector may be as little as 10 per cent on average in industrialized countries. However, major hotels in large cities are often unionized, even in countries where smaller units or hotels located outside the centres of large cities are not. For example, in Canada (Vancouver, Toronto and Montreal), an estimated 80 per cent of large full-service down-town and airport hotels were unionized in the mid-1990s. In the United Kingdom, the role of trade unions is stronger in institutional catering, mainly in the public sector, and in a minority of large hotel groups.
- *The mainly young workforce:* Most workers in the HCT sector lack experience with labour issues as they are in their first formal employment, which in most cases is still of a transient nature.
- *High staff turnover:* Even those workers who stay in the sector will change employers frequently or leave work altogether during certain periods of their life; this is notably the case with women when their children are small.
- *Prevalence of part-time and casual work, irregular hours:* Part-time or on-call arrangements, as well as irregular working hours, keep communication between workers at a low level. In particular, the increasing number of students working in the sector are not necessarily inclined to join trade unions.
- *Varying employment contracts:* Subcontracting, fixed-term employment, and internships in many modern hotel and restaurant enterprises split workers up into several segments with different employment conditions, even when they perform the same tasks. This results in individualization of workers and competition between them.
- *Gender:* Weak affiliation to workers' organizations is more common among women workers since they are

disproportionately represented among part-time, casual and young workers and in small enterprises. As they form the less qualified and less well-remunerated segment of the labour force, they also tend to have less access to information and are less able to contribute to workers' collective bargaining power.

- *Attitude factors:* Low self-esteem among the workforce as a collectivity is specific to the hotel and restaurant sector. This is due, firstly, to its generally poor image from which only modern enterprises are immune. The sector is still associated with service in the traditional sense, which involves a "submissive" relationship. Secondly, success in hotel and restaurant services is hard to measure objectively, as it depends on the subjective feelings of customers. The modern customer relationship is built on individual capacities, skills and style, and there is little collective kudos to be had from excellent service.

These factors are reflected in the attitudes of many employers who do not favour the organization of workers in independent bodies with roots outside the enterprise. This is particularly marked in small and medium-sized enterprises and in multinational enterprises whose central management is not used to a trade union culture. Some observers stress the paternalistic management style prevalent in small hotels and restaurants as a factor working against any collective workers' representation.

Subcontracting and Franchising

Trade unions in the hotel and restaurant sector take the view that subcontracting is a method increasingly used to divide workers and thereby weaken collective bargaining power. Moreover, subcontractor enterprises are normally less unionized or belong to a different sector from that of the contracting enterprise. As a result, they tend to pay lower wages and provide less stable employment conditions. Increasingly, subcontracted services relate to security and surveillance, maintenance, cleaning, catering for hotel personnel and restaurant services for guests. As profit margins are considerably lower for restaurants than for hotel operations, subcontracting of restaurants is being increasingly used in large and medium-sized hotels.The Hotel Employees and Restaurant Employees International Union in the United States and Canada acknowledges that leasing out a hotel restaurant is economically attractive where the hotel is unionized and the leasing enterprise is not. The phenomenon is "exacerbated [for the unions] because in most major North American cities the restaurant industry is largely non-union". At the "New York-New York" Casino in Las Vegas, for example, where virtually all food and beverage services have been subcontracted, HERE represents 900 workers; it would represent 2,700 workers in the hotel if food and beverages were not leased out.

Safeguarding workers' interests in the context of subcontracting has become one of the main objectives of collective bargaining in the hospitality sector. Trade unions are not opposed to subcontracting in principle but want to negotiate the modalities in order to protect workers against dismissal or deterioration of employment and working conditions. The IUF regards subcontracting as a priority area.

Some of here's local affiliates bargain to establish joint liability of the employer and the subcontractor. Agreements include a commitment on the part of the (old) employer, e.g. "to require such contractor to offer employment to existing personnel, to recognize their length of service, and to recognize the union as the collective bargaining agent".

The franchising system creates similar difficulties with regard to worker representation as subcontracting, especially where legislation provides for company-wide workers' representative bodies based on minimum numbers of employees per unit. Franchised units have the legal status of independent employers, although in terms of their workplace activities they are an integrated part of a larger company. Trade unions therefore believe that there is an imbalance between the actual size of a company and the legal status of its smaller units. Franchised units benefit from the support of central management in areas such as labour relations, marketing, technological innovation and standardization of procedures. However, agreements concluded between trade unions and companies such as Accor or McDonald's apply only to those units that are owned centrally, not to other franchised units which may well represent the majority of all units, as is the case with McDonald's. The IUF therefore proposes to its affiliates a strategy aimed at creating the same social conditions for workers in franchised units as for the workers in units fully owned by the multinational company in question, in accordance with the principle "same brand-same rights".

Workers' Representation at the Enterprise Level

It has been pointed out in previous sections of this report that the hospitality sector, with its subdivision into relatively small units, its service industry character and its flexible orientation towards the customer, has been guided by teamwork for a long time. Bodies that organize workers within the enterprise on the basis of teamwork structures, such as quality circles, are therefore more common than formalized works councils.

Workers' representation at the employer's initiative rarely addresses fundamental interests such as pay or working time. It is intended more to improve communication between staff and management and among staff members, and to deal with questions concerning the improvement of day-to-day business operations and staff training. For example, the British Hospitality Association (representing 25,000 establishments in the United Kingdom) advises that the issues dealt with in consultation with the workers should be selected at the discretion of the employer and as required by legislation.

The actual presence and activity of employees in non-elected workers' participation structures seems to vary considerably depending on the subject dealt with, whether the meeting takes place during working hours, at what time of day, and other factors. Participation is therefore largely on an ad hoc basis. An Accor hotel manager in Paris, referring to meetings with staff on hotel refurbishing options, stated that as a rule one-third of the staff had participated actively, another third remained rather passive but were present at the meetings, and the rest did not attend.

Collective Bargaining

Collective bargaining in the hotel, catering and tourism sector varies according to the social dialogue culture of a country or region. Collective agreements often differ from each other according to local conditions or enterprise cultures. Trade unionists say that the great variety of collective agreements in the sector may reflect a low level of coordination across geographic and enterprise borders and ultimately follows from low trade union density. Collective agreements are not yet fully applied to ensure decent working conditions for all and competitive human resource development, even where appropriate clauses are contained in the text. They normally cover mainly remuneration and working conditions, as well as non-discrimination and, more recently, the prohibition of child labour. Training provided by the employer is mentioned only in a minority of collective agreements. Among the working conditions reflected in most agreements, working time predominates owing to the prevailing irregular working hours and the difficulty of assessing overtime and guaranteeing rest periods. Works councils, where they exist, are often given ad hoc power to agree to changes at short notice.

Remuneration is determined in collective agreements according to occupational group, hierarchical level and personal criteria such as age and seniority. The definition of these criteria often creates difficulties, as classifications of occupations are not generally agreed by the social partners in all countries. Especially in the HCT sector, the definition of occupations is becoming increasingly fluid as phenomena such as multiskilling and flexible distribution of tasks in the enterprise prevail as a result of restructuring and new management methods imposed by competition. Trade unions are concerned with providing, through collective bargaining, minimum definitions in order to prevent salaries from deteriorating as a result of unclear notions of new work patterns. The classifications of occupations reflected in collective agreements are generally established by bipartite or tripartite bodies, often within the framework of vocational training policies.

The structure and scope of collective bargaining in the HCT sector varies according to legislation and national practice. In North America, Asia and Africa, the workforce of an enterprise tends to be the representative group for the purposes of bargaining. In European countries, on the other hand, negotiations are frequently undertaken on behalf of all workers in the sector or of a subsector on a geographical basis, i.e. at national or regional level. In Germany, collective agreements with geographical coverage at the regional (Lander) level stipulate minimum regulations and are complemented by collective agreements at the enterprise level. Recently, there has been a tendency to negotiate more issues at the enterprise level than was done in the past in order to take account of sharper differences between the economic performance of individual enterprises.Collective bargaining in the HCT sector is based on the subsectors covered by employers' organizations, so that separate negotiations are often held for hotels and restaurants, catering and the tour operating and travel agency subsector. Chain enterprises may engage in collective bargaining, leaving small and medium-sized enterprises behind; this has been the case in France, where collective agreements were concluded for a number of years for hotel and restaurant chains, while the independent hotels and restaurants adopted the procedure only recently. As many as 80 per cent of independent (predominantly small) enterprises are covered by the collective agreements, although their workers are normally not unionized. In addition, the collective agreement is regularly extended by Government decree to cover all enterprises and all workers in the sector.

Collective bargaining and collective agreements have been useful in mitigating the negative effects on workers of increased competition between enterprises resulting from globalization, and in preventing an unbalanced distribution between employers and workers of the burden resulting from rapid changes. A common challenge arises when ownership of an enterprise changes. In such cases, a general clause is sometimes introduced in collective agreements to guarantee the preservation of employment contracts and other arrangements for a certain period.

One example of this is an agreement between the Italian-based company, Autogrill and the Dutch trade union federation, Horecabond in 1998. Following Autogrill's purchase of the Dutch company AC Holding, the agreement guaranteed that no worker would be dismissed within a period of two-and-a-half years and that existing employment conditions and workers' rights would remain in force during that period. Collective agreements addressing similar situations have been concluded in other European countries.

Trade unions have had difficulties in bargaining on the continuity of working and employment conditions in cases where they are faced with a weak local interlocutor and the acting party behind the change is a multinational enterprise based outside the country. This situation may arise in cases of franchising or in cases of management contracts with strict decentralization of power with regard to labour relations. It is generally the policy of transnational companies to leave labour relations to the local level to ensure that local conditions are taken fully into account. Trade unions object to this policy, however, where it puts workers in a subsidiary of a multinational enterprise in a less favourable position than other workers of the same chain, or where the mother enterprise's absence from labour relations leaves the local employer in a weak position or unwilling to assume contractual responsibility.

Social Dialogue Plus: Community Involvement

Organizations involved in campaigning for changes in the hotel, catering and tourism sector can find partners and supporters in different segments of the community because the sector overlaps with many others. This is more likely in countries where tourism is the most dynamic sector or where it is the major source of foreign exchange income, as is the case in many small island States, such as those of the Caribbean. An interesting example is the "living wage campaign" conducted in the 1990s in the hospitality sector in Los Angeles.

Regional Social Dialogue: The Case of Europe

At the level of the European Union and the European Economic Area (EEA), employers and workers of the hotel, restaurants and cafes sector engage in social dialogue at the sectoral level within a framework provided by the European Commission. A formal social dialogue committee at sectoral level was set up in 1999 after social dialogue activities had been launched by the social partners (ECF-IUF and HOTREC) in the early 1990s. The group meets four times a year for sessions conducted by the European Commission.

The results of sectoral social dialogue at European level include various joint declarations adopted by the social partners since 1995. The most recent one, dated 3 May 1999, is the Joint Declaration for the promotion of employment in the European hotel and restaurant sector. It reflects the major social issues concerning this sector at present. In order to achieve improved competitiveness and efficiency of European enterprises, provide better qualified and motivated staff and create new job opportunities, the social partners propose to adopt certain measures concerning, in particular, the reduction of taxes and non-wage costs, and improved training and certification to enhance workers' employability and mobility. Issues of part-time employment and flexible working hours are also addressed. The creation of full-time jobs remains a priority; the intention is that flexible working hours should be applied within the framework of agreements between the social partners and adapted to the respective needs of companies and employees.

An Agreement on vocational training in the European contract catering sector was reached by FERCO and ECF- in October 1999. The Agreement covers joint initiatives in the area of continuous vocational training, commitments to equal treatment for men and women and for full-time and part-time workers, and commitments to non-discrimination against workers involved in training. It also stimulates joint action at the company level to identify training needs, elaborate programmes and evaluate their effectiveness.

Employers' and workers' representatives also participated, through individually named experts or the European Trade Union Liaison Committee on Tourism (ETLC), in the High Level Group on Tourism and Employment convened by the European Commission in 1998. The resulting recommendations have reportedly been useful in many bipartite or tripartite debates on the development of tourism as an employment-creating activity. They cover issues such as: negotiation of flexible employability systems and a dynamic approach to social protection; promotion of vocational training for career development; mutual recognition of qualifications between European countries to enhance workers' mobility; and structured, sectoral social dialogue.

European Works Councils

Social dialogue within multinational companies at European level is provided for by the EU Directive on European Works Councils (EWCs), which has initiated cross-border meetings between workers' representatives and managers of companies having business in more than one country within the European Economic Area (including the United Kingdom since the 1997 Amsterdam Treaty).

The essential requirement of the Directive is the creation of a European Works Council in every active enterprise with at least 150 employees in each of at least two countries and a total of at least 1,000 employees within the EEA. A procedure for consultation and information sharing must be established if at least 150 employees from at least two countries request it. Those meetings are not so much collective bargaining sessions as information and consultation procedures, and employee representatives cannot block management decisions.

Most of the European Works Councils in the hotel, catering and tourism sector were created by multinational companies that established "voluntary agreements" for a transitional period before full implementation of the Directive in September 1996. Those agreements could be concluded with appointed employee representatives instead of those determined in accordance with national law or practice, as required by the Directive. At present, there are 14 EWCs of which only two were established after the deadline for voluntary agreements (by Sodexho, the world's largest institutional caterer, and in American Express)., The achievements of the EWCs so far have only partially lived up to the expectations of the trade unions involved. This seems to be mainly due to the infrequency of (annual) meetings.

Internationalization of Information on Labour Issues

Communication technology makes it possible to post information for an international audience without delay. Labour disputes in hotels or restaurants are increasingly drawn to the attention of the public through trade unions websites. Those sites also contain recommendations on hotels to avoid and those that should be patronized in the light of management attitudes to trade union activities and workers' interests. Detailed accounts of labour disputes are given in cases of non-recommendation by the IUF. Employers' associations object to the practice, which they maintain does not adequately distinguish between labour relations disputes which do not necessarily involve any illegal actions and acts which are "illegal and socially reprehensible".

In response to the limited success of collective bargaining, trade unions have also resorted to international solidarity campaigns. A major labour dispute in the Lotte Hotel in Seoul came to an end on 21 August 2000 after several trade unions posted information on the dispute and the workers' claims on their website and representations were made by trade unions in different countries to Korean diplomatic missions. The agreement provides for an automatic mechanism to stabilize precarious employment of staff.

Information and communication technologies also increase the potential for pressure on tourism destinations that fail to comply with minimum standards. An example of this is the tourism boycott against the military regime in Myanmar pursued by the

IUF through the Internet. A number of companies involved in tourism activities in that country and engaged in social dialogue with trade unions affiliated to the IUF have responded by discontinuing their engagement until the social and political situation in the country is stabilized and pending civil rights issues are resolved.

Social Dialogue on Tourism Development Policies

Workers' and employers' organizations are involved in tourism development policies in many countries where tourism boards include workers' and employers' representatives. In a number of cases, the structure was established following ILO technical cooperation.

At the international level, workers' and employers' organizations are represented at the annual meetings organized by the United Nations Commission for Sustainable Development (CSD) as a follow-up to the 1992 United Nations Conference on Environment and Development (UNCED), which identified tourism as one of the key economic sectors which could make a positive contribution to achieving sustainable development.

At the Seventh Session of the Commission for Sustainable Development (CSD-7, 1999), which dealt with sustainable tourism development among other topics, business and industry was represented by the International Hotel and Restaurant Association (IH&RA) and the World Travel and Tourism Council (WTTC). Workers were represented by the International Confederation of Free Trade Unions (ICFTU) and the Trade Union Advisory Committee to the OECD (TUAC). During the discussions, the social dimension of sustainable tourism development was widely recognized. Both groups called for training of hotel and tourism personnel in environmental protection, and emphasized the importance of making tourism sustainable so as to maximize its potential for job creation.

The workers and trade union representatives noted a deterioration of working conditions and labour rights in tourism arising from globalization and from competition among countries for foreign investment. The business group presented its environmental initiatives – WTTC's "Green Globe" label and the annual environmental award "Green Hotelier" given by IH&RA and UNEP – and set out its views on the criteria for sustainable growth in the industry and many voluntary initiatives undertaken by it.

Summary and Suggested Points for Discussion

Summary

The hotel, catering and tourism sector, as defined by the ILO in 1980 within the framework of its sectoral activities, includes enterprises most of which fall under sections 55 (Hotels and restaurants) and 6304 (Travel agencies and tour operators, etc.) of the International Standard Industrial Classification of All Economic Activities (ISIC), Revision 3, 1990. However, owing to the strong development of the tourism economy in the last decades both in developed and in developing countries, many other organizations focus their activities on the United Nations definition of tourism as all economic activities providing products and services to travellers or tourists. The ILO definition of the HCT sector differs from this in including not only services provided to travellers but also those used by residents. Although in national accounting the tourism ratio of hotels and restaurants, i.e. the proportion of their services provided to travellers, may range from one-quarter to three-quarters, it is normal practice to subsume the sector under "tourism". On the basis of a United Nations recommendation of 1993, national statistical offices are starting to prepare Tourism Satellite Accounts in accordance with a methodology worked out jointly by the World Tourism Organization, OECD and EUROSTAT. An extension for tourism labour statistics is being contributed by the ILO. The private World Travel and Tourism Council (WTTC) has been issuing simulated Tourism Satellite Accounts based on input-output analysis of a number of countries.

The economic concept of tourism includes personal travel (for leisure and other purposes) as well as business trips, international as well as domestic travelling. The industry's direct or "face-to-face" services to tourists represent between 3 and 4 per cent of GDP in most of the world economy and employ about 3 per cent of the world's total labour force, although in some countries tourism employs up to 10 per cent of the workforce. Currently, the industry is growing worldwide by about 3 per cent annually, with Europe showing a lower than average growth rate of 2.3 per cent, and the Asia-Pacific region having the lowest, at 1.4 per cent in the aftermath of the Asian crisis. The highest annual growth rates have recently been seen in South Asia (9.1 per cent) the Caribbean (6.8 per cent) and Central and Eastern Europe (5.2 per cent). However, the travel and tourism industry's share in the world's GDP has been fairly constant because the largest tourism volumes are still in the regions where growth is in line with economic growth in general (according to the WTTC in 2000).

If we include the industries that serve tourists indirectly, i.e. those that do not involve face-to-face contact with tourists but provide infrastructure or inputs to the direct tourism industry, the total tourism-related economy has been estimated to produce as much as 11 per cent of GDP and to employ 8 per cent of the labour force worldwide (WTTC, 2000). Worldwide, one job in the direct tourism industry induces roughly one-and-a-half additional (indirect) jobs in the tourism-related economy. The figure has been estimated to vary from 1.2 (in North America and Latin America) to about 2 (in the Caribbean and Europe), while falling somewhere between those values in Asia and Africa (WTTC, 2000).

Border-crossing tourism has grown faster than tourism overall. According to statistics published by the World Tourism Organization, international tourist arrivals have grown at an average annual rate of 7 per cent since 1950 and will grow at an average annual rate of 4.5 per cent over the next 20 years. In recent years, however, the growth of international tourism has been no more rapid than the growth of the world economy as a whole, i.e. about 3 per cent. During the year 2000, almost 700 million tourists crossed a border and spent over US$500 billion while abroad. Border-crossing tourism adds about 25 per cent to domestic tourism GDP worldwide, with certain regions depending more markedly on international tourism than others. In the Caribbean, a fifth of GDP is produced for tourists, directly or indirectly, by one out of every seven workers. Latin America and Africa have increased their market shares recently, while that of Asia has declined but is recovering rapidly.

The demand for tourism services is also changing qualitatively. Travelling is increasingly becoming part of the lifestyle of a substantial proportion of some nations' populations, including the better-off in developing countries. Trips have become shorter but more frequent. New market niches are being exploited, such as nature tourism, ecotourism and adventure tourism. Tourists are becoming more knowledgeable and aware of issues such as the protection of the environment. The spread of information technologies enables tourism providers to cater more efficiently for a more diversified clientele.

Globalized tourism has been strongly supported by the deregulation of air transport. In developing countries, no less than 80 per cent of international tourists arrive by air. Air fares are falling drastically as a result of increased competition and the abolition of national monopolies. The General Agreement on Trade in Services (GATS) has had an impact on the liberalization of the international tourism economy. Most countries have made tourism-related commitments under GATS concerning issues such as commercial presence or access to technology. The liberalization of the "presence of natural persons", however, is not far advanced.

Economic blocs also promote the increase of tourism activities among their member countries and support their development as global tourism destinations. In particular, the European Union (EU) and the Association of South-East Asian Nations (ASEAN) are known for having specific tourism promotion policies, whereas in the Caribbean, regionally coordinated tourism is developing.

Concerns have been raised about the relatively low participation of developing countries in electronic distribution and reservation systems run by large air carriers, which do not sufficiently take into account the needs of small and medium-sized enterprises. However, the Internet is increasingly being used to market destinations worldwide, including by associations of independent enterprises. Tourism is among the most important application domains in the World Wide Web. It is estimated that up to half of all online transactions are tourism-oriented, but these still represent only a tiny proportion of total travel business (as yet not more than 1 or 2 per cent). However, this amount is increasing rapidly as Internet sales of travel products reduce costs and present low entrance barriers in terms of financial investment and know-how. E-commerce therefore clearly increases the opportunities for developing countries to reap the benefits of their competitive advantage as tourism destinations.

Large hotel chains are constantly increasing their business through mergers, as well as franchising and management contracts. The largest hotel chain, Cendant, operates 6,000 hotels with a total of 500,000 rooms. The four next largest chains operate half as many hotels each, but still offer between 300,000 and 460,000 rooms. The 20 largest chains together operate as many as 27,000 hotels with 3.26 million hotel rooms out of an estimated world total of 15 million. Some operate in almost 100 countries (Bass Hotels and Resorts in 98 countries; Best Western in 84; Accor in 81; Starwood in 80). The value of the capital involved in a single merger or acquisition can amount to US$14 billion. The last five years have witnessed nine major hotel merger and acquisition transactions involving a total of US$40 billion. In Europe, only about 30 per cent of all hotels are affiliated to chains in some way, whereas the proportion in the United States is as high as 79 per cent. A large majority of five-star hotels in developing countries are managed by international chains. Some of the largest international hotel chains run all their affiliated hotels through management or franchising contracts. Most large hotel chains, however, own a majority of their hotels. Management contracts and franchising often raise questions regarding the identity of an employer in labour relations, as chain companies may be composed of large numbers of legally independent enterprises.

Tour operators are consolidating their operations through vertical integration as well as horizontal takeovers in order to have better control over their forward and backward linkages such as air companies, hotels, travel agencies and retail distributors. As the tour operating business generates only small profit margins, economies of scale represent only a few (if relatively important) percentage points of revenue.

Capital consolidation is also important in the institutional catering subsector, where the largest companies employ respectively 212,000 workers (Compass) and 125,000 workers (Sodexho). The institutional catering subsector has good expansion prospects, as its market is far from saturated. Catering is also growing in the restaurant subsector through the sale of pre-prepared meals.

Whilst large chain enterprises are growing dynamically, independent enterprises tend to be left behind. Small and medium-sized enterprises (SMEs) employ at least half of the sector's workers and represent a majority of its enterprises; in Europe, the figure is more than 90 per cent. Almost all of them are micro-enterprises with up to ten workers, often family members drawing little or no remuneration for unmeasured working time. They are hardly able to compete in global markets, as they suffer from low productivity, poor product quality and a lack of access to credit and training. Their strongest comparative advantage comes from low labour costs. In order to benefit from other advantages, such as presence in niche markets and adaptability to customer demands, they need to boost their technology and training. This is being undertaken by special schemes or through associations of entrepreneurs. Legal deregulation and lower taxation also make their survival easier.

Most HCT enterprises, large or small, employ only a core of permanent and full-time staff. Other staff are employed under atypical contracts including part-time, seasonal and casual labour arrangements. Flexible employment is convenient for many young workers who are studying or aim eventually to move to other sectors, and for female workers with children, but these workers are often unable to make a living as head of a family. Up to half the workers in the industry are under 25 years old and up to 70 per cent are women. However, women are much less represented at management levels, where they occupy just over 40 per cent of posts. The higher up in the hierarchy one goes, the fewer women are present, and women occupy a low percentage of the top earning posts in the industry.

The HCT sector pays its workers on average at least 20 per cent less than other economic sectors, as it employs a higher proportion of unskilled workers. Tips increase the income of workers with customer contact. However, little is known about overtime payments and remuneration for irregular work. Performance-dependent remuneration is not yet common in the HCT sector, although it has been introduced in some restaurant chains. Payment is in general less attractive in small enterprises and in enterprises performing subcontracted services. Large enterprises in general pay their core staff better.

Staff turnover is costly to employers, who have to find new staff for up to half or more of their posts every year, and is estimated to cost several thousand US dollars per employee. It is tempting to presume a correlation between unattractive working conditions and high turnover, a correlation frequently cited by employees. There are in fact a variety of reasons for employee turnover, of which poor career prospects, low pay, unsocial working hours and physical stress appear to play a part. Working hours are irregular for half of all employees in the HCT sector, most of whom perform work on Sundays and in the evenings, and almost half of whom also work at night. However, employees now also have a greater say in the choice of hours and can thus adjust them better to their needs. Chain employers have started to implement personnel development strategies, including training and career development plans, in order to improve staff retention.

Part-time and fixed-term work is increasing. However, the social partners stress that the creation of full-time jobs should be a priority, that workers in part-time and fixed-term jobs should not be subjected to discrimination and should receive all available benefits on a pro rata temporis basis. Casual workers are included in this category. In Australia, they account for over half of all employees in the sector. Atypical employment relationships, however, entail a weaker link between the partners, and trade union affiliation is rare.

Certain forms of tourism, such as nature tourism, rural, agri- or ecotourism and adventure tourism, have grown over the past decade. Populations living in remote areas, or peasant farmers with diminishing incomes, benefit considerably from employment opportunities and income generated by tourism. However, ensuring that the benefits exceed the potential damage is a delicate task. Indigenous populations need training to resist cultural destruction, natural parks need the proper involvement of local populations to guarantee their preservation, and agritourism needs regulation in order to reduce or prevent unfair competition with professional lodging. The sustainable exploitation of these "soft" forms of tourism therefore requires participatory institutions and social dialogue in the communities concerned.

Very young children work in all kinds of HCT occupations, particularly in family-based enterprises, but also on their own as vendors or helpers. Probably the worst form of child labour in tourism is seen in the sex trade. The international community has expressed its concern at this phenomenon at a number of meetings. A task force against the commercial sexual exploitation of children, involving the participation of international employers' and workers' organizations and the World Tourism Organization, is promoting appropriate counter-measures. The industry is also engaging in innovative programmes to prevent and combat child prostitution in tourism. Migrant workers are another vulnerable group over-proportionately employed in the HCT sector, mostly in the lower paid, less stable segment of the sectoral labour market. This is often due to language problems or inadequate knowledge of the host culture.

The hotel and restaurant industry is very conscious of the fact that human resources are becoming more valuable to the sector, given the new customer demands, new technologies, intense competition and continuing shortage of job applicants. Additional efforts are needed to make working conditions more attractive to a range of age groups, not just young workers, to increase worker responsibility and to make employment in the sector a prestigious lifetime engagement. The need to value labour is also reflected in the fact that output per worker has increased dramatically in recent years, as employment in the sector continues to grow more slowly (about 2 per cent a year worldwide) than its value added (about 3 per cent).

The best performers, as far as hotels are concerned, are in the European Economic Area and the Caribbean. New forms of work organization are certainly an important factor boosting productivity. They include multiskilling, flat hierarchies and subcontracting of ancillary or specialist tasks. At the same time, a growing number of occupational profiles demand higher skills, especially among managers and staff in direct contact with customers. Some managers need to carry out planning exercises in order to identify and exploit market trends more rapidly, while others need to improve their knowledge, including ICT skills, in order to satisfy customers' demands for more meaningful experiences when travelling. All employees need enhanced social skills in order to play a full part in organizational teamwork, as more customer contact and more teamwork have brought about a shift away from operational or vocational skills towards personal and social skills.

Within the hotel chain industry, there is a trend towards greater investment in staff training, up to 1 per cent of revenue being earmarked for this purpose. In general, however, both employers and workers often fail to recognize the need for training. Employers often prefer to select staff on the basis of personality rather than formal qualifications, although, at management level, post-secondary education is generally required. Tourism-related degree programmes have proliferated all over the world and are on their way to recognition as an academic discipline.

Continuous training beyond initial vocational training is becoming increasingly important for workers at all levels, in response to rapidly changing skill requirements. There are proposals that initial training should be reduced to a multisectoral learning platform. However, continuous training schemes are still very limited and benefit only a tiny percentage of workers, even in the most advanced countries. Policies on continuous training have been the subject of social dialogue far less than initial training policies. Standardization and certification of competencies is essential if continuous training policies are to make full use of workers' efforts and capacities in a context of flat hierarchies, teamwork and labour mobility. The new paradigm of competencies is replacing traditional occupational qualifications. Competencies are described in terms of the results to be achieved by a worker instead of tasks, reflecting the underlying concept of problem-solving responsibilities of workers at all levels. Their international recognition and certification will also help in the global marketing of quality services.

Tourism education and training is provided by a wide range of institutions, public, semi-public, such as trade associations, or privately owned. Distance training systems with worldwide outreach, based on CD-ROM and interactive Internet technology, are starting to operate and are changing the training business profoundly, raising quality and lowering costs despite the huge investments made in the new training instruments.

New training technologies will also be accessible to small and medium-sized enterprises. This will allow more training to be extended to lower skill groups which at present are largely restricted to spontaneous on-the-job training.

Social dialogue in the HCT sector still needs to be developed further. The primary concern of trade unions is to be recognized as genuine partners in social dialogue throughout the world, whereas many employers, while favouring greater social responsibility of enterprises, also expect trade unions to understand the pressures arising from increased competition. Trade unions are concerned with the anti-union attitudes shown by some multinational companies in countries where trade unions are traditionally strong and with the adverse impact on workers' representation arising from subcontracting, franchising and management contracts which split large enterprises into small units that are too weak to be effective partners in social dialogue. Among the positive developments from a trade union perspective is a collective agreement concluded with the Accor Group which guarantees recognition of free trade unions in all units carrying the group's brands around the world.

The largest international organizations of social partners represent, either directly or through their affiliates, some 750,000 establishments and 10 million workers in most of the world's countries. The SME subsector is under-represented in employers' associations and trade unions, but employs as much as half of the labour force. Among other factors limiting the trade union density in the HCT sector are the young workforce and the low level of education and training, the high proportion of women, high staff turnover, frequent atypical employment and working patterns, employment by different employers acting in the same unit through subcontracting, and the generally low degree of identification of workers with the sector owing to the poor image of personal services. Trade union density is generally not greater than ten per cent, although it is higher in a few European countries and in large enterprises located in urban areas, where it can reach as much as 90 per cent of the workforce.

Some workers' representation is initiated by employers at the enterprise level in various forms, including quality or safety circles or communication groups to comply with legal requirements or to promote improvements in day-to-day life in the enterprise. Where freely elected bodies exist, however, trade union presence is the rule. Works councils generally do not exist in small enterprises, whose workers are therefore largely left out of social dialogue, although they may be covered by any agreements that may be concluded.

Collective agreements in the HCT sector vary considerably even within countries and from enterprise to enterprise. They mainly concern remuneration and working time. Detailed matrices of occupations and hierarchies are used to reflect the value of the labour force, and these are challenged by flexibility requirements such as multiskilling, new forms of work and new "soft" skills. Ad hoc collective agreements have been important instruments for mitigating the negative effects on workers of increased competition and frequent changes of ownership in the context of globalization. They have provided workers with a certain minimum continuity of employment and working conditions. Collective bargaining is not conducted at the international level, but other forms of international social dialogue are being developed. European Works Councils derived from EU legislation provide for yearly communication between the multinational companies and local trade unions from different countries.

The meetings are considered an important means of dealing with questions of principle concerning possible redundancies or workers' training.

Sectoral social dialogue between regional employers' and workers' organizations in the European Union has resulted in common statements on flexibility or the promotion of employment in the HCT sector. The sectoral social partners also engage in international forums not directly concerned with labour issues, such as those provided by the United Nations to promote sustainable tourism development or by the European Union to promote employment in tourism.

Information technology is starting to open up a new dimension of internationalization in the form of workers' solidarity campaigns and calls to boycott destinations or hotels that do not comply with established or perceived rights. In view of the dangers of biased or distorted information through the Internet and the possible economic losses involved, industry representatives have voiced concern at boycott appeals in general.

Suggested Points for Discussion

1. Globalization;
   a. What strategies should be pursued in the HCT sector to reap the benefits of globalization?
   b. What measures should be adopted to help developing countries to enhance their capacity building in relation to market access and to the promotion of human resource development and employment in tourism?
2. *Employment creation and working conditions;*
   a. What are the barriers to employment creation in small and medium-sized enterprises and what role can the tripartite partners play in removing those barriers?
   b. In view of the increasing importance of subcontracting, what measures should be taken to ensure that

minimum working and employment standards are applied?

c. What are the reasons for the existence of seasonal, casual and on-call employment in the HCT sector and what measures should be taken to improve the conditions of such employment?

d. What measures should be taken to enhance the employment of women in the HCT sector?

e. What are the obstacles to the ratification and implementation of the Working Conditions (Hotels and Restaurants) Convention, 1991 (No. 172), and what measures should be taken to address them and to promote the ratification of the Convention?

3. Human resources development.

   a. What strategies should be adopted for human resources development to ensure that workers are attracted to and retained in the HCT sector?

   b. What should be the role of the tripartite partners and the ILO in the provision of training in the HCT sector? What measures should be taken to increase training opportunities for workers in small and medium-sized enterprises? How can vocational training be enhanced particularly in developing countries?

4. Social dialogue.

   a. What measures should be taken to promote social dialogue, including collective bargaining, in the HCT sector?

   b. How can the tripartite partners and the ILO contribute to sustainable tourism and employment?

The Hospitality Executive's Guide to Reducing Labour Costs & To Improving Customer Service

1. Forecast major volume indicators seven days out by day and by shift to anticipate employee workloads for the next weekly work schedule. Establish a weekly "Forecast" meeting with department heads that lasts a maximum of 20 minutes, to specifically discuss upcoming business.
2. Identify and analyse hourly customer traffic patterns by day on an annual basis.

3. Develop employee-staffing guidelines that identify "fixed" (non-volume related) and "variable" (volume related) labour requirements by job.
4. Make sure that all employee staffing guidelines/labour standards are related to a realistic frame of time for completion. Quantify the work.
5. Report and analyse actual daily employee hours worked, versus scheduled daily employee labour hours, versus target daily employee labour hours (what labour hours should have been used based upon the actual volume that occurred).
6. Measure current employee productivity levels weekly versus historical productivity levels to see if improvement occurs or gets worse.
7. Observe and rate customer service and quality levels for all departments.
8. Experience what your customer goes through in all aspects of your operation on all shifts.
9. Get to know all of your employees on all shifts. Let them see you.
10. Stay out of your office and be "on the floor" as much as possible.

6

Delivering Excellence: Tourism Industry in Perspective

The contribution of tourism and trade industry towards a nation's economy is manifold. It not only makes its impact on the economic growth of the country, in terms of revenue generation and employment opportunities, but also in terms of the cultural enhancement of the nation and its people.

What differentiates one country from another is the kind of service that is offered to the visiting population; and also the customer-centric approach of the government and the natives to the influx of tourists to their country. The paper analyzes the position of India in terms of the various yardsticks that define any great tourist destination across the globe.

The paper is singularly India focused analysis of the potential way forward for the native travel and tourism industry. It critically examines the current scenario of the Indian tourism industry with its pitfalls and then strategizes for the future.

Importance of Tourism Industry

A strong travel and tourism network system spanning the entire nation has the potential to pull off a multiplier effect on the economic growth of the country. It necessitates employment opportunities in direct interfaces of tourism such as hotels, restaurants, travel agencies and related services. The industry is fundamentally responsible for diversifying the economic activities in the country and opening up new means of trade and commerce. Corporate travel is the new buzzword and any amount of investment into the existing businesses and creation of new business will only favour the local economy in terms of increased trade through exports and internal job creation.

However, the biggest gainer in terms of travel and tourism industry is the mutual exchange of culture and ideas and most importantly, the way of life. A keen knowledge of another culture throws open a wide variety of prospects in terms of not only commerce, but also perspectives and practices of a group of people that is worthy of emulation by the visiting nationals. Besides, the natives incorporate foreign nuances into the ethos of the local culture.

The paper analyzes the performance and possible areas of improvement for the Indian tourism industry. It would objectively looks at a) domestic tourism b) international tourism c) medical tourism d) corporate travel. A nation's ability to provide a standardized tourist experience will reflect its ability to provide professional services to the visiting population.

Indian Tourism Industry–A Snapshot

India was ranked as the 42nd most desired tourist destination by the United Nations World Trade Organization {UNWTO} in the year 2007. The same report mentions India as the 6th best in terms of price competiveness and 39th in terms of safety and security.

The global tourism industry is expected to touch $7.2 trillion in the next two years in economic activities, together with a generation of 260 million jobs across the world. India is expected to command 1.5% of this mammoth figure by 2011. It has also been observed that although corporate travel has taken a hit, the tourism industry has not suffered heavily because domestic travel and medical tourism have been as buoyant as before.

Currently, tourism and travel contribute about 6% of the Gross Domestic Product of our country, while in the world the industry contributes an average of 10.2 % of the GDP. International tourism contributes 6% to the total exports of the nation, and 6.4 % of the total employed force of India belongs to tourism and related services. It is expected to jump to 7.2% in a decade's time.

India Tourism Industry Forecast 2007-2011 reports some interesting facts about the nation's travel and tourism perspective. Some of the key findings are as follows:

- In India, inbound tourist expenditure per head is the third highest in the world and even more than the global average tourist spending.
- India has been promoting its healthcare tourism by providing the visitors with private healthcare facilities. It is expected that the number of tourists visiting India for the purpose of medical treatment will reach one million by 2012, representing a CAGR of 28.09% from 2007.
- Indian outbound tourist flow is expected to increase at a CAGR of 12.79% over the five-year period spanning 2007-2011.
- Tourist influx to India is expected to increase at a CAGR of 22.65% between 2007 and 2011.
- India's share in global tourism is expected to reach 1.5% by 2010.

There are several fear factors that inhibit tourism to a country. Some of those that could be potential threats to Indian tourism could be as follows:

A) Political instability: although the UPA government has come back to power, Indian politics has a long way to go before they stabilize into real governance and professionalization of politics.

B) Shock factors: Terrorist activities could be a major deterrent to tourism in any country. The 26/11 attacks in Mumbai targeted the foreign tourists who were residing in premium hotels such as The Grand Oberoi and the Taj Mahal Hotel. The fear factor could seriously create a dent in the image of the nation.

C) Corporate infrastructure: Considering that corporate travel is an indirect effect of general tourism and factors that are beyond immediate influence, it is imperative that India builds on an infrastructure that would facilitate corporate travel.

Strategies for Success

Five strategies that should propel India's tourism industry in to the limelight are:

1. Segregated Tourism: Although an emphasis can be made on the pan-India initiative, segregation of tourist types

could be done in order to attract differentiated tourist base. India should concentrate on the following areas with specific advertising and promotion:

A) Medical tourism: although it has been touted as the next big thing for tourism, it has had a lacklustre performance so far. Even within medical tourism, orthopaedic-, neurological-, cancer-and cardio-treatment could be dealt with and promoted separately. This will also depend very heavily on the available infrastructure for stay; as well as the medical facilities available. Yoga could be promoted extensively. There could be two aspects to this. One, for the ailments and their treatments and the second, for rejuvenation-centric tourism.

B) Adventure tourism: To showcase the cascading waterfalls, the rocks and valleys, adventure sports could be a brilliant medium to promote. River rafting, Bungee jumping, trekking, rock climbing, paragliding amongst others could be focussed on, to attract sport enthusiasts from both within and outside the country.

C) *Coastal Tourism*: Amongst travellers, a majority have been found to love the sea. With a mainland coastline of 5700 kilometres and an added 1800 kilometres of coastline of the Andaman and Lakshwadeep, India has a huge coastline to boast of.

D) *Historical Tourism*: Steeped in rich history of a civilization older than 5000 years, India's march down the annals of history can be packaged interestingly. The forts of Gwalior, Jodhpur, Udaipur; temples of Madurai, Caves of Ajanta and Ellora are exemplary locations that attract tourists in herds. Tourism can also be segmented region wise.

2. IT-based infrastructure: Aimed at corporate tourism as well as high-end travellers for leisure, IT-enabled solutions could turn out to be a great service differentiator. India should especially, in mid-sized and premium hotels, enable Wi-Fi connectivity with good and robust bandwidth. Not only does it facilitates business decisions and deals but

also allays work-related tensions that could possibly be communicated through the Internet.

3. Safety: The recent spate of incidents that question, in many ways, the strength of the police and safety infrastructure in the country has to be a prime area of concern. The 26/11 attacks on the Taj and Oberoi hotels had terrorists targeting foreign tourists. There has to be safety cells with greater decentralization and fast track courts that cater to tourism related incidents specifically.
4. Pan India Integration: The Incredible India campaign was a brilliant exercise which successfully roped in greater number of tourists to India. However India, being so diverse a nation, cannot be packaged into a single ethos that can be described by the word 'Incredible'. There has to be a differentiation in terms of pan India packages and regional packages.
5. Public Private Partnership: There are several advantages that can be listed about such an initiative between public sector involvement (for their available funds) and private sector (through professional management of services). Some of the advantages are:
   - Acceleration of Infrastructure Provision
   - Faster Implementation
   - Value for Money
   - Genuine Risk Transfer
   - Performance-Related Reward
   - Improved Quality of Service.

Conclusion

One of the obvious conclusions about the Indian Tourism industry is that it has great potential to be one of the best tourist destinations of the world. The need of the hour is to milk the opportunity and apply a two-pronged approach. One, for first time visitors of other nationalities, there could be India wide tours and two, a segmented approach towards niche category of tourists, who should be served according to the specificity of their needs. In an increasingly customer-driven approach, the training of professional staff for serving the customer, who dictates the needs and the delivery, is aptly rewarded.

It represents not just an opportunity to showcase the true hues of Indian landscape and culture but also an immense platform to break the jinx of India as the land of snake charmers and black magic to a land of true beauty.

Use by Industry

There are three essential conditions for revenue management to be applicable:

- That there is a fixed amount of resources available for sale.
- That the resources sold are perishable. This means that there is a time limit to selling the resources, after which they cease to be of value.
- That different customers are willing to pay a different price for using the same amount of resources.

If the resources available are not fixed or not perishable, the problem is limited to logistics, i.e. inventory or production management. If all customers would pay the same price for using the same amount of resources, the challenge would perhaps be limited to selling as quickly as possible, e.g. if there are costs for holding inventory.

Yield management is of especially high relevance in cases where the constant costs are relatively high compared to the variable costs. The less variable cost there is, the more the additional revenue earned will contribute to the overall profit. This is because it focuses on maximizing expected marginal revenue for a given operation and planning horizon. It optimizes resource utilization by ensuring inventory availability to customers with the highest expected net revenue contribution and extracting the greatest level of 'willingness to pay' from the entire customer base. Revenue management practitioners typically claim 3% to 7% incremental revenue gains due to revenue management activity. In many industries this can equate to over 100% increase in profits. A competent revenue management analyst with good decision support tools can generate $10,000 per hour.

Yield management has significantly altered the travel and hospitality industry since its inception in the mid 1980s. It requires analysts with detailed market knowledge and advanced computing systems who implement sophisticated mathematical techniques to analyse market behavior and capture revenue opportunities. It has evolved from the system airlines invented as a response to deregulation and quickly spread to hotels, car rental firms, cruise lines, media, and energy to name a few. Its effectiveness in generating incremental revenues from an existing operation and customer base has made it particularly attractive to business leaders that prefer to generate return from revenue growth and enhanced capability rather than downsizing and cost cutting.

Airlines

In the passenger airline case, capacity is regarded fixed because changing what aircraft flies a certain service based on the demand is the exception rather than the rule. When the aircraft departs, the unsold seats cannot generate any revenue and thus can be said to have perished. Airlines use special software to monitor how seats are being reserved and react accordingly, for example by offering discounts when it appears that seats will remain unsold.

Another way of capturing varying willingness to pay is to attempt market segmentation. A firm may repackage its basic inventory into different products to this end. In the passenger airline case this means implementing purchase restrictions, length of stay requirements and requiring fees for changing or canceling tickets.

The airline needs to keep a specific number of seats in reserve to cater to the probable demand for high-fare seats. The price of each seat varies inversely with the number of seats reserved, that is, the more seats that are reserved for a particular category, the lower the price of each seat. This will continue till the price of seat in the premium class equals that of those in the concession class. Depending on this, a floor price (lower price) for the next seat to be sold is set.

Hotels

Hotels use this system in largely the same way, to calculate the rates, rooms and restrictions on sales in order to best maximize the return too. These systems measure constrained and unconstrained demand along with pace to gauge which restrictions e.g.. length of stay, non refundable rate, or close to arrival. Revenue Managers in the hotel industry have evolved tremendously over the last 10 years and in this global economy targeting the right distribution channels, controlling costs, and having the right market mix plays an important role in Yield Management. Revenue management in hotels is selling rooms and services at the right price, at the right time, to the right people.

Rental Cars

In the rental car industry, yield management deals with the sale of optional insurance, damage waivers and vehicle upgrades. It accounts for a major portion of the rental company's profitability, and is monitored on a daily basis.

Inter City Buses

Yield management has moved into the bus industry with companies such as Megabus and BoltBus, which runs a low cost network in the UK and parts of the US, and more recently, nakedbus.com and Intercape, which have networks in New Zealand and South Africa.

Index

I

K

L

M

N

O

P

Q

R

◆◆◆